P9-APA-666

Sister Rosita

Nazareth College

Rochester 18

N. Y.

Guiding Junior-High-School Pupils
in Music Experiences

Guiding
Pupils in Music

Illustrated by Joe Smith

1953 · New York

Junior-High-School Experiences

FRANCES M. ANDREWS

The Pennsylvania State College

JOSEPH A. LEEDER

The Ohio State University

DISCARDED
LIBRARY

PRENTICE-HALL, INC.

PRENTICE-HALL EDUCATION SERIES

Harold Spears, Editor

44982

Copyright, 1953, by PRENTICE-HALL, INC., 70 Fifth Avenue, New York. All rights reserved. No part of this book may be reproduced, by mimeograph or any other means, without permission in writing from the publishers. Printed in the United States of America.

L. C. Cat. Card No.: 53-10164

780172
And

Prentice Hall. June 1961- 6/5/1—

To the Children

Preface

The authors of this book have long been aware of the interesting and challenging situations faced by the music teachers of junior-high-school pupils, and realize that these teachers evidence unusual concern and eagerness in their search for improved teaching methods, understanding of their pupils, and materials with which to work. They have also noted, in their teaching and observation of junior-high-school pupils, a need for vital and enlivened music situations.

Throughout the writing of the book, the authors have held steadfast to the purpose of supplying materials and methods that may be put to practical use. Discussion of educational theory and philosophy has been limited to the extent necessary for the clarification of controversial issues and the furnishing of background information. Because both authors realize that the success of procedures suggested depends upon the individual teacher who uses them, they urge that the teacher in no case regard these procedures as rigid, but rather that he freely adapt them to his own ability and situation.

The book was originally outlined by Dr. Andrews, who wrote the "Overview," the second part of Chapter 1, Chapters 2, 3, 6, 7, 10, and the discussion of music reading that appears in Chapter 5. In some cases both authors have treated the same topics, because such treatment was deemed necessary to make clear the particular relationship of the topic to the chapter's area.

The authors wish to acknowledge the assistance of many junior-high-school teachers, music consultants, supervisors, and directors. Their stimulating influence, their deep interest in pupils of junior-high-school age, and their devotion to the field of music education have been kept constantly in mind during the book's preparation.

The authors express appreciation to all persons who, directly or indirectly, assisted in the preparation of the manuscript, and in particular to junior-high-school teachers who contributed to certain of the materials lists; Janet Leeder Scheeler, for her aid in the preparation of Professor Leeder's chapters; Hummel Fishburn, Jo Hays, M. Claude Rosenberry, G. William Henninger, Elizabeth Reynolds, and Willa Taylor, for their encouragement and assistance in offering advice and constructive criticism with regard to certain of Dr. Andrews' chapters; and the illustrator, Joe Smith, a high-school junior, who executed with both humor and insight the ideas presented for illustration. Thanks are due also to those authors and publishers who gave permission to quote from their works.

Obviously, the use of the book is not limited to the teachers in a formal junior-high-school organization; its material is intended for teachers of this age-group in any school organization. Beyond this, many of the suggestions in the book may be adapted for other age-groups.

The whole intent of the writers has been that their book should serve, in a practical way, the needs of today's music educators, whom they look upon with respect and admiration.

FRANCES M. ANDREWS
JOSEPH A. LEEDER

Table of Contents

ix

An Overview

The prime function of every junior-high-school teacher is to guide the development of the children who, as individuals, bring together a rich variety of human individuality in the classroom. This variety of boy and girl individuality is what the music teacher endeavors to nourish and help grow through the extensive range and variety of musical materials at his disposal. To do this, he must reach far beyond the walls of the classroom into the everyday lives of the boys and girls he teaches, into the community and the world around them. The child is the first factor, the music is the second factor. Between stands the teacher, bringing them together. Of the two factors, it is obvious that the child is the live one and that the music lives only when it becomes part of him through his own absorption of it. The word "absorption" has a peculiarly apt signifi-

1

cance here, since in definition it implies a drinking-in process, a mental process of engrossment in the materials at hand, and a physical process of "reception and transformation into heat of radiant energy which falls upon a surface."[1]

The role of the teacher in modern education is well established as that of a guide, familiar and well informed about the land through which he guides his students, but able to view it with understanding and sympathy through the eyes of each new traveller. Each child comes into the junior-high-school music class with his own set of musical standards. The child must never be sacrificed to the different standards of the teacher but must be approached through his own standards, which are the result of eleven, twelve, thirteen, or even more years of his preceding life. Each child brings with him, and could not leave behind him if he would, a level of musical knowledge and an attitude toward music as part of the school curriculum. Unfortunately, attitudes toward music in the classroom and music in out-of-school life are in some cases different. Boys who see no point in the classroom music program are sometimes those who are scarcely outside the school door before the harmonica is whipped out of the hip pocket, and the reedy tune is floating back into the deserted music classroom. We cannot successfully disregard the child's own level of musical knowledge and his attitude toward music. We may test, evaluate, and survey his musical background, but whatever the results of such evaluation, the child is now the center of our work, and our take-off point must relate clearly to him in his present status. For some teachers this is merely common sense; for others it is a radical departure from a former concept of education which stressed the acquisition of knowledge and skills above all other goals, with emphasis on the goals and not on the child. A concomitant to this latter viewpoint had to be an attitude of indifference or resigned fatalism toward those children who did not achieve the teacher's goals.

---

[1] *The Winston Dictionary, Encyclopedic Edition* (Philadelphia, The John C. Winston Company, 1952), p. 5.

The philosophy of this book is based upon a viewpoint of child first, music second, and teacher as intermediary. The book's purpose is to suggest specific materials and techniques through which the philosophy may be implemented.

The practical application of the philosophy revolves first and always around the already identified object of our teaching, the child himself — all the children. This at once establishes the differences in the way we must go about our teaching. Traditionally, methods used on the college level (academically speaking) or the conservatory level (musically and technically speaking), either have been handed down intact for application on the secondary and even the elementary level or have trickled down through the hands of the teacher simply because he was doing what he himself knew best: teaching the way he had been taught. This has prevailed notwithstanding the many methods courses to which teachers are exposed and has so prevailed because such methods courses often are taught on a "do-as-I-say, not-the-way-I-am-doing-this" basis. Verbalism has defeated the purpose of methods courses; the teacher has proceeded on the basis of familiar and known methods which he himself has experienced. This vicious circle must be attacked at the source; tomorrow's teachers, now in the public-school classrooms, must be taught the way we hope they will teach. It must be attacked also at a higher level, in teacher-training institutions. But to do so, today's college teacher must exercise great resourcefulness and planning in classroom procedures. Modern teaching methods (referred to as "modern," although it is likely that superior teachers have used these same methods in whole or in part since time immemorial) are more complex than traditional ones. They require that the teacher be immersed in understanding of the teaching environment, which again is based upon understanding of the children involved, and which means a number of different teaching environments varying according to the number of different classes taught by each teacher. They require a mind and personality tremendously alive and inquiring on a day-to-day, year-to-year basis. They require that the teacher exercise great ingenuity and flexibility in choice and use of materials. The underlying philosophy regards students realistically as inconstants, possessing varying growth potentials, and continually casting about and reaching out for new experiences, new ideas, and new ways of doing things — all as part of the growth process.

Routine, repetition, drill, and step-by-step processes, typical procedures and mainstays of the traditional classroom teacher, must be reconceived and re-evaluated in their classroom use. For the most part, they have a use in the classroom, but only where and when they may be used as a means to an end, and not as an end in themselves. In former practice, these procedures became a means of attempting to impose a body of knowledge, or in music, of performing skills, upon the student — *all* students, ready or not. Today's philosophy, with its insistence that such knowledge and skills develop from within the student, requires that the forced acquisition of knowledge and skills be discarded. All effective learning is creative; it involves the absorption and transmutation of the materials with which the teacher and the students concern themselves. But music particularly is an area where the pupil should learn willingly and of his own volition.

We are primarily concerned with the question of how all of this shall come about. Growth in music and a favorable attitude toward it are inseparable as far as effective learning is concerned. The chief requisite of both is a rich, stimulating musical environment. This is the teacher's responsibility. The child is continually responding to forces outside of himself. The teacher, in part at least, is able to determine what these forces shall be. Where he provides forces which are in balance with the needs of the student, a three-way relationship is established, reverting to the "child first, music second, teacher-intermediary" idea. Where forces not in balance are attempted, no real basis of communication is established. For example, the rural child whose musical standards are based upon the hill-

billy music he has heard coming over the radio in the early
morning hours while helping with farm chores cannot adjust to
Beethoven, Mendelssohn, or even Victor Herbert without a
great amount of help and understanding from the teacher.
The teacher's standard is one thing, the student's is another.
Each must be respected, neither sacrificed. But the pupil's
growth in musical values is the teacher's responsibility. He is
not successful until understanding progresses past the hill-billy
music already known and accepted, or in general, expands in
appreciation beyond the status quo and in the direction of a
more eclectic viewpoint.

The reader will find no discussion of creative activities under
a separate heading in the following pages, for this reason: The
authors believe all the activities described should be approached with a creative philosophy. Whatever is a new
experience for the child, whatever he accomplishes with an
attitude of individual interpretation and a spirit of personal
participation is creative — for him. Thus, a child who assists
in working out square dance steps, who hears and recognizes
for the first time an oboe tone, or who offers an original and
constructive suggestion when learning a song is developing and
showing evidence of creative spirit. Eventually, out of such
activity he may bring forth work traditionally considered to
be creative, such as musical compositions or song texts. This
will be encouraged. But we must not believe that the child
who fails to produce such work is lacking in creative urge. All
individuals must build a framework of reference in knowledge
and interpretation of materials before they strike out in highly
original paths. Building such a framework is the task of most
concern to the teacher. Encouragement, patience, the ability
to point out relationships, willingness to allow attempts at new
and different ways of accomplishing tasks (even though these
may result in failure), and a spirit of enthusiasm are indis-
pensable characteristics of the teacher who wishes to engender
a creative atmosphere in his classroom. Rather than through
a few days devoted each year to its development, the creative

spirit is nurtured in a school climate.

To summarize the preceeding discussions, we are concerned with effective musical learning. This means that we must set up classroom situations which consider and encompass as well as possible the student's out-of-school environment, his personal needs, his present interests and attitudes. Using these factors as a springboard, we introduce the student and the musical materials to each other. Then, if our approach has been well planned, something similar to the chemical reaction referred to in the definition of absorption takes place; the "radiant energy," which is the music falling upon the "surface," which is the child, is transformed into "heat," which is the creative process in which the child makes the music a part of his total understanding.

The reward of such teaching is the richer life of the boy or girl whom it reaches. The purpose of this book is to suggest ways and means of going about the business of such teaching. But all suggestions contained within the book must be adapted by the teacher to his own classroom situation; they will succeed only when they are interpreted by the teacher in the *live terms of the boys and girls he teaches.*

1. The Junior High School and Its Pupils

THE DEVELOPMENT OF THE JUNIOR HIGH SCHOOL

The junior high school, including grades 7-9, is the framework of reference for the boys and girls whose musical experiences are the subject of this book. But whether the school in which we find pupils in these grades is labelled "Junior High," or whether they are part of an 8-4, 6-6, or other organization, is not the important factor. Foremost in our thinking is the developing relationship of the pupil with music. If this relationship is one through which he better adjusts to, understands, and enjoys the world in which he lives, the school organization matters little; the teacher, in whatever school, has accomplished his purpose.

For purposes of definition and clarification, however, let us look briefly at the traditional junior high school, its reasons for being, and its organization.

There were many early influences for reorganizing secondary education at the turn of the twentieth century. There was at that time a decided interest in reorganizing the 8-4 plan since

7

many educators believed the eighth grade, usually housed with the elementary school, should be connected with the high school. It was thought this might facilitate the elimination of the prevalent "review" subjects and aid in reducing the high percentage of pupil withdrawals from school at the ninth-grade level. In brief, the reasons why the 8-4 plan needed reorganization as stated by Gruhn and Douglas [1] were as follows:

1. The need for economy of time in the program of elementary and secondary education.
2. The need for closer articulation between the elementary and the secondary school.
3. The need for an educational organization and a program which is suited to the nature of adolescents.
4. The need for increased retention-rate of pupils, especially in grades 6-9.
5. The need for earlier differentiation of instruction in terms of the needs, interests, and capacities of individual pupils.

Various educational committees developed, between 1892-1912, the basic concepts of the present-day junior high school,

[1] William T. Gruhn and Harl R. Douglas, *The Modern Junior High School.* Copyright 1947, The Ronald Press Company. Pp. 46-47.

and a few school systems attempted school reforms. It was during the school year 1909-1910 that the junior high school had its beginning in Columbus, Ohio and in Berkeley, California. Due to growing school enrollments and a desire for an educational system geared to adolescent needs, the movement spread to other cities.

ITS FUNCTION

The many factors which influenced the organization of the junior high school developed into basic ideas, which emerged in terms of the following functions:

1. To develop a better articulation between the elementary school and a program geared to adolescent needs and interests.
2. To provide a flexible program to meet individual differences in ability, personality, interest, aptitude, and background.
3. To guide pupils in making wise judgments concerning vocations, and social, emotional, mental and personality problems.
4. To nurture integrative educational experiences which utilize basic knowledge and skills in developing favorable social attitudes and acceptable behavior.
5. To furnish opportunities for pupils to explore their special abilities, aptitudes, and interests.

In order that the foregoing functions might prevail, the following type of junior-high-school program was organized and developed in varying degrees, as noted by Davis.

1. Grades 7, 8, 9 or 7 and 8.
2. Separate buildings.
3. Separate staff of teachers and supervisors.
4. Different program of studies.
5. Departmental organization of subject matter.
6. Plan of vocational guidance.
7. Elective studies.
8. Socialized recitation.
9. Supervised study.
10. Promotion by subjects.
11. New methods of instruction.

12. Student activities to meet needs and interests of adolescent pupils.[2]

Teachers will find it interesting to compare today's junior high school with the early ones. In this way we may see to what extent we fulfill the hopes of the educators who pioneered the beginning junior high schools. Whereas it would be difficult to state in exact terms the amount of progress which has been made in the better education of boys and girls through the junior-high-school movement, we can point to certain accomplishments resulting from it:

1. Attention has been focused on the problems of boys and girls of the junior-high-school age, and attempts are constantly being made to find solutions for these problems.
2. A broader curriculum is offered in the junior high school than was characteristic of the traditional 8-4 organization, with greater emphasis on courses which actually meet the needs of its pupils.
3. More pupils remain in school through the ninth grade.
4. Greater emphasis has been placed on meeting the social and emotional needs of junior-high-school-age pupils.
5. Pupils are encouraged to consider possible vocations at an earlier age, and to prepare for them accordingly.
6. Growth of the junior-high movement has emphasized the special need of its pupils for highly skilled and understanding teachers. As a result, educational institutions are attempting to develop improved programs of teacher-preparation in this area.

In the final analysis, it might be said that today the purpose of the junior high school is to afford the best possible educational opportunity for the many pupils it serves. These boys and girls present a bewildering variety of abilities, interests, and attitudes, which confront the teacher of music in every class he meets. Yet, confusing as this presentation of the many facets of their personalties may be, its variety gives the teacher a rich source of material through which he presents his *musical*

---

[2] Calvin O. Davis, *Junior High School Education* (Yonkers-on-Hudson, New York: World Book Company, 1924), pp. 13-14.

materials. Since no book dealing with the teaching of junior-high-school students would be complete without some discussion of their nature, a brief summary of some important characteristics is included here.

CHARACTERISTICS OF ADOLESCENTS

Looking over a class of thirty or forty junior-high pupils on a single grade level, the teacher at once recognizes certain obvious outward differences. It is noticed that pupils vary in size and physiological development. Some are better clothed than others, some are neater, even cleaner, in their appearance, some look healthier and better nourished than others, and some are more alert and interested in the activities of the classroom than are their fellow students. These are important matters; no teacher is competent unless he is constantly aware of such points and their implications. But other factors which should determine the teacher's procedures in his day-to-day teaching may be concealed wholly or in part. These have to do with the child's intelligence, emotional maturity, social adjustment, interests, and previous experiences with the subject which is the teacher's special area of education.

In order that a school may carry out the basic functions of the junior high school, teachers and administrators must know the adolescents they serve and know them thoroughly with regard to all their characteristics. Often schools are concerned only with subject matter, but a modern school devoted to the genuine functions of the junior high school is obligated to make its program fit its consumers. Although today we consider pupils foremost as individuals, there are certain characteristics common to most adolescents. It is important that the successful teacher know these, and the music teacher is in a strategic position to use such knowledge, since music is an excellent vehicle through which adolescents may be offered needed avenues of expression.

Not all pupils in the junior high school are adolescent; some are preadolescent (prepubescent). These children may be accelerated. The following table, compiled from the University of New York Annual Report,[3] shows the average ages for grades 7, 8, and 9. One can easily see that each grade level presents considerable differences in age, a variance which adds to the music teacher's problem.

Grade	Age 10-11	Age 11-12	Age 12-13	Age 13-14	Age 14-15	Age 15-16	Age 16-17
7	.001	.287	.475	.137	.057	.048	——
8	——	.006	.233	.504	.168	.089	——
9	——	——	.011	.249	.477	.189	.054

Yet adolescence does not begin or end suddenly at a fixed point, and its advent is foreshadowed in the youngest of junior-high-school pupils. We may consider, therefore, that it concerns all the children with whom this book deals and assume that it is vital for us to become familiar with its characteristics. First we need to know what adolescence means. Here is a useful definition for educators:

Adolescence is a period of growing up that comes between childhood and adulthood. It may be thought of either as the actual growing-up process or as the time during which this process takes place. In either case, it is usually regarded as covering the years 12-20, or the "teen age." [4]

EMOTIONAL CHARACTERISTICS

We have all noticed that adolescence seems to be for some boys and girls a period of "storm and stress." There is no doubt that glandular (endocrine) changes have an important part to play in the emotional upheavals of adolescence, but we must not forget that environmental conditions, too, have a great

[3] University of the State of New York, "Education Department Annual Report" (Albany, New York: State Education Department, 1950), Vol. II, pp. 14-15.

[4] *Guiding the Adolescent,* Children's Bureau, Publication 225 (Washington, D. C.: Federal Security Agency), p. 2.

influence on emotional stability. Emotional upsets influence a pupil's social relationships both at home and in school.

Hurlock [5] says that adolescent emotions are intense and moody, and pupils lack steadiness, consistency, and control of expression. This accounts for much of the quarreling, teasing, giggling, sudden likes and dislikes, great tensions, shyness, and feeling of inferiority. Here we have hero worship, love of adventure and excitement, reverence for God, and great emotional capacity as dominant characteristics of the adolescent junior-high-school pupil. Understanding these characteristics the wise music teacher selects his music to fit the wide range of his pupils' emotional needs.

SOCIAL CHARACTERISTICS

The adolescent becomes intensely socially conscious. He feels the need of belonging to a group. But he may resent and resist parental and teacher control, even though he develops a feeling of being unwanted through the lack of it. Dollard says:

From the child's standpoint, adolescence is a problem because during adolescence he becomes as big, as emotional, and as intelligent as he will ever be, and yet he is still looked upon as a child and made to stand waiting at the door of life. To be sure, he lacks something very important — experience. But how is he going to get that if he cannot try out new things? [6]

Social adjustments with the peer-group and the achievement of prestige through group acceptance are most important. This process may be accompanied by intense emotions. Here the social set, the crowd, and the gang become very important, and being a part of one's group is basic in developing a feeling

[5] By permission from *Adolescent Development*, by Elizabeth B. Hurlock. Copyright, 1949. McGraw-Hill Book Company, Inc. Pp. 113-117.

[6] Reprinted by special permission from The University of Chicago Round Table, *What Parents Should Know*, broadcast April 25, 1948, from a statement by John Dollard, Professor of Psychology, Yale University, who was one of the participants on the program.

of security. The adolescent will often stand by his crowd, notwithstanding parental or school interference.

The extrovert goes to extreme lengths to show off in order to attract attention, while the introvert retires within himself to avoid drawing attention and possible ridicule from others, especially from his peers. Finding a place within his group is a definite problem for the adolescent, so we find him satisfying his gregarious needs by joining various kinds of gangs and clubs.

Worthwhile organizations can do much to develop leadership and democratic social ideas, and to break down social, racial, and intellectual prejudice. Musical organizations can be of great value here since they act as mixers, leaveners, and a means of vigorous self-expression.

PHYSICAL CHARACTERISTICS

In early adolescence there are changes in body development accompanied by changes in behavior. At the age of 13, girls, on the average, are taller than boys, but by the age of 15, boys may have caught up with and passed them. Rapid muscle and bone growth results in some boys and girls becoming awkward. At times some individuals are unwilling to participate in square and folk dances for fear of embarrassment. Such behavior as stumbling, slouching, falling over furniture and dropping objects is often due to faulty co-ordination, not wilful misconduct. Adults are prone to forget their own adolescent difficulties and reprimand adolescents for awkward, seemingly rude, behavior. Then, when such behavior is involuntary, the boy or girl becomes defensive, and may cover up by even more boisterous, at times aggressive, conduct.

The "overgrown" or early-maturing adolescent may find himself a social misfit, and can easily become isolated. He may try to establish leadership and in so doing become a "bully." The "runt" may also try to win the spotlight by pushing, pulling hair, or by displaying other socially unacceptable behavior.

Changes in endocrine as well as in sex glands may result in

a period of becoming easily fatigued and having an over-abundance of energy, of having headaches (real or imaginary), stomachaches, or nervousness.

Many adolescents are bothered by acne, which may cause shyness. Boys are extremely sensitive to ridicule by adults or their peers, particularly when bothered by lack of control over their lowering voices, caused by the lengthening of the vocal cords. With some, this "shifting of gears" (going down approxi-mately an octave) comes rapidly, while with others it is a slow process lasting from one to three years. Girls' voices change in range and quality, but do not drop an octave.

INTELLECTUAL AND OTHER CHARACTERISTICS

In addition to the physical development of the adolescent, we must consider the mental, social, and emotional character-istics out of which his interests and aptitudes grow. These are more difficult to measure or estimate than is physical develop-ment. The many tests which in the hands of a trained adminis-trator are helpful include tests of intelligence, emotional and social maturity, interests, and vocational aptitude. The chief value of such tests lies in their diagnostic and prognostic use, however, and they should not be used to place boys and girls in an arbitrary category.

Administrators and teachers in some schools attempt homo-geneous organization of classes, for example, on the basis of pupils' intelligence rating. While such procedure has as its objective the facilitating of intellectual learning, its weakness lies in its tendency to neglect social learnings. The intelligence quotient (I.Q.) signifies the ratio between the mental age and the chronological age in years and months. Thus pupils are found to be, approximately speaking, average, above average, or below average in intelligence.

The general music class which is not organized according to I.Q. will contain all three levels of intelligence. Ordinarily, due to individual differences, no two classes will cover or be interested in exactly the same learning activities. Pupils should not be pitted against each other; rather, many educators believe that a flexible standard should be used to meet the needs and abilities of these various levels of intelligence. This is a functional problem of the junior high school. Music, because of its many types of activities such as listening, creating, playing on simple instruments, rhythmic activities, singing unison and part songs and sight reading, lends itself well to developing the abilities of the varied degrees of intelligence and ability found in the junior-high-school grades.

PRESENT-DAY PRESSURES AND TENSIONS

To add to the complex problem of teaching adolescents and preadolescents, the teacher is likely to find himself beset by conflicting educational philosophies and practices. His pupils are children of parents also confused by shifting viewpoints with regard to child-rearing. All parties concerned, including the children, are part and parcel of a high-pressure, break-neck-pace civilization where the very preservation of existence in a war-torn world is an everyday topic of conversation. Each one of these factors affects the teacher-pupil relationship. Yet, the teacher may have as little as one period a week to learn about his students, or at the most, four or five periods when he is meeting a large number of boys and girls.

Pressures and tensions have existed in the world since men first congregated and began working out the problems of living together. Though each generation's children adjust somehow to the environment in which they find themselves, today's children are part of a world which must seem very insecure and unstable when they reach an age where the broader aspects of living concern them. (This age is likely to correspond to the junior-high-school years, which are the years of preadolescence and early adolescence.) Certain signs that some boys and girls are faced with problems which they find unsolvable are obvious in our world, as witness the per-

centage of teen-age drug addiction and the high rate of teen-age delinquency. Even the percentage of teen-age automobile accidents indicates the inability of our boys and girls to cope with the tools of today's civilization. The adolescent realizes, and the preadolescent has begun to realize, that he must establish himself as an individual in a world that is not only highly competitive but dangerous and unpredictable as well.

Margaret Mead, in discussing the rapid pace at which our changing civilization moves, notes that children at the age of five years already accept as commonplace certain ideas to which many adults will never quite be oriented. In a brilliant development of this topic, and with particular reference to the idea that teachers are faced with a difficult problem in understanding today's children, she says:

Within the lifetime of ten-year-olds the world has entered a new age, and already, before they enter the sixth grade, the atomic age has been followed by the age of the hydrogen bomb, differentiated from the atomic age in that many of those who failed to understand the dangers of the atom bomb are painfully beginning to take in the significance of the hydrogen bomb. Teachers who never heard a radio until they were grown up have to cope with children who have never known a world without television. Teachers who struggled in their childhood with a buttonhook find it difficult to describe a buttonhook to a child bred up among zippers, to whom fastnesses are to be breached by zipping them open, rather than fumblingly feeling for mysterious buttons. From the most all-embracing world image to the smallest detail of daily life the world has changed at a rate which makes the five-year-old generations further apart than world generations or even scores of generations were in our recent past, than people separated by several centuries were in the remote past.[7]

The home always reflects to some extent the stress of the world situation, and pupils similarly reflect the pressure and tensions of their homes. At times we find adolescents excited, and again, depressed; such emotional fluctuations affect school behavior. Pupils bring to the classroom the whole gamut of human emotions including joy, hate, anger, enthusiasm, disgust, love, shame, and humiliation. The fact that music is an art which is chiefly emotional in appeal puts into the hands of the music teacher a great power for influencing the behavior of his pupils.

Lack of understanding between parents and children may be the cause of outbursts in the classroom; an unthinking teacher may wrongly consider such behavior as personally directed. Too much parental control, or the lack of it, is often the cause of unacceptable behavior patterns. The teacher should explore and allow for the home pressures and social tensions which cause the otherwise inexplicable actions of some class members. He will find that, for example, broken homes and situations where one parent is away from home for extended periods — such as a father in military service, or a mother at work — may influence conduct.

---

[7] Reprinted by permission of the publishers from Margaret Mead's *The School in American Culture* (Cambridge, Mass.: Harvard University Press), 1951, pp. 33-34.

The present-day feeling of national insecurity is reflected in our pupils, many of whom see resulting problems reflected daily in newspapers, movies, and television programs. Jittery feelings and insecurity developed through such sources force the music teacher into a more encompassing role than he has faced at any previous time. His materials and methods must be chosen with the idea of helping children to find acceptance and security, despite such problems.

VARYING COMMUNITY AND SCHOOL INFLUENCES

To understand his pupils, the teacher must know the type of community served by the school. The community which offers few recreational facilities causes boys and girls to seek excitement, which can easily result in conflict with the law. For normal desires, every community must supply such outlets as playgrounds and youth centers if it wishes to develop law-abiding, responsible youths. Low economic home status, as well as unstable home situations, often contributes to youthful delinquency, while on the other hand the overprivileged community may unwittingly cause its youth to feel superior and unwilling to assume responsibility.

The music teacher must join forces with other teachers and administrators in studying the causes that shape social patterns in school and community. Where we find the cause for delinquency and unacceptable social behavior to lie within the home, our work with the parents may be more beneficial than punishment administered with a revengeful attitude towards pupils. Schools today are finding it necessary to take over much of the social training that once was given in the home. Mort and Vincent, in discussing the increasing share carried by the school in this respect, have this to say:

Our purposes in bringing up children have always been the same. They are two. The first is an individual one: to develop each youngster to the highest degree which he is individually capable of attaining — in body, mind, spirit, character, and feelings, and in personal, economic, home, and civic competence. The second is a social one: to replace our generation with a rising generation that is *at least* as competent to cope with the problems of community, state, nation, and world as the older generation.

Schools have not always been charged with a big share of this job. Today they share it with the home, the church, the university, and similar groups, and with other less formal agencies and influences. The 1900 school was entrusted with a very slim share indeed of the total job. But as the job itself has grown more complex, and as the informal agencies and influences which helped to shape children back in 1900 have gradually left off with their work, the modern school has filled the gap with newer practices consciously designed to round out the growth of its youngsters.[8]

Where the home, school, and community fail to provide situations which favor and recognize the desirable development of boys and girls, poorly adjusted children are a direct result. For example: The natural desire of boys and girls to win approval of their classmates turns out, at times, to be the basis of unacceptable behavior. This develops from an attitude that could be stated thus: "If I can't get attention and win social approval by desirable performance, I'll get it by displaying unacceptable behavior." Sometimes this is so successful a device that pupils who, for example, defy authority become gang or group leaders, chiefly because their peers believe they are not afraid to challenge adults (a desire which lies close to the surface in the minds of many boys and girls). Winning over the leader of the gang or set is a technique every successful teacher must master. That school which is geared to the needs of its pupils and the community serves best educationally. No two communities are exactly alike, thus identical educational programs cannot be followed. In fact, *we must learn that no two classes can be taught alike, nor can we slavishly follow a single, prescribed routine. The program must be adapted to the community, not the community to the program.*

The community with a transient or shifting population offers

---

[8] Paul R. Mort and William S. Vincent, *A Look at Our Schools.* Copyright 1946, The Ronald Press Company. Pp. 64-65.

a special challenge to the music teacher. Pupils who move many times from school to school often have difficulty in making new friends and adjusting to new school programs. In music classes during the fall, one teacher considered this problem and asked newcomers to the community to identify themselves. He then asked children who had been newcomers to the school in previous years how other children and teachers had helped them to become adjusted. In each class, children volunteered their experiences and told freely of their feelings of loneliness, their difficulties in finding a place in the group. Then the class members discussed ways in which to help the newcomers. Feelings of tension, always present when children are trying to adjust to a new situation, were eased, and the established pupils were put on their mettle with regard to helping new students. Class morale was instantly lifted by these friendly discussions. The class suggested group singing and folk dancing as a means of breaking the ice and helping new pupils feel part of the group. Perhaps a few worries were relieved, and life made a bit more pleasant. Music teachers need to take cognizance of such problems as this, not only in their relationships with pupils, but also in the selection of musical materials and activities.

PRESSURES RESULTING FROM MASS MEDIA OF COMMUNICATION IN THE WORLD COMMUNITY

In a preceding paragraph, the factor of various mass media of public communication was mentioned. Today radio, television, and motion pictures afford boys and girls greater information and knowledge on almost any subject of interest than has been afforded any previous generation. Yet, the length of dependence of these children on their families for financial support has increased, if anything, so that their experiences, vicarious and otherwise, urge them toward an independence they are unable to exercise in real life. It is not intended to suggest that children of junior- or even senior-high-school age are ready to be independent individuals, but rather that they are pulled by the artificial means of mass media in the direction of many things which are made to appear highly desirable. This pull may range from the advertising of particular brands of toothpaste and cigarettes and the plugging of current song hits to the demonstrating of particular styles of dress, ways of conduct, and so on. In the music class, the teacher is competing, willy-nilly, with the radio and television musical productions heard and seen by his pupils. These are, for the most part, geared to fit popular taste with no thought for the upgrading of such taste. Yet, the teacher's work entails the responsibility of helping the child grow and expand in his musical tastes. When the teacher finds himself in competition with media which readily expend thousands of dollars on half-hour shows, the implications are at times overwhelming. In every age, the urge of the young to be modern and up-to-date is strong; today's pressures make it all too easy to abandon values in everything from music to morals in order to be in the front ranks of those impressed by the excitement of standards artificially created through the media mentioned.

In the classroom situation, which results from such pressures ("classroom situation" used here means any group of junior-high-school students learning under the school instructional program), the teacher must reflect in his teaching procedures all the attitudes and interests of his students, however acquired. Still, he must be keenly aware of the fact that some of these are short-term interests of little real value. Those of real importance must be nurtured, and thus, without making any child feel that his opinions and values are inferior, gradually substituted for those which are momentary. This should be done by the simple process of opening up new worlds to the child.

As an example, consider the way boys and girls often test new teachers by asking whether or not they will be permitted to sing popular songs in class. The wise teacher knows that there are popular songs of both good and dubious value; he also realizes that, on the whole, there are many songs which are more rewarding musical experiences than the fleetingly popular songs of the moment. Children cannot always be expected to grasp this, however. Refusal to incorporate such songs into the classroom program not only negates the pupil-teacher planning idea, but also constitutes an adverse commentary on the pupil sense of values. It seems logical that some popular songs should be included for recreational as well as other values (such as rhythmic content). Overemphasis of such songs may be eliminated by developing a wide repertoire of well-arranged folk, art, and other composed songs which have stood the test of time, and are interesting, attractive, and vital in musical content. Teachers should face the fact that popular songs are "loaded" in their appeal to children because they are backed in most cases by radio, television, motion picture, or recorded presentations representing investments of thousands of dollars. The obvious implication is that classroom presentation of song material must be so vital that children will enjoy singing many songs in addition to the popular songs of the day. Notice that the authors neither condemn nor urge the inclusion of popular songs; when serving the purpose of stimulating musical interest growth the use of such songs in the classroom appears to be justified.

Though we have referred to this as a "simple process" we are aware of the fact that such teaching requires a teacher of skill and wide cultural horizons. It may be said that children seldom fail in the total growth process, but that instead teachers often fail to help them achieve even the minimum possible growth. Why? Usually it is because of a failure to evaluate the individual and class potential. Sometimes, however, the growth process is stunted through the teachers' failure to continue throughout their teaching careers an expansion of their own horizons. When children are taught by an adult whose spiritual and mental growth is at a standstill, they are faced with a barrier which blocks their own development.

But if it has been implied that the forces of mass media work against the teacher's attempts to develop certain standards and values in the consciousness of his pupils, some factors at least in this situation are working in favor of the teacher. The pupils' wider acquaintance with the world around them means that the teacher has many avenues of approach to his subject. This is in sharp contrast to the former textbook approach. In the case of music, it serves to disperse some of the atmosphere of the sacrosanct which has caused the false belief that the real enjoyment and understanding of "good" music is for the talented few. So it may be, if we begin and end our approach with music which is remote to the understanding and taste of the average consumer, who appears in the classroom as our pupil, but who has already formed his ideas and tastes about music. Take the case of Bill, for example. Bill was a member of an eighth-grade music class. He had trouble singing on pitch, and his classroom difficulties were complicated by a slight speech hesitancy, noticeable particularly when he made oral contributions to class discussion. Judging by his music class behavior, he tried to be interested, but often found his attention wandering, especially in the singing activities of the class. One day in talking with Bill outside school, the instructor found that he was an enthusiastic Boy Scout. He also learned that Bill was working on certain merit badges and was particularly eager to obtain the Indian merit badge. This led to a discussion of Indian music. The next time music class met, he asked Bill whether or not he would be interested in hearing some music based on Indian melodies. Eager to do so, Bill took the records, chose a friend, and went to the instructor's office with a portable phonograph to listen. On his return he commented that he did not like the music very well; it was not really Indian music. The instructor then arranged for Bill to hear some recordings of authentic Indian chants, which he and his friend listened to while the rest of the class proceeded with their regular activities. After Bill's listening was finished, the instructor asked him to make an oral report to the class on the portions of the music he liked, and why. Bill was very willing to do this and gave the class an interesting account of his listening activities from which he drew some good conclusions. The most significant feature of this report, however, was that in making it he did not hesitate once; his interest in the project was enough to carry him through any speech difficulty.

Where did Bill receive his initial impression of what was and what was not authentic Indian music? Probably from motion pictures or television; at least enough of an impression to enable him to have some kind of basis of judgment. And how did the instructor find a way of establishing Bill's security in the class? By bringing his out-of-school world into the classroom. The line of demarcation between in-school and out-of-school worlds is almost imperceptible in present-day schools; a basic idea, as illustrated in the case of Bill, is to take over into the classroom the activities which make life interesting and vital to boys and girls. Where the greater experience and wider horizons of today's children are useful springboards to classroom learning, they should be utilized to the utmost.

RESULTANT ATTITUDES AND SOCIAL ADJUSTMENTS

The junior-high-school pupil brings to the classroom many varied attitudes toward music and toward life itself. No teacher should expect a pupil to be highly co-operative if he comes from a home where he has been badgered into submission by parental threats. Often such pupils feel unwanted, this feeling showing itself in non-co-operative and antisocial actions. A feeling of insecurity affects the overt behavior of adolescents.

Negative attitudes toward songs which are sung by certain religious sects or concern minority groups are especially noticeable in some communities. Nevertheless, music teachers may use music effectively to develop understanding and tolerance where racial and religious problems are concerned.

The good music class helps pupils adjust socially to the activities of the group. In fact, music can be one of the important factors in helping the adolescent adjust to his environment. The skilled teacher will not demand the same standards in each type of classroom activity; we must consider social differences in the selection and use of the many types of materials.

THE SCHOOL'S RESPONSIBILITY

The educational progress of pupils is one of deep concern to pupils, parents, and teachers alike. The standards of some classrooms often are geared to the superior student, and as a result the average and the slow learner finds school increasingly more difficult and distasteful as he goes from grade to grade. Some are trying to carry intellectual loads beyond their ability, with frustrating results that manifest themselves in antisocial and belligerent attitudes. In other situations, the superior pupil is the more neglected student, since there are few challenging activities offered him, and he has little interest in what the average or slow learner can do.

Often we find ourselves trying to teach pupils who have had little or no experience with music in the same class with those who have a rich background in the art. This situation, found in most classrooms, demands varied musical activities, which, through their different appeals, cause the class to become a pleasurable experience for all.

The effective school adjusts its curriculum to the abilities and needs of all pupils. To meet the classroom situation, music must be taught as experience, as activity learning, and not as *memoriter learning*. No teacher who believes in social, emotional, physical, and intellectual education for the whole child can teach otherwise.

Never before have pupils had such a varied, and often rich, musical experience available in their daily living as they have today. The radio, the movies, television, and the phonograph have brought faraway places and their music into many homes. As a result, pupils are no longer satisfied with a note reading program. Instead, they are interested in an enriched program that is a part of today's living. Community resources, current magazines, newspapers, and musical events should be utilized as music materials in the modern school.

SUMMARY

The junior high school came about as a result of a definite need for the consideration of the nature of prepubescent and adolescent boys and girls in relation to their education. Today it has reached some of its original objectives in part, chiefly in the way of meeting individual needs and of understanding the boys and girls involved. To an increased degree the school organization has become subservient to the pupil; therefore, more pupils are remaining in school and are better prepared to face life situations when they leave. Courses are taught by teachers who keep in mind, to the best of their abilities, both the mental and physical characteristics of each student, his emotional nature, his social needs, his individual interests, and his out-of-school life. With particular regard for the latter, the superior teacher is conscious of tensions existing in today's world and tries to help pupils by considering their in- and out-of-school problems in relation to these anxieties. The teacher also bears in mind the influence of the home and community on the boys and girls he teaches, and the effect of such forces as radio, television, and motion pictures. It is as important for the music teacher as for the guidance counsellor to consider such influences in his teaching, since each child reflects them in his classroom attitude. The materials and methods of the music teacher cannot be effective unless they are chosen and used with a total picture in mind of the child and his background. The teacher's job today is more important than at any time in the past, because of the larger part played by the school in the shaping of each child's character and personality. In effect, the music teacher no longer has the single responsibility of teaching music; he, with his fellow teachers, is responsible to a large extent for what the child becomes as a citizen.

2. Music in the Life of the Pupil

LET'S FACE IT — THEY HAVE THEIR FAULTS!

No group of pupils is more spirited, enthusiastic, and rewarding in terms of return on the teacher's investment than is a junior-high-school group. They rush into class bubbling with energy; they are early instead of late to rehearsals. Put them well-prepared in front of an audience and they will sing and play their hearts out, abandoning themselves wholeheartedly to the music and the director. They will, that is, if the teacher has won them over to music and to his teaching. They are sensitive, responsive, loyal, and grateful.

Yet, there seems to be an opinion prevalent among teachers to the effect that the junior high school is a "hot" spot in which to teach; too hot for comfort, in fact. Music teachers are no exception to those holding this opinion. No file has yet been designed which would hold all the complaints about our junior high schoolers. Teachers say, "They won't sit still — they don't pay attention — they're rude — they talk all the time — they push, shove, kick, throw paper-wads, and giggle until they're reprimanded, then unexpectedly burst into tears; they won't

28

assume responsibility — they can't read, write, or spell. . . . " The list is endless. Even the parents join in the chorus of complaints.

All the accusations are true — of some pupils at some times. Nearly all of them hold true *only* when these boys and girls are in a group situation. People who are expert at getting along with small groups sometimes learn this in a hurry. Anna Perrott Rose points this out in a passage from the story of her experiences in taking so-called problem children into her home:

In between times, when we needed a little extra money, I did substitute schoolteaching. This is not a restful pastime. I picked up a note on the schoolroom floor one day which read: *"I see we have a substitute. Let's take her for a ride,"* and the battle was on!

There is, unfortunately, something about schoolteaching that rouses a hostility between child and grownup not found so frequently in other relationships. This is partly because the teacher is obliged to hold the young nose to the grindstone until sparks fly, and it is also due to the necessity of handling too many children all at once. I really like to teach children, but I do not like to teach classes. In the confusion of numbers it is easy to suppose that a child is "bad" when he does not conform to a class pattern. There is not much time to find out why he won't conform.[1]

Mrs. Rose relates her experiences in a way which should enlighten many teachers, and finally says, in discussing a ninth grade:

. . . any woman who remains competently, steadfastly at her post in a classroom, year after year, deserves the Congressional Medal, at the very least. I am no medalist and I gave up. There are easier ways to earn a living than by being thrown to the lions five days a week.[2]

Unfortunately, it is most often the undesirable traits of junior-high-school pupils which attract attention. The majority of pupils who are co-operative and helpful in the group are taken

---

[1] Anna Perrott Rose, *Room for One More* (Boston: Houghton Mifflin Company, 1950), p. 102.

[2] *Ibid.*, p. 105.

for granted by teachers, as are the many good traits of all the boys and girls who make up these troublesome classes.

The complaints of music teachers follow the same pattern as those of other teachers and parents, with a few such specific irritants added: "They can't read music — they don't know key signatures — they won't sit still long enough to listen to a record. . . . "

Listening to the remarks about these children, it is easy to get an impression of premeditated mass assault on civilized standards of conduct. In some junior high schools where unrest is characteristic, teachers report that at the end of a day's teaching they are emotionally exhausted — victims, we might say, of combat fatigue.

On the other hand, some readers may blink at the preceding paragraphs and say, "It never happened to me. My classes are perfectly quiet and obedient; they do just what I tell them to do. I never have discipline problems." Taking a quick look at the latter situation, it seems possible that it may lean toward regimentation, and at times, may tend to stifle the pupil's initiative and growth in self-expression in order to save the teacher's disposition.

Perhaps the key to this junior-high-school dilemma really has something to do with a teacher's case of combat fatigue. The answer may lie in *what* we are trying to combat.

First, when we object to certain obnoxious traits — obnoxious to adults, that is — exhibited by adolescents and preadolescents, we are simply objecting to a natural part of the child's growth process. Let's look at a few statements by Fritz Redl, authority on adolescent and preadolescent psychology. In discussing pre-adolescents, Redl says:

By pre-adolescence I mean the phase when the nicest children begin to behave in a most awful way. This definition cannot exactly be called scientific, but those who have to live with children of that age will immediately recognize what I am talking about.[3]

Redl also points out that these children are extremely restless physically, that they apparently need to be kept busy:

Their hands seem to need constant occupational therapy — they will turn up the edges of any book they handle, manipulate pencils, any objects near them, or any one of the dozen-odd things they carry in their pockets, pull at parts of their own bodies, whether it be nose or ears, scratch their hair or parts of the anatomy usually taboo in terms of infantile upbringing.[4]

Now does this, from an authority on child development, plus our discussion of adolescents in Chapter 1 give you an idea of the reasons why teachers tend to shrink from teaching in the junior high school? It should make one thing very clear; we can't succeed by struggling against nature — that's where the heavy cases of combat fatigue occur. We have to get this tremendous force working on our side.

---

[3] From the chapter by Dr. Fritz Redl in the book *Our Children Today* edited by Sidonie M. Gruenberg. The Viking Press, Inc. 1952. P. 161.

[4] *Ibid.* Pp. 163-164.

The problem is — how? Some teachers say it can be done by damming up the child's reactions. True, sooner or later he must learn to behave as a stable and agreeable human being in order to get along. So these teachers argue, "The sooner the better!" *If we force the issue*, however, and do artificially what the process of maturing will take care of less painfully, we don't succeed in all cases. If we do, the child sacrifices something of his personality, even though it be only a passing phase and one which adults are perfectly willing to have him sacrifice. Consider it this way: Driving along the countryside, we are often charmed by a brook which meanders along through meadows, woodlands, and pastures, winding in and out, probably being a big nuisance to many a farmer. At great cost and effort it could be channeled into a straight canal. Only it would no longer be itself, the charming, meandering brook we liked in the first place. A brook cannot do the work of a stream or river. So the hastening of a natural process is not only frustrating to the child (and probably to the teacher during the process), but it may also leave a somewhat bitter residue.

No . . . this is not what we want. There must be a better way. We *want* to preserve this intense activity, because this is good. We want to preserve the interest, the alertness, the tremendous *aliveness* of our preadolescents and their older fellows, who have reached the real struggle of adolescence. Understanding boys and girls, we teachers really do not want to thwart or abort their birthright of growing up at a natural pace; we see around us too many bitter, frustrated adults who suffered this indignity at the hands of previous generations.

In order to look around for this better way of handling our pupils, let's leave the teacher's desk and sit down in the classroom, getting what the boys and girls themselves sometimes call the "worm's-eye view."

To begin with, why should we expect boys and girls to like music and to find a place for it in their lives? What thoughts go through their minds about music? Let's tune in on the thinking of a ninth-grade boy.

TAKE A LOOK AT THE "WORM'S-EYE" VIEW

"Music is fun, or should be. We have more parties in ninth grade than we did in eighth — more boys are dating girls, too — don't know what we'd do without music for dancing and pepping things up. About all you can do with a nickel nowadays is get music out of a jukebox. When the music is going it gets you over awkward pauses in conversation, helps you feel at ease, and actually seems to make it easier to manage clumsy hands and feet if you're thirteen or fourteen or even older.

"Singing is *always* fun . . . outside of school. You don't have to bother with struggling to read notes, or following dynamics in the music . . . you just sing. Around the campfire, at a picnic, or in Joe's rumpus room somebody begins singing, and everybody joins in. Soon a girl adds an alto part and a fellow with a budding tenor voice slips up a third above the melody . . . there may be some sour notes, but it's somehow satisfying, and anyhow, remember when your Dad's college quartet last let loose with some barber-shop? Some of it was *too* close, but did they have fun! They weren't singing the *Pilgrims' Chorus* from *Tannhäuser*, either.

"In the third place, when you're eleven or twelve or even thirteen and fourteen, it's very important to be a part of a group. Now in music there are some fine groups, like the junior-high choir and band. Maybe you're really scared at having to walk into a roomful of people and speak to each of them when you come home after school to find your mother's bridge club is still there. But when you get behind your baritone horn and forty or fifty other kids are all around you, the music begins, and you forget everything but fitting your own special part into the big sound . . . well, you never even think of being afraid. Somehow, hanging on to that horn helps. Then one of those marching scale-wise passages comes along, and you can give it all you've got . . . this is one of the times when you can really get rid of a lot of energy, and no one yells at you to be quiet. There are times, too, when everybody seems to be wrong but you, and days when the whole world is against you. You can take that horn and go into your room and . . . *blow!* After awhile you're not mad at people any more, and when you come out, they don't seem to be as irritated with you.

"Fourth . . . and it's hard for you to say this because you're only a junior high schooler . . . music does strange things to you. Sometimes, after practicing a long time in band or orchestra or choir, just when you've about decided that you're tired of this darned old piece and the oboe keeps squawking on that one note the player can't seem to control, all at once everything clicks; all the fellows and girls seem to jell into an inspired team, and the music comes out the way it's supposed to sound — then suddenly you feel a chill run up and down your spine, just because the music is beautiful, and it says something you feel and want to put into words for yourself, but haven't been able to. You think it's because every kid in the group is giving everything he has . . . everyone is playing over his head, maybe. Then you wonder whether the math teacher isn't wrong . . . because the whole seems to be equal to *more* than the parts!

"This is like the time you went to the county music festival with a gang of kids from your school and played and sang with kids from eight or ten other schools, kids you'd never met before, except when you were trying to beat them at soccer, football, or basketball. There were all kinds of kids in the big band and chorus; some of them were a bit on the sad side as musicians, and the first rehearsal scared you because it was pretty rough. But the night you gave the concert, the hall was jammed with parents and relatives . . . some of them had driven thirty or more miles just to hear the music and see all of you up there on the stage. Funny thing, even though you were only one of a hundred kids, your knees were shaky when the band marched up on the stage, and you had butterflies in your stomach when the director raised his baton.

"Then the first march started, and all the kids were playing away as though nothing else in the world mattered! You didn't know it could sound so good . . . and when you had that two-

measure solo part to play, it came out sweet and kind of relaxed, and it was fun. The guy next to you nudged you when
you finished and you knew he liked it, even if you'd never seen
him until you started playing next to him. All the people liked
the whole thing, too; you could tell, because they clapped and
clapped until the director had you play the last number over
again. Afterwards, riding home with your director in the car
with four other fellows and girls — each fellow had asked
whether he could bring along one particular girl for the ride
back — you asked, 'Are we going to have another of these
festivals next year?' The director sounded pleased, and said,
'Yes, but why? You kids will be in tenth grade next year, and
this is a junior high festival.' You were dead earnest when you
said, 'We want the others to have a chance at this; it was great
meeting the kids from other schools. Did you hear that one
bass from Scottsville and that clarinet player from Smithtown?'

"And the rest of the way back you sang, whatever songs you
wanted to. You kept hearing the music of the concert, though,
for a long time, and the good feeling stayed with you.

"Sometimes it makes you feel good, too, just because you
know something about music. Remember in eighth grade, when
your voice got quite low, and the teacher began showing you
what the bass staff was all about, and how to follow the good,
meaty bass part of the harmony? Then singing hymns in
church, you tried to fit in the bass part, and it sounded good —
the notes you could reach! The other kids in the class noticed
you more, too, when the teacher assigned parts and said, 'Dick,
you may sing the bass part . . . I think you can reach that low
B flat, now.'

"After football practice, too, in the shower room when the
older fellows were harmonizing, you tried singing with them
once or twice, and when they noticed you were singing, they
slapped you on the back and said, 'Come on, kid, help us out!'
Even the coach liked it when all of you sang on the bus coming
back after games; and when you lost a tough one, he said, 'Well,
even if you couldn't play ball tonight, you sure can sing!' "

As teachers, we wish our pupils would tell us, once in a while, the thoughts that are going through their heads about what makes utilitarian sense in our music classes. But junior-high boys and girls are not very articulate in their day-to-day living. True, gradually the extreme restlessness of the preadolescent vanishes, if sometimes only through the sheer force of adult authority; even the difference between seventh graders and eighth graders is marked. If the unrest has not found constructive channels of expenditure in keeping with the nature of junior-high-school pupils, it finds others not so desirable. So, behavior which is generally diffuse and rather incoherent in seventh grade appears more consistently patterned in the eighth; extremes of emotional color are obvious both inside and outside of the classroom. The frustrated ones are more likely to be sullen and withdrawn, or openly rebellious and indifferent. The insecurity of the changing voice may produce dubious musical results in a formal situation, yet the same group, singing happily without a teacher, in a comfortable self-chosen key, will "give out" to their hearts' content.

LET'S LOOK AT AN UNHAPPY "WORM'S-EYE" VIEW

"I don't like music class. But I have to sit there twice a week. I wish the teacher would let us do something I can do. At home I always turn on the radio, and I never forget to listen to my favorite programs. But the teacher doesn't seem to like my kind of music . . . at least we never have any of it in class. I never heard any of these symphonies and tone poems before I came into this eighth grade . . . The teacher in the last school I attended only had class once a week and just seemed to notice the kids who were good at music and could play an instrument or read notes. Anyhow, we mostly just sang all period. Once or twice this year I thought I was going to catch on to what all those de-re-mi's were about, but I was afraid to ask for fear the other girls in the class would think I was dumb. I don't think all of them know what it's about, either; the teacher keeps calling on the same few all the time when he asks what the key-signature of a song is. If one person knows, he's satisfied. Anyhow, he seems more worried about the boys' voices than the girls', and I guess he doesn't care whether I can't sing the high notes . . . Guess girls' voices are supposed to stay the same, but I used to be able to sing high, and now I feel better when I sing low. Maybe there's something wrong with me.

"I don't think I can ever catch up with all the things the teacher seems to want us to know. A page of music is full of signs I don't understand. Once a boy[5] who was a caddy in his spare time asked the teacher what that sign was that looked like two golf clubs, one right side up and one upside down. Everybody looked to see what it was, and the teacher seemed to have some trouble finding it. But after he did, he explained to us that it was a "natural" and showed us on the piano how it worked. We took turns finding natural signs in songs, and the teacher helped us sing them and play them in the song; we used the piano, too. Everybody got interested, and I was surprised when the bell rang at the end of the period. That was something I could understand — it did look like two golf clubs!

"I wish I could get in the Glee Club. Maybe I'd get to know more of the kids that way. But only a few were asked to try out for it. I'd be too scared anyhow, I suppose. But Dad says my voice sounds pretty when I sing around the house. Probably isn't good enough for Glee Club. I wonder how it feels to be up on the stage singing for the whole school in assembly . . . ."

This might be a sample of the things an eighth-grade girl thought were nonutilitarian in her music class.

The truth is that if through atomic energy or a related force some machine were invented which would permit teachers to X-ray what was going on in the minds of their pupils during the class period, there would be hundreds of cases of shock and disillusionment, and teaching would thereupon improve one

---

[5] This incident is discussed again in Chapter 5, from the teacher's viewpoint in relation to the development of music reading skills.

hundred per cent in a startlingly short time — out of sheer necessity! We do not help our boys and girls develop their musical potential as they should and could simply because we do not know them well enough. Yet, they are our job and at least one of our reasons for taking up space in the world. When a teacher complains that his work is a thankless task, perhaps it is because there is not very much his pupils *can* thank him for.

LET THEM SOUND OFF — IN MUSIC!

Someone has observed that our junior highers are wired for sound. Most of us would agree that, in addition to this, they possess an abundance of self-generated power. In the music program this should add up to a forceful musical sound-off. But the key factor is the teacher's role: He must connect the power to the music and release it. Some teachers flick the switch, and the music pours out. Others do so and get only a series of clicks, grumbles, and other unpleasant adolescent (and preadolescent) sounds.

Perhaps what these unsuccessful teachers forget is that learning is a two-way process: *from* and *to*. Most music teachers have three strikes against them to begin with, like other teachers; first, they are already interested in the subject they are paid to teach, and second, they are adults, and have learned, presumably, the fine art of getting along in school. Junior-high-school children are still naive enough to ignore the latter for the most part and let the chips fall where they may. With regard to the first strike, as music teachers we are likely to assume either that the children *are* interested in music since it is so interesting to us, or that they should be, for the same reason. Unhappily, this assumption does not prove itself in practice: Children are interested in many things, one of which *may* be music. It doesn't have to be.

The very fact that children are involuntary participants in our music classes is a third strike against us. If you stand outside a junior high school at 8 A.M. on a school day and watch the children approaching the school, then return at 3 P.M. and watch them leaving, there is an obvious difference in the situation. To be on the safe side, we teachers must assume that it's our job to capture and hold the interest of our pupils in music. It is something like getting a hold of the lion's tail and being afraid to let go except that here, if we stop holding on for a day, the less interested may slink away to the solitude of their own thoughts, instead of exhibiting active antagonism, and begin to watch the trucks go by outside, or count the number of television antennae on nearby houses. Remember, they don't *have* to be interested!

WHAT TEACHERS MUST KNOW ABOUT PUPILS

The business of trying to remember how it felt to be of junior-high-school age is a difficult one. One reason for this is that both adolescents and their slightly younger fellows differ as individuals. The state of adolescence is a highly introverted one, and while we may remember how we ourselves felt during that period, we cannot remember too clearly, or know too certainly, how many of our classmates felt. All that remains is an impression of the way the fellows and girls in our particular gang behaved — most of their deep feelings were kept secret. During adolescence, putting up a front is very important; even if we don't feel self-confident and secure, we pretend. So a process of memory-searching and retrospection cannot help us teachers to tell much about our pupils.

Yet, to start the music pouring out, we must know a great deal about these children who sit in our classes. To accomplish this, to get to know about them as soon as possible, there are a number of techniques which may be employed:

1. We can get them to tell us about themselves. This is very important in the kind of teaching which will be discussed in the following chapters. Individual interviews are helpful because as we have said, adolescents, in individual behavior, display different traits than in groups. The group behavior they have learned from their earliest school days follows them into

adult life. This behavior is quite often a play between dominant and less decisive personalities; as stated in the first chapter, the latter follow along at times because they admire traits which they themselves lack, especially when it comes to challenging an adult who represents authority. Person to person, we are much more likely to obtain a clear picture of the child than by observing his group behavior, although both are significant. Therefore, the individual conference or interview is likely to give us a better glimpse into the true nature of our pupils.

Here is an example of what may be learned in an individual conference: In an eighth-grade class the teacher noticed that one boy consistently refrained from joining in singing activities. After a few weeks, he asked the boy in a conferᵉnce after school why he did not sing. He received a straightforward answer when the lad replied, "Last year I went to a different school. There was a big boy in our class, bigger than most of us, and he kept singing lower than the rest of the class. That old witch of a teacher kept making him stand up and sing alone. All the other kids used to stare at him. I made up my mind that when my voice got lower I wasn't going to sing any more — I don't want any of that stuff to happen to me in front of the rest of the kids!"

This is the kind of thing no boy would tell a teacher in front of a class. But after he learned that no one would be forced to sing alone, and that the teacher understood what was happening when boys sang lower than the rest of the class, he was reassured enough to begin singing.

Unfortunately, classes are often so large that several months of the school year may pass before a teacher is able to schedule interviews with all his pupils. An inventory technique is useful in helping the teacher form an immediate general picture of the individuals in his class. Pupils may be asked to fill out an inventory form similar to the one illustrated. (See example.) This is an inventory of background, interests, hobbies, leisure-time activities, and reactions to music.

Occasionally, individuals may resent some of the inventory

PUPIL'S MUSIC AND INTEREST INVENTORY FORM
JUNIOR-HIGH-SCHOOL MUSIC

Name_____Grade_____Home room_____
Age_____Home address_____
Father's occupation_____Mother's occupation_____
(if employed)
School attended last year_____
Have you ever taken lessons on a musical instrument?_____
Instrument_____
If so, for how many years?_____
Do you have a piano in your home?_____A phonograph?_____TV?_____
A radio?_____Name any other instruments in your home._____
If your father or mother or any of your sisters or brothers play an
instrument or sing, please tell about them briefly._____
_____
_____
_____
Would you like to learn to play an instrument?_____If so, does any
particular instrument interest you?_____
What things do you like to do most, in school and out of school?_____
_____
Tell about your hobbies, games you enjoy, books you have read and
liked, or anything that seems to you to be fun and worth doing._____
_____
Do you like to sing in class and outside of school?_____What kind
of songs do you enjoy most?_____
Do you enjoy listening to records?_____Why?_____
_____
What would you especially like to do in music class?_____
_____
What radio or TV programs do you like best?_____
_____
_____
_____
_____

questions. One boy asked, after examining such a form, "Aren't
you getting a little personal in some of these questions?" The
teacher assured him that he need not answer any question he

considered an invasion of his privacy. Interestingly, this boy was a new pupil in the school who afterwards came to the teacher and, in an individual conference, told a long history of never having been able to sing "in tune" with other children.

Teachers must be careful to present the inventory in such a way that pupils will not feel they are being put in a spotlight for the purpose of revealing their weaknesses. It is quite possible to discuss the matter with the class sympathetically so they will realize that, in giving information, they are really helping the teacher. (In passing, it should be noted that pupils like a fair exchange; the teacher should tell every new class, when the right time comes, something about himself. One girl was overheard saying to a friend, as they watched two teachers laughing and talking in the hall between classes, "Teachers seem different outside of class; they laugh and seem to have fun." A wistful and revealing comment on a teacher was once made by a little girl who had been in the first grade for only a week. She said, "Our teacher never smiles at *us*. She only smiles when the principal comes in the room.") Pupils are more likely to give complete and accurate information if rapport has been established between class and teacher.

2. With an extroverted class, a group discussion of the interests of the class, their homes, brothers and sisters, and so forth, helps the class members to discover mutual interests and become acquainted with one another. This seems to be more effective with seventh- than with eighth- or ninth-grade pupils. For the purpose of putting the class at ease it may be used as a preliminary step to filling in the inventory form.

In both the written inventory and the preliminary group discussion techniques, pupils sometimes deliberately withhold information. Boys who have had piano lessons, but are afraid other boys may think it is a "sissy" activity, may make no mention of such musical experience. Pupils who are afraid they may be called upon to perform will conceal information about playing ability, usually because they have had unhappy experiences in being "pushed" into playing for groups.

On the other hand, pupils at times may put down some items of information concerning their musical experiences that have no basis of fact. In organizing a class "play-day" (each member of the class was asked to do either individually or as part of a group whatever he felt he could for a musical program), a teacher noticed on a pupil-inventory form that one girl had said she played the harmonica. He talked with the pupil privately, and she volunteered to play a solo. Fortunately, before the class period arrived, the teacher asked the girl to bring her harmonica in at noon for a private rehearsal and discovered that she had never played one in her life! Together they worked out a substitute activity using the Autoharp. (Later the girl bought a harmonica and learned to play it, with the help of a few lunch-hour lessons from the teacher!) Desire for status and prestige in the opinion of the teacher and classmates may occasionally lead to overstatement on the part of a few students.

Making allowances for such possibilities, the teacher has in his hands a potent tool for reaching his class through the inventory technique. By tabulating the various items he arrives at a composite picture of the class. He can quickly note which pupils are about average in their background of musical experience, and which are definitely above or below. He can note groups with special interests. For example, a "blood and thunder" group often appears in the eighth grade. This shows in the pupils' selection of radio and television programs — mysteries, westerns, and stories of high adventure. It also shows in the choice of books read. With regard to these boys and girls, teachers commonly take one of two viewpoints. They may say, "This group is already being overstimulated by their radio and television experiences," or they may say, "Since this seems to be a gripping interest, perhaps we can relate it to some of the songs we sing and the music we hear in class." The first reaction may be a good one; perhaps they *are* overstimulated. But at this age, it accomplishes little to ignore their likes and dislikes, because the background from which they have been developed cannot be replaced in a week or a month.

It may be, too, that such tastes develop from use of devital-ized music in the classroom. Many of our junior-high-school students are typically restless. The teacher must meet fire with fire in the choice of vigorous materials; the "blood and thunder" group may respond better to Moussorgsky's *A Night on Bald Mountain* than to a symphony, or prefer the exciting *The Erl King* (*Der Erlkönig*) of Schubert to *Who Is Sylvia?* (*An Silvia*).

It may be that we overlook the correlation of music with active interests of junior-high-school pupils. Take the matter of hobbies, which are often at their peak in junior high school in the form of collections. Here the teacher may find both boy and girl stamp and coin collectors, and girls who have collections of dolls in different national costumes. A boy or girl who is asked to bring his collection to class, display, and discuss it, is re-ceiving salutary recognition. The correlation with music is obvious; each of the above-named collections represents dif-ferent countries and is a starting point for a unit or project during which the class may study the folk and composed music of various nations.

Other items on the inventory will furnish the teacher with many leads he can follow in learning to know his pupils. Some teachers like to note in their roll-books a few items from these inventories, so that there is a ready means of individual identi-fication and relation of interests to music during the class. Like adults, children are happier when they are made to feel a bit "special." By remembering particular interests and accomp-lishments, it is easy to give pupils a feeling of individual im-portance instead of the feeling, so frustrating to a child who is beginning to realize that he must eventually stand on his own feet, of being just another name on the roll.

When we use pupil-interests in connection with our teach-ing of music, we are more likely to get a musical sound than just the click — or a series of grumbles — when we try to re-lease pupil-power in music.

3. In addition to the inventory and discussion techniques

the anecdotal record is often used. This consists of jotting down behavior and achievement observations of individual pupils and is a valuable means of learning to know how pupils are similar and dissimilar, what they are like in the classroom and, when observation is possible, outside. A convenient way of keeping anecdotal records is to have a 3" x 5" card for each boy and girl; as often as he can, the teacher writes on the card items which seem significant. Such comments as the following might be included:

Rockham, John   Age 12   Grade 7   Section III
    9/27/52   Brought in record of his favorite march.
    9/30/52   Volunteered to sing in trio.
  10/14/52   Disturbed boy next to him by excessive talking.
  10/16/52   Told me after class he had a "new baby sister."

By adding notes on behavior which seem significant, and even by noting regularly items which do not seem too important at the time, the teacher builds a composite picture of the behavior patterns of his individual students. If, in going over such anecdotal records, he finds that for several students he has made very few entries, this very fact indicates to him that they may need more individual attention. In fact, they may be unnoticed because of co-operative, routine behavior, or they may purposely withdraw from the class situation to avoid attracting attention to themselves. Pupils in the latter group may be said to have adopted "protective coloring" — they go through the motions of classroom activities, but without much real interest, and often are facing more serious problems of personal adjustment than are pupils who display the annoying type of behavior which most teachers associate with so-called problem children. Anecdotal records do consume time, and the observations of the teacher must be recorded while still fresh in his mind. They are, however, invaluable in their potential for constructive use as signposts pointing to individual needs.

    4. A more remote source of information about the members

of music classes and musical organizations lies in the cumulative record of each pupil kept by many schools from first grade on. This record folder, passed along from grade to grade as the pupil advances, contains information relating to his scores on intelligence and other standardized tests, academic achievement, behavior patterns, and any items teachers have thought significant enough to record, plus the usual information relating to age, place of birth, other schools attended, home, parents, nationality, siblings, serious illnesses, et cetera. When such a cumulative record has been conscientiously kept, it can help the junior-high-school teacher locate the roots of behavior and adjustment problems. (Teachers should not allow themselves to be prejudiced by information in such records, however.)

5. A fourth source of information about pupils lies in teacher and parent interviews. In junior high school, pupils have many different teachers. Sometimes we find that a pupil is apparently well adjusted in one class and poorly adjusted in another, a fact that should suggest constructive channels of action to the teacher. Or we may learn that a boy or girl is seemingly out of step with the whole school situation. In either case, where several teachers work together in an attempt to find ways of helping a pupil, results are likely to be better than where each teacher hews strictly to his own lines.

Parent interviews are as valuable as pupil and teacher interviews. But by the time a boy or girl reaches the junior-high-school age, he is often no longer eager to have his parents visit the school. The pupil peer-group frowns upon this; too often parent visits are associated in the child's mind with trouble or, just as bad, with apple-polishing. Distrust and suspicion of adults is often a part of the adolescent and preadolescent pattern of development. . . . If our parents visit the teacher, it means that we cannot stand upon our own feet — "that's baby stuff!" Parents, too, are likely to be somewhat on the defensive when sought out by teachers, due to the fact that most of the times when this happens it is because the child is having trouble in school. *Too few teachers seek out parents to report favorably on a child's progress;* likewise, the attitude of many parents is that the school's business is its own, and that "no news is good news." Yet, the disturbing problems of junior high schoolers can be solved best when teachers and parents work together harmoniously from a positive basis of preventing problems, rather than from a remedial basis after problems have arisen.

6. A fifth source of information about boys and girls should not be overlooked — observation through association with them outside of the school situation. By attending school-sponsored social affairs, canteens, Teen-Age Community Clubs, and by organizing class parties or picnics, teachers can learn more about the adolescent patterns of behavior than they can ever hope to learn through classroom observation in the school situation. In informal activities, teacher pressure is off, and boys and girls are mainly concerned about their relationships with the peer-group. Here their guards are down, and they are more likely to reveal themselves in characteristic action and attitudes. Although they may scoff at the idea of interest in teacher attendance at such affairs, they often inquire of teachers whether or not they "are going to be there." This is really asking, "Are you our friend, or just our teacher?" The teacher who is truly interested in his pupils will manage to attend some of their social functions.

KNOWLEDGE OF PUPILS AS A GUIDE TO TEACHING

From the sources mentioned, the teacher can obtain and organize information about his pupils so that he has available three guides to his teaching:

1. A clear picture of individual differences.
2. A composite picture of the fundamental group interests.
3. Some conclusions regarding the outstanding characteristics of the age-groups he is teaching.

In the materials chosen for use in his classes, and in the methods used to develop them, these three guides will help the teacher bridge the gap between his adult views and values, and those of his students. To go back to the opening discussion of this section of the chapter, pupils have no way of getting to their teachers, although learning is a two-way process, *except at the will of the teacher.* Once the teacher opens the circuit through the above means, the current begins flowing from the teacher *to* the pupil, and just as important, from the pupil back to the teacher. This is a chain reaction, too, in that it flows from one pupil to another, making possible an infinite number of varying and interesting reactions to musical materials. Through his understanding of and use of the three guides we have cited, the teacher simultaneously creates a unity in the class and a security of environment. It may be true that junior-high pupils are ready for a musical sound-off, but a three-way switch is in the hands of the teacher; he is the only one who can connect music to each pupil's self-generated power.

INTERESTING PUPILS IN THEIR VOICES

As an example of this, let's take one of the age characteristics that would be a part of guide number 3 (listed previously). We know that boys and girls in the junior high school are intent upon establishing themselves as individuals. This means that they are interested in what is happening to them personally. Changes are taking place in the voice of each adolescent pupil. Each, whether or not he is in the band or orchestra, possesses the most personal instrument of all — a voice. This may be suffered as an embarrassing and undependable part of adolescence, or it may be accepted as an interesting and normal part of the growing-up process. A changing-voice chart may be designed to interest and help each child follow the changes taking place in his voice and in the voices of his classmates. Picturing clearly the voice in its relationship to the staff and the keyboard, this project should be initiated by a frank discussion of what happens when voices change. Each pupil is then helped to locate the range of his voice and draw it on the chart. (In one class pieces of colored yarn attached to the cardboard chart were used.) The chart is kept in a conspicuous place in the classroom. As a voice changes in range, the pupil indicates the change by adjusting his range-line on the chart. Boys and girls become interested in their individual voices. Boys who have been reluctant to sing now learn to follow their voice range on the piano keyboard, and a few may even go to the piano the first thing each morning to check their singing range; some members of the class may do the same thing upon entering the classroom. As soon as the range of voices appears upon the chart, a wide difference is apparent, and no one worries about what is happening to his voice; those boys, for instance, who have a limited range understand that this is only temporary. Not only does this project help the teacher to follow the changing voices more accurately, but it results in certain musical learnings in connection with associating the range of the voice with staff and keyboard. Above all, it gives each pupil an interest in something which is his alone and different from that possessed by anyone else: his voice. Yet, at the same time, each is reassured to find that his vocal problems are shared by others.

ESTABLISHING CONTINUITY AND UNITY
IN THE MUSIC CLASS

Another point which makes the preceding type of activity desirable in the junior-high-school classroom is that it may sustain interest throughout a whole school year, thus lending continuity and unity to classes which meet only once or twice a week. This is desirable since we know that boys and girls of preadolescent and adolescent age need to be identified with groups or gangs. A music class can hardly be considered a gang, but it is a group, although membership is involuntary. If the activities of the class are attractive and interesting enough to form a real part of the child's life, and if the group is unified through a high level of self-activity and identification with the class on the part of its members, the adolescent desire to belong is partly satisfied. To be more explicit, boys and girls must want to come to music class and must look forward to it as pleasurable activity rather than as just another forty-five or fifty minutes of school time which they must endure.

This is one reason why units and projects have been used so successfully in music classes. Here is a type of activity which not only continues from class period to class period, but it also stimulates self-activity and initiative on the part of the pupil, thus helping to develop his power of expression.

An example of a unit that provides a means of personal identification and also a sense of continuity might be called the "Emigration Unit," or "From What Country Did Your Ancestors Come to America?" Using a large wall map of the world, map pins are inserted in the countries where parents, grandparents, or other relatives were born. The class then hears a composition or sings a song chosen by each student to represent the national origin of his family. This finds an association in class discussion with the difference in folkways of the United States and other countries; it may, with skillful handling by the teacher, establish pride in national heritage in children who represent minority groups.

The use of folk music in this unit is important because of its emphasis on universal human experiences. Through it boys and girls begin to understand that whatever the country from which their forefathers came, its people are not altogether different from the people of our own country, and their emotions, fundamentally the same as ours, have also found expression in music. All of us are involved in similar problems, so the family relationship, love, hate, war, and death, which concern us today, are not new song subjects; people have been singing about them for hundreds of years. The torch singer wails that her love went away and left her; this is the burden of a popular song. But the troubadour sang a similar refrain eight hundred years ago.

This same unit readily develops a fundamental principle of democracy as it exists in the United States; we are comparative newcomers, as history judges time, to our land. If we go back far enough, we find that all our forefathers were immigrants, and all of them had one goal in mind: living in a country where a better way of life was possible. The descendant of a Jamestown settler and the newest refugee from a totalitarian state have this in common. This is what the United States means.

Continuity over a series of classes is also provided by projects that occupy only a small part of each class period. Sometimes attitudes or statements by pupils help to cue the teacher in initiating such projects, as in the case of one used with a class of seventh-grade pupils who announced as soon as they reported for their first music class that they did not want to learn anything about reading music. The teacher, instead of reacting negatively, discussed the matter in a friendly way with them, as he would have discussed the observation that they did not like spinach, and discovered they were not convinced that there was any good reason why they should learn to read music. He thought that they were not quite sure just what the process of reading music was, and that the root of their aggressive attitude lay partly in lack of motivation and partly in insecurity. From the frank attitude and open discussion he decided that they had failed to accomplish enough in their previous music reading efforts to satisfy themselves, and being thus frustrated, had become defensive. (Children sometimes do naturally what great generals have advocated; the best defense is an attack. So — the announced resistance: "We do not want to learn to read music!")

After several weeks, during which no direct reference was made to the reading of music, the class came in one day and immediately noticed that measures of music, labelled "Mystery Tune," had been written on the board. This happened to be a very active seventh-grade class, and the boys and girls crowded together around the board. Some attempted at once to hum the tune, and some began firing questions about the "Mystery Tune" at the instructor. In response he told them that every time they came to class there would be a mystery tune on the

44982

board for them to "decipher." "The musical notation is a code," he told them, "and it tells us how a tune sounds. This one is a tune you all know; by noticing the direction in which the notes move on the staff, perhaps you can figure it out."

Nothing was said in direct reference to the reading of music. The first tune proved to be *America,* which several pupils recognized after two or three minutes. A few classes later, questions began to come from the class members who had not succeeded in identifying a tune: "How can we tell what tune it is?" "How is it that John (a member of the class) always knows what the tune is before anyone else?" Here was a direct invitation from members of the class to help them develop reading ability.

This chapter does not include a discussion of reading skills; rather, the example has been used because the "Mystery Tune" proved to be something the majority of the class looked forward to identifying in each meeting, and also because the "Mystery Tune" title was a means of interesting pupils in a learning process that they thought they had decided to reject. Naturally, it did not take much of the time of each period; after several months the class had transferred techniques, learned in solving these tunes, to the regular song learning activities of the class, and the "tune-guessing" was discontinued.

For this particular class, the mystery tune routine was a "natural"; it provided the incentive for a continuing experience in learning the significance of music notation. Like the weekly radio programs some of the class listened to, it was always there at the same time, but always different. (The first few tunes were very familiar, and easily recognized, to insure success on the part of the majority of the class.) We believe that the use of the popular terminology was justified in that it made the music class a more interesting place to be, remained in the minds of the pupils from class to class (almost a week elapsed between meetings of this class), and led to musical learnings.

It is easy to see that the teacher of this class might have incurred a severe case of combat fatigue if he had attempted to force these pupils to continue their music reading efforts at the time of their announced resistance. Instead, he looked at his pupils, analyzed their situation, and found a solution which everyone enjoyed. This was a class to which pupils really did rush because they wanted to try deciphering the "Mystery Tune." It is an excellent example of releasing energy, or tapping the source of power, through constructive means.

Continuity in classes may be developed by relating the out-of-school activities of pupils with music class. In a class which was working on a voice type unit, this conversation took place at the beginning of the period:

First pupil: Mr. Brown, did you see the cover of *Life* magazine this week? Patrice Munsel's picture is on it! We heard a record of her singing last week!

Teacher: Yes — and did you open up the magazine and see what was written about her?

NAZARETH COLLEGE
LIBRARY

Second pupil: There were colored pictures of opera — I saw them.
Third pupil: Once I saw Risë Stevens on television at my grandmother's . . . . We heard her on a record last week, too.
Teacher: I didn't see her on television, but I have heard her on the Firestone program on the radio. Has anyone else in the class heard her?

This carry-over from radio and television undoubtedly made the classroom musical experiences seem more vivid, and in this case served as a review of previous classroom experiences while leading into immediate ones.

The problem of maintaining continuity from one class to another will always be particularly important for classes that meet only two or three times a week, but music teachers *can* find musical threads interesting enough to run through the week-to-week activities of any class, and so hold them together. Unless this is done, the class is likely to feel that its meetings are a series of stones set in a stream where the current is so fast there is no means of progressing from one to another. Life does go on at a rapid pace for junior-high-school pupils whether or not music class is meeting.

SEX DIFFERENCES IN ATTITUDES TOWARD MUSIC

The majority of experienced teachers will tell you that most of the dissenters in music classes are boys. Girls seem more willing to go along with the classroom activities, even when they do not enjoy them. This is easy to understand; from their earliest training, the majority of boys are encouraged to be aggressive and to display qualities of leadership — the fact that some do and some don't still does not negate this. Generations of getting their way by less overt means still show in the girls' surface display of consent to authority. Such assentation does not mean that they are always happier in music class than are the boys. At adolescence the girls' nervous energy finds different outlets than does that of the boys.

Another factor which works toward a more boisterous attitude on the part of the adolescent boy is the fact that he is being pushed toward participation in body-contact sports as a means of establishing himself in the group, so we can scarcely expect him to display aggressive, masculine behavior on the football field and passive, "ladylike" behavior in the classroom. Typically feminine traits tend to produce one type of classroom behavior in girls; typically masculine traits work to produce another type in boys. Both are part of the natural process of maturing. Unfortunately, the masculine pattern in its noisier aspects is harder for teachers to accept than is the feminine pattern. Yet, the tremendous aliveness and vitality of adolescent boys is the most potent kind of energy for the music program. They are fully as sensitive as the girls in their reactions to music, and once they find in it a source of emotional satisfaction, it serves as a compensating force for the many times they must make a show of rough-and-tumble behavior they really do not feel, but must pretend to feel because they are trying to prove to themselves and the rest of the world that they can fit the masculine role.

We must give boys virile material in music — "muscled" material. A boy who learns to sing the tenor or bass part of a song has succeeded in doing a masculine thing, that is, he has established himself with credit in a manly role. This makes him feel good, and he is then willing to go along with other classroom activities. He definitely wants to be different from girls, so he wants his songs to reflect his masculine role and his singing to be robust and solid. However, just at this time his voice has become a somewhat unpredictable instrument that is likely to betray him when he would most like it to support his intense emotions.

If a teacher does not understand what is happening to boys at this point, their self-generated power is short-circuited into undesirable behavior, and the music class becomes an unhappy place for teacher and pupil alike. Again we say, teachers should speak the language of the pupils in terms of activities and interests they already know and like. A teacher may say to a boy, in explaining how he goes from his changed voice into his falsetto, "This is like shifting gears on a car!" and the boy immediately understands what is meant. In explaining the rhythmic feeling of singing a sixteenth note followed by a dotted eighth, he may say, "The sixteenth note is like a feint in boxing," and demonstrate it . . . the boys will feel what is meant, and the girls will be interested as spectators. Or the teacher may say, "This phrase lifts like a plane taking off." Technical terms may bore them, particularly if they lack an apperceptive background of musical experiences. We music teachers can so easily talk over the heads of our pupils, or — so easily speak in a language they understand!

A boy rejects more quickly what does not interest him than does a girl. Again, this goes back to a life pattern; he is often busier outside the home and school than a girl, and less closely supervised by parents. From the time he first leaves home to attend school, the limits of a boy's activities may be more extensive than are those of a girl. He has a wider choice of activities in many communities and schools, so he can better afford to take his choice. If he does not like one thing, he may simply withdraw mentally from it and spend the classroom time he is forced to allot it daydreaming about the activities which do interest him. The withdrawal pattern is just as hard or harder to solve than the aggressive pattern, since the former does not display itself in overt action.

The solution seems to lie in an understanding of what makes boys tick. They are interested in action rather than verbalism. They want the "muscled" songs to which we have referred to approximate the satisfactory outlet of a stiff baseball game or wrestling match. They want to be allowed to use initiative and self-direction in the choice of materials, and they particularly want to feel that engaging in musical activities is a manly thing to do.

In brief, we help boys establish themselves in music by relating it to their other activities and interests, by choosing material they can sing and hear with personal satisfaction, and by treating them as growing young men rather than as children. Through music we can help them psychologically in their growth toward adulthood.

The problem with regard to girls is almost exactly the opposite to that of boys. We must be careful not to neglect them in the classroom. This happens frequently when teachers are so busy with the problems of the boys' changing voices and their more openly expressed likes and dislikes that there is little time left for the girls. Many teachers overlook the fact that girls' voices change, and due to the more restrained behavior of girls in general, also overlook the urgency of the problems faced by adolescent girls. It is a strange phenomenon of adult psychology that a group of boys appearing before the public in musical performance is likely to receive much greater attention and applause than a group of girls, even though the girls may do a better musical job. Perhaps this is due to the less inhibited manner of boys; they often seem more natural than do the girls, despite the obviously freshly scrubbed appearance and unusual suits and ties. In all fairness, we must admit that the girls deserve at least an equal amount of our time and attention, since growing into well-adjusted womanhood is just as difficult a problem as is growing into manhood. They, too, need materials related to their interests and activities, which furnish emotional outlets.

But the real facts of the boy-girl situation in music classes are that girls will go along with what the boys like because the mores of our culture push them in this direction, and that if we must veer to one side or the other in our choice of musical materials, it should be to the side of the boys. Girls like the materials boys like when it is vigorous and musical. *But remember, it should be musical.* There is no justifiable reason for using "cheap music" with these boys and girls. Gradually boys want more and more music which does not have to be characterized by lively melodies; this is a sign of musical growth. But it, like all growth processes, is gradual.

INTERESTS OF JUNIOR-HIGH-SCHOOL PUPILS

One of the best ways of learning to know a boy or girl is through out-of-school interests. Since we believe that everything about the child is important in giving us clues to the most expedient ways of attracting his attention musically, it is suggested that each junior-high-school teacher should survey these interests and relate them as often as possible to the selection and development of musical materials. Hobbies and interests of junior-high-school pupils include the following: looking at television, listening to radio programs (mysteries are very popular); sports, hiking, camping, fishing, riding horseback; owning dogs, cats, and other pets; games of many kinds, dancing, collecting (including stamps, hotel soap, postcards, dolls, miniature horses, seashells, coins, books, cards with pictures of movie stars or baseball players); handcraft, building model planes or automobiles, drawing, music, radio repairing, cooking, reading, movies, and sometimes items such as mathematics. Listening to music on the radio or television is neither at the top of the list in popularity nor at the bottom.

The list as a whole indicates that these boys and girls enjoy doing things which engage their physical energies, and a high level of interest in collecting suggests that this meets a definite need for ownership of something peculiarly the property of the collector — "This is something I have gathered together myself; it is *mine*." It also suggests that there is a feeling of satisfaction in building a collection over a period of time, perhaps due to the fact that it furnishes concrete evidence of achievement.

How can these diverse interests be related to music? Through knowledge of materials, imagination, and the ability to perceive relationships — all three on the part of the teacher. Sports, for example, can be related to form in music, or to the part music plays in building up spectator spirit — most children see bands at football games or at circuses. Nature lovers are easily interested in the great wealth of music that stems from the composers' love of the outdoors. Those hobbies based on working with the hands can be used in making simple instruments. *For every interest or hobby there is a relationship with music* which will make some child say to himself, "*Now* I understand it. . . ."

The nature of junior-high-school pupils' interests shows that they will be satisfied only if their musical activities afford avenues of personal expression, engagement of physical energy, and evidence of achievement. In Chapter 3 the discussion of the classroom program, pupil-teacher planning, and evaluating achievement with the class covers this.

LIMITING THE ACTIVITY PROGRAM

As pupils progress through the public schools, their out-of-school activities increase. Junior high school may be for many children the period when they find it difficult to continue with private music lessons because of the pressure of other activities. They tell their parents, "I don't have time to do my homework, go to Boy (or Girl) Scouts, take care of my paper route, and do my practicing too!" It is certainly a good time for teacher, parent, and child to look at the extra-school program and decide just what should be the weight of the load carried. One thing is certain: Most of the junior-high-school boys and girls have more energy than is constructively used, so they need to be busy. That they do not want to be lectured into learning follows in music class as well as in other activities. In fact, they cannot, and will not be. Action is the key to learning for junior-high pupils, and the teacher must provide musical situations in which they can be wholeheartedly active. However, when a child is overloaded he may become tense and nervous, or he may develop a habit of doing things in a sloppy fashion. Some limits should be set for the number of activities carried, but these depend upon the individual. There cannot be an arbitrary limit for a group as a whole.

PUPILS AND CLASSROOM DISCIPLINE

Some readers may be saying to themselves, "All this discussion is well and good, but what we *need* are practical suggestions for handling classroom discipline." For these readers a brief discussion follows.

It is now generally accepted by teachers that the ultimate in discipline is self-discipline. This develops *from the child's desire* to co-operate and conform. Highly desirable as this may be, it is much more elusive in practice than the traditional strong-arm methods which apparently assume that, because an adult supposedly knows what is best for a child, he holds an automatic license to enforce conformity. When applied to certain rebellious individuals (remember that the pupil is usually either smaller than, or inferior in status to, the teacher) this often forces a *show* of conformity which leaves pupils seething within themselves and results in repeated outbreaks of the same undesirable behavior.

Teachers employing such methods have had to resign themselves to a certain disturbing but inevitable number of battle casualties. Few of us actually believe that this is good educational practice; none of us would have it if we knew how to avoid it.

Experienced teachers, by a trial-and-error process, usually acquire techniques of controlling pupil-groups which, they assume, make them "good disciplinarians." But sometimes these techniques are no more than a "bag of tricks" designed to keep pupils in a state of submission, contributing little or nothing to the child's growth in self-discipline. Observers often say of such a teacher, "How well he manages the class!" *They do not say,* "How well the children manage themselves!" Yet the latter is our goal.

If true learning must have a basis of motivation, so must true discipline. This rests upon a mutual understanding and acceptance existing between teacher and pupils. Considerable discussion in this chapter and Chapter 1 has been devoted to the matter of understanding, because it fosters acceptance, which may exist without it, but only on a somewhat shaky basis. After all, any time thirty junior-high-school pupils want to defy a teacher and, for instance, walk out of a room, they can. In numbers and energy they exceed the physical ability of any one individual to prevent it!

Obviously, it is both unrealistic and undemocratic for one person, without regard for the nature, interests, or desires of others, to impose a standard of behavior upon them. Yet, pupils need guidance and rely upon the moral stamina of the teacher to help them develop self-discipline.

Genuine discipline problems are those in which pupils are in conflict with the best interests of the group. Such problems, if unsolved, result in a chaotic classroom situation and certainly work against educational goals.

On the whole, there are as many answers to the problem as there are teachers and pupils. However, a few general suggestions may be offered:

1. Be sure that pupils understand the reasons why certain classroom behavior is expected, and what this behavior is. Talk it over with your pupils. If it makes sense, the majority of the class will accept it. Furthermore, they will assist in developing and maintaining it.

2. An aggressive attitude on the part of the teacher may produce withdrawn and stubborn pupils, or pupils who adopt only an outward semblance of conformity. Expect the best. Look for and build upon good behavior traits, rather than fight undesirable ones. Be generous with praise and approval.

3. The rebellious or defiant child is a troubled child. Seek the underlying causes.

4. Children need to be needed. The noncontributing members of a class, lacking this feeling, may seek self-esteem and group prestige through undesirable behavior channels.

5. Children who are interested and active are rarely behavior problems.

6. Keep class activities moving. Confusion and behavior problems often arise in music classes when going from one activity to another. But don't keep the lid on all the time! (During band, choir, or orchestra rehearsals, remember how

you used to talk with your neighbors between numbers?)

7. De-emphasize the importance of minor behavior problems. No one behaves perfectly all the time; why expect it of pupils?

8. If you find yourself involved in a real discipline problem with a pupil, *let him talk out his side of the problem.* Don't force him into a defensive position. Try to arrive at a solution through mutual understanding. Many teachers find that pupils can, and will, propose satisfactory solutions for such difficulties. A receptive attitude is disarming. Teachers, whom we assume to be mature adults, should behave as such.

9. Be fair — be firm. Pupils expect and need to rely upon these qualities in their teachers. Pupils do *not* expect to "get away with" major offenses.

10. Be consistent. Pupils go from teacher to teacher and must adjust to many different types of classroom discipline. Don't confuse them by vacillation. Instability in the teacher breeds instability in pupils.

In conclusion, notice that expert teachers develop a sensitivity to tension existing within their classes. By this means they note storm warnings and many times prevent major crises, or at least are prepared to handle them if they occur.

SUMMARY

Teachers are disturbed by the restlessness of junior-high-school pupils, yet this is a natural part of the growth process. Seventh graders are typically open-minded about their restlessness but are at the same time willing to be attracted to constructive outlets for it. Eighth graders who have not found a constructive channel for their restlessness may become somewhat resentful of teacher authority and display aggressive attitudes if there is an attempt to force them into musical activities for which they see no reason. Most ninth graders have either found an interest in music or have decided that there's not much use trying, since their previous efforts have been unsuccessful . . . real belligerence may develop in this grade and cause teachers unhappy hours in classes they dread meeting. In such situations all the fun and joy of music vanishes.

Sheer force of authority accomplishes worse than nothing in the junior high school because it leads to the development of negative attitudes. Exerting undue pressure on junior-high-school pupils may cause unhealthy tensions.

Music must make sense to junior-high-school pupils in its relationship to their everyday lives. To learn what makes up these everyday lives, use of conferences, interviews, inventories, anecdotal records, and cumulative school records is suggested. Here we must be careful not to put the child in a category and label him, for he changes, grows into different interests and attitudes, and finally loses those obnoxious traits which caused us such concern. He learns to get along with people. One conference, one parent interview, one inventory may be indicative, but it yields no final, unchanging sum. The challenge of junior-high-school pupils is not to understand them . at any fixed point, but rather to develop an understanding of their growth processes, and to remember that they change from day to day, week to week, and year to year.

Pupils are interested in themselves first of all, because they are striving to become independent. Teachers must find musical activities in which they can succeed; through this, group prestige and security is gained.

Teachers who sidestep the natural interests of boys and girls and attempt to teach music in isolation from these interests are likely candidates for heavy cases of combat fatigue. Almost every junior-high-school pupil has more energy than does the teacher; multiplied by thirty or forty, it is hopeless to struggle against the current; the voltage is too high. When this same power is used to reveal the meaning of music, the junior-high-school years find children achieving musical satisfaction never surpassed in terms of contribution to pupil adjustment.

Boys need virile musical materials and a special understanding of their vocal problems. But in the pressure of this situation, the girls' problems must not be forgotten.

Every child is interested in something, and every interest has a musical implication for the teacher. For some, the music itself is enough, but for others, the relationship between music and other interests must be clearly established before it assumes meaning and importance. Remember, boys and girls *may* like music; they don't *have* to!

3. The General Music Class

It is a source of concern to some teachers that the music work done in the first year of the junior high school appears in some instances to be of lower calibre than does the music work in the last year of the elementary school. But what seems to be retrogression actually may be part of the total adjustment of the child to a new situation. Assuming that the child enters the junior high school after sixth grade, he must adjust to some or all of the following factors:

1. A new school building, bringing with it the problem of becoming familiar with its plan so that he may locate classrooms and reach his assignments on time. Often the factor of a longer distance to travel to school is added, plus a different route.

2. More departmentalization, more teachers. This means more personality adjustments, and adjustments to different ways of teaching.

3. New groupings of classes. (Both this and item 2 lead to a feeling of insecurity in the group until the initial adjustment is made.) This factor has the effect of disturbing the group

65

singing spirit that a class of pupils may have built up over a period of years. The leaders have been dispersed, and new leaders in the class must be established before the singing will proceed with enthusiasm. Also significant here is the apparent drop in level of reading ability. This, too, may be due to the disruption of class leadership. What appears to be good group sight reading in the sixth grade may be good class organization; that is, a case of each singer who is not a good reader knowing, almost unconsciously, whom to follow.

4. Longer class periods, requiring a lengthening of the child's attention span.

5. The appearance of changing voices in the seventh grade.

The shift from grade to junior high school may be likened to moving into a new home with new parents. The period of readjustment involved calls for great patience and understanding on the part of the teacher, who, faced with many new pupils, is having to make his own adjustments to them. Standards of performance and achievement must not be too high but must be adjusted with the total situation in mind. It is difficult for the children themselves to understand why their group morale has changed.

The teacher should not be disturbed if classes entering junior high school do not produce good musical results at once, especially in singing performance. Seventh-grade classes may be disappointed by their apparent retrogression, and part of the classroom planning should include a discussion of the situation.

As a part of the bridging-the-gap process, it is a good practice to invite entering junior-high-school classes to visit the school sometime during the semester preceding their entrance. During this visit they will meet with junior-high-school teachers, explore the building, and learn something of the program they will follow. Such visits build confidence and remove the fear of the unknown, which at times worries children. In such a visit, musical organizations may well find a place on an assembly program.

To summarize this problem, the teacher should bear in mind that he must not only know what the previous musical experiences of the class have been *but also make it evident that he is interested in them.* He must not set a standard beyond the ability level of the class members and must reassure them about their lapse in musical performance (if there is a lapse). Junior-high-school music should be a continuation and expansion of the elementary-school music program; teachers should build upon the latter wherever possible and make evident to pupils the relationship between the two situations.

DEFINITION, SIZE, AND TIME ALLOTMENT

By "General Music Class" is meant the class in which we find a group of junior-high-school pupils on a particular grade level meeting together to study music. The size of such classes varies considerably from school to school, as does the number of times per week the class meets. These two points are important ones, however, so far as the success of the class is concerned. A class of more than thirty pupils is undesirable, because it makes individual evaluation of the pupil difficult for the teacher. A class meeting less than twice a week is undesirable, not only because of the inadequate time limitations it imposes, but also because of the length of time elapsing between the meeting periods of the class. If a class of approximately thirty pupils can be scheduled to meet *three* times a week, the teacher is presented with a favorable situation in which to work.[1]

Although not always required, it seems highly desirable that all pupils in the junior high school should participate in general music classes. The reasons for this are fairly obvious. The junior high school is exploratory in nature; it offers pupils a wide variety of courses in an effort to acquaint them with their own abilities, interests, and talents. As has been noted in a previous chapter, the preadolescent and adolescent years are characterized by emotional needs that music by its very nature is suited to meet. Moreover, music on the senior-high-school level is largely elective; the junior-high-school years are often the end of the pupil's opportunity to identify himself with music. Thus, it is important that he be given an experience with a wide variety of musical activities and experiences during the junior-high-school years and that this opportunity be made available for all students through the required music course.

The suggestions included here for general music classes may be adapted for use either in required or elective classes.

OBJECTIVES OF THE GENERAL MUSIC CLASS:
PUPIL-TEACHER PLANNING

What should be the objectives of the general music class? Certainly they must be broader than those of the traditional, stereotyped general music class (more often known as the "vocal music class"), which seemed to include not much more than the singing of songs, learning (or attempting to learn) to

---

[1] The recommendations discussed herein concerning size and number of meeting periods per week are in substantial agreement with the *MENC Junior High School Curriculum Consultants Report,* September, 1950.

read music, and the memorization of principal themes of well-known musical compositions.

Any good list of objectives should be drawn up by the teacher and class, discussed, and understood by all. Doing this brings the matter into the realm of reality for the child and makes objectives specific and workable. However, it is desirable (and probably inevitable) for the teacher to have in mind a number of general objectives for each class and, in the role of guide, to steer the activities of the class so that both the general objectives, important in the development of continuity of musical growth, and the more specific class-planned objectives and activities, important in self-evaluation and immediate motivation, are compatible. For example, the teacher might have as objectives a list equivalent to the following:

1. Helping each child find some musical activity in which he can participate with satisfaction and some degree of mastery.
2. Building a repertoire of songs the class can sing with musical enjoyment.
3. Building a listening repertoire that is both immediately satisfactory and of lasting musical significance.
4. Developing musical learnings, including reading skills and familiarity with the materials of music-making (instruments of the orchestra, voice types, technical information) through singing, rhythmic, and listening activities.
5. Correlating music with other areas of school activity, and with the child's out-of-school world.

While such objectives as these may be clear in the teacher's mind, in this form they are beyond the child's grasp and interest because they are objectives in the long-term view. The junior-high-school pupil lives from day to day, not as much as do his younger brothers and sisters, it is true, but still to an extent which causes him to place heavy emphasis upon his immediate activities. In clarifying objectives in the child's mind, pupil-teacher planning is an important aid. It utilizes the child's desire, normal at this age, to have a voice in determining his activities. Since this is a democratic procedure, the pupil is encouraged to participate in it actively. Such planning should help the work of the class develop from the intrinsic interests of the children.

Whereas occasionally a pupil by making suggestions which are obviously inappropriate may test the teacher's sincerity in conducting the classroom activities on such a basis, usually the other class members will reject such suggestions. Even in the face of such suggestions, it is important that the teacher, having invited ideas from the class, should treat them with respect. Secure in such respect, the less aggressive and confident members of the class will be encouraged to make their contributions. If we suppose, for the sake of illustration, that the music teacher asks the members of a seventh- or eighth-grade class to list activities in which they are interested, some of the suggestions which might be expected to come from the class are:

1. Singing songs, especially lively songs, or "fast" songs; singing "popular songs."
2. Learning about instruments.
3. Hearing records, especially of music that tells a story (program type).
4. Learning to read music. (This may be difficult for some readers to believe, but it is often forthcoming in a good situation.)
5. Square dancing.
6. Reading stories about music and composers.
7. Having classroom concerts with live performers.

Probably not all these suggestions would come from any one class; perhaps none of them would appear. Certainly there would be wide variations in the wording of the suggestions. The wise teacher, however, will have prepared the class for its planning discussion by talking over with them some of the possible activities of the class and by telling them something of the work of other classes. Teachers inexperienced in the use of the pupil-teacher planning technique sometimes limit their efforts to asking pupils what they would like to do in music class. Because of the wide differences in musical experience and background among junior-high-school pupils, this is much like asking a man who has never been to China how he likes the scenery there. A child in the music class does not know what he would like to do until he has been exposed to a variety of musical adventures and experiences. He reacts in terms of specificities rather than generalities.

How does a teacher go about initiating pupil-teacher planning? This question may be answered by an example: When a music class comes into a room for the first time, its members are curious about the equipment, what their activities will be during the periods the school says they must spend there, and, if he is a stranger to them, what their teacher is like. The teacher, too, should have a lively curiosity concerning the nature of the class; in fact, one of his first objectives will be to learn as much as possible about its members as soon as he can. A good beginning point is to explore the music room's books, musical instruments, pictures, phonograph, and other accessories. This may be done informally, perhaps through a "how many musical objects in the room do you recognize" game, with a time limit, after which the members of the class explain the use of these objects. Or perhaps the teacher will prefer to explain to class members the various equipment with which they will work. The former approach has the advantage of bringing about class participation. The teacher will want to discuss with the class previous activities in music classes and also to get from them their reactions to school in general.

After such an exchange of viewpoints, the teacher and his pupils should feel at home with each other; for example, the boy or girl who sees an Autoharp in the room and shows the class how it is played has immediately gained security in the situation and has helped his classmates to do so. The teacher can pick up many leads through such a procedure, all of which will help him in planning with and for the class; in fact, through it pupil-teacher planning often has a good beginning.

Another specific example may help clarify our discussion.

Boys and girls like to see concrete evidence of class achievement. It is also believed that a desirable method of raising the level of class participation and achievement is to have constructive criticism come from the pupils as well as from the teacher. One example of a way to satisfy both objectives is through the use of a class "Song Bag." As carried out in one school where several junior-high-school music teachers have worked with the idea, the procedure is this: A "Song Bag" is made by covering a cardboard form with burlap, bound at the neck with brightly colored twine, and labelled "Song Bag." The class then discusses the project and its objective, which is to place the name of each song, printed on a cardboard note (which may be half, whole or otherwise) on the song bag when the song is sung acceptably by the class. In this way the cumulative repertoire of the class becomes visible. The next step is to decide just how the class will interpret "sung acceptably." The class may set up certain standards, such as these:

1. The song must be sung correctly, and with good tone quality.
2. Everyone in the class must join in singing the song.
3. One verse should be sung from memory.
4. The song should be sung in the right mood, according to the composer's markings and the spirit of the words and music.

These requirements or standards vary according to the class that is setting them up. The teacher participates in the discussion, which may be led by him or by the class chairman.

Once the standards are agreed upon and accepted by the entire class, a committee is elected to judge when the song is ready to go "into the bag." This committee is changed frequently, so that all members of the class will have a chance to serve on it. When the class indicates its singing is ready to be judged, the committee listens to the singing of the song and renders a verdict, giving reasons why it does or does not believe the song is "sung acceptably."

In addition to developing values with regard to singing, this procedure is democratic. Members of the class who do not co-operate often find class pressure working to help them get into the right spirit. In the classes where the project has been used, the "Song Bag" has often proved to be one of the proudest posessions of the class. One of the authors once walked into a classroom where members of other subject classes had been amusing themselves by removing the notes bearing the song titles (usually thumbtacked on the "Song Bag"), and found a large and angry sign posted by the class members on the bulletin board: "We enjoy our Song Bag. Please do not disturb it!" Ample proof of its success!

Pupil participation in planning has been criticized as leading to "aimless" and "spotty" learning. But this can be avoided if the teacher keeps in mind the general goals for the class and guides the work at hand so that it is progressing in terms of these goals while using the activities and materials chosen by the pupils themselves. Certainly, children seem to learn most effectively in situations where they are free to express their own ideas, make their own discoveries, develop insights, and perceive relationships through active participation.

Furthermore, the teacher with a background of experience and careful observation can determine approximately what the content and procedures of the general music class will be, and this without eliminating the element of pupil participation. Through the pupil-inventory blanks discussed in Chapter 2, the teacher has a rough evaluation of his class with reference to musical background, basic interests, hobbies, and music in the home. He is aware of the range of musical activities which may be carried on in the general music class. He knows the amount of time that is available for the class work. For more information concerning individual pupils he may refer to the cumulative records which most schools keep for every pupil. He knows, or has access to, the intelligence scores of his pupils.

All these sources of information provide him with a broad framework within which he, with the aid of his pupils, sets up a class program where the three basic activities are singing, listening, and rhythmic activities. From these many others may develop naturally. A characteristic of this type of program is that in different music classes on the same grade level activities may vary considerably with regard to the choice of materials used, the difficulty of the materials, the learning emphasis in the use of these materials, and the approach to the materials. This need not interfere with the continuity of the learning procedure; it is possible to operate from a required minimum course-content, which is expanded by the teacher to fit the needs of each class. This prevents injudicious repetition of the same materials at different grade levels. For example, in a school where there are eight or ten sections of eighth-grade music classes, taught by several teachers, it is sometimes difficult for each to know just what musical materials have been used the preceding year and almost impossible to know what recordings children have heard in their elementary school experience. Children *should* hear the same music more than once if the time limit of the music class permits. But they should not be expected to listen to *Danse Macabre* year after year simply because of lazy or inefficient planning, which does not provide for presentation of other tone poems. (Some teachers, instead of allowing *Danse Macabre* to become a Hallowe'en warhorse, have used effectively selections such as the de Falla *Ritual Fire Dance.*) *New* experiences are vital to interest, whether in song, listening, or other activities. Through them children grow.

It is to be hoped that each class, through the planning of the teacher and its members, will hear various types of music. A whole semester spent studying overtures or singing spirituals might be very interesting but would limit the pupils' opportunities to become acquainted with other forms of music. "Request" days several times a semester allow boys and girls to choose favorite compositions they wish to hear again; many teachers provide for the singing of favorite songs by taking the requests of pupils each time the class meets and singing these favorites sometime during the following meeting of the class.

Whether a grade is made up of twenty or five hundred boys

and girls, they should have certain musical experiences in common. In comparing notes with each other, one youngster often asks another, "What are you doing in music class?" Mutual experiences provide a basis for comparison of reaction and are social and intellectual means of communication.

The minimum course-content outline is simply a basic list of materials sung or heard by all the children in a certain grade. This is *not* a limiting factor which says to the teacher, "Teach these materials, and no more." Rather, it says, "See that every boy and girl in this grade has an *opportunity* to sing these songs and hear these compositions and expand their musical activities from this basis. In such expansion, consider the particular class you are teaching, their reaction to the materials you are using, and their needs; above all, let them work with you in the choosing of materials."

Even such a minimum course-content outline should be characterized by flexibility rather than rigidity in its classroom use. If a visitor walks into eight seventh-grade music classes on the same day, he should find a variety of activities taking place; no two sections may be doing the same thing. But all may be making progress toward their objectives. In terms of pupil differences, it would be unusual to find all eight sections listening to *Till Eulenspiegel* on the same day or singing an identical song group, even though these were part of the minimum course outline. In such a plan there would be no instructions telling the teacher he *must* or *must not* use certain materials at a certain time. The minimum course-content outline *does guard against the criticism that pupil-teacher planning leads to inefficient and "spotty" learning experiences. But it does not confine either teacher or pupils so that there is lack of breadth in these experiences.* Having presented one tone poem, the teacher may present more of the same, if this seems wise.

In considering illustrative lists of materials, such as presented in the following pages, it is important to bear in mind that good planning considers the school situation for which the plan is made and builds from there. *In no case should a plan drawn*

up for one school situation be imposed upon another. The
whole process of drawing up a plan of procedures and materials is as important as the final plan itself. All teachers who
are to use a plan should have a voice in making it, as should
the children for whose use the plan is intended. It should be
in keeping with the work of other school departments, and
teachers in these departments should be given an opportunity
to react to it in terms of their own subject and teaching areas.
The plan should be flexible, but strong enough in its broad
outline so that its adaptation in order to meet needs of different
classes will not destroy basic objectives.

The actual approach to the *use* of such a course-content outline may be made through discussion with each class involved.
The remainder of the materials (supplementary or expansion)
should be chosen by the class and the teacher together, on the
basis of class interests and needs. The entire plan should be
approved by administrators who are concerned with the
situation.

The availability of song source-materials in the form of textbooks varies markedly from school to school. One school may
have only one set of songbooks; another may have four or five
sets of different songbooks. Therefore, instead of having an
example of a basic song list in this chapter, a list of procedures
to guide the teacher in drawing up such a list is included. Song
textbook libraries are unlike the record library; a single record
suffices for the listening of an unlimited number of pupils,
while song textbooks must be in the hands of pupils — at least
one book for every two pupils. Furthermore, a record library
accumulates over a number of years, and with good care does
not wear out, while textbooks must be replaced, a fact which
automatically limits the cumulative song textbook library.

For these reasons we have included record lists illustrative
of the minimum course outline and omitted lists of songs which
draw upon particular song textbook sources. The only song
list included is one of songs found in many different books and
intended for general group singing. Two record lists are in-

cluded in the following pages. These lists are cited as illustrating the planning technique, which has been discussed in this chapter. Teachers of seventh- and eighth-grade music classes in one school (each grade met in four or five different sections) met together and worked out the minimum listening experiences they believed boys and girls in these grades should have in common. No attempt was made to say how each should be presented or to what extent it should be developed.

It is not suggested that music teachers in other schools should use these lists exactly as they appear here; in fact, such a procedure would violate the principles involved in the underlying philosophy.

COMPILING A BASIC SONG LIST[1]

1. The purpose of such a list is to provide a song repertoire, which pupils in all sections may enjoy singing and from which musical learning may develop.

2. All teachers who have sections of the grade help compile the list.

3. The ability and needs of the pupils (musical, emotional, and physiological with respect to changing voice) are analyzed through group discussion by teachers. Prior to this, teachers should have discussed with children their attitudes toward musical materials. Their likes and dislikes should be considered in choosing songs for the list.

4. The list should be balanced as well as possible by choosing unison and part songs. Folk songs, composed songs, and art songs should be represented on the list. Range of songs should be considered with respect to the changing voices of the class.

5. Correlation with listening, rhythmic and creative activities, other subject areas and activities, and with world events should be considered.

6. The factor of time limitation should determine the length of the list. The basic song list for a particular grade should be

---

[1] A similar procedure may be followed for basic listening lists.

no more than one-third of the total number of songs the class sings during the year.

7. Songs chosen for this list should have great appeal with regard to melody, rhythm, harmony, and text. They should not be so difficult that the class will have to overwork in order to enjoy them, and the text should be one that is well within the understanding of the boys and girls who are to sing it, preferably a text which can be related in some way to the present life of the pupil.

8. After each song is learned, the teacher should try to judge the reaction of the class to the song. This is useful in making the list for the succeeding year.

9. The list should be remade, or at least revised, every year, as the needs of classes and the level of ability vary from year to year.

10. Songs which supplement the list should be chosen with the direct co-operation of pupils and should be specifically chosen by each section of the grade, should it be made up of two or more sections.

11. Songs should be chosen from a variety of textbooks, if possible, to afford the best possible choice.

Example I: Minimum Course-Content Outline Planning: A Basic Junior-High-School Song Repertoire, Grades 7-9 Inclusive. (Developed by their teachers) (In the school for which this list was planned, all junior-high-school music classes learned these songs as a *basis* for group singing in and outside of the school. Other songs, among them popular songs, were also sung in assembly.)

The Star-Spangled Banner (first and last verses)	Rounds: *Scotland's Burning* *Row, Row, Row*
America	*O Worship the King*
America the Beautiful	*Follow the Gleam*
Levee Song	*Grandfather's Clock*
Home on the Range	*Ain't Gonna Grieve My Lord*
The Caisson Song	*No More*
Cielito Lindo	*Dixie*
Camptown Races	*Yankee Doodle*

Red River Valley
The British Grenadiers
Funiculi, Funicula
Blow the Man Down
Battle Hymn of the Republic
Short'nin' Bread
Joshua Fit de Battle
Swing Low, Sweet Chariot
Jacob's Ladder
Hand Me Down My
    Walking Cane
Old Folks at Home
The Boll Weevil
Walking at Night
Down in the Valley

Big Corral
Marianina
Sourwood Mountain
A Bicycle Built for Two
The Band Played On
The Man on the Flying
    Trapeze
Polly Wolly Doodle
Drink to Me Only with Thine
    Eyes
Christmas Carols
Oh, Susanna
Loch Lomond
All Through the Night
The Blue-Tail Fly
Prayer of Thanksgiving

Example II: Basic Listening Repertoire for All Seventh-Grade Music Classes. (Developed by their teachers)

1. Demonstrations of instruments of the orchestra in the classroom.

2. Showing of music films illustrating uses of these instruments in orchestra and band. (See list — Chapter 9)

3. Use of records illustrating these instruments in different instrumental compositions.

4. Demonstrations of voice types by records and live performances when available. Choral music is timely before Christmas.

5. Use of records to illustrate different forms in music.

6. Use of records to illustrate different schools of musical composition used as an orientation to further study in Grade 8.

INSTRUMENTS OF THE ORCHESTRA

The Young Person's Guide to the Orchestra (Variations and Fugue on a Theme of Purcell) (Used in
conjunction with motion picture)   Britten
Peter and the Wolf   Prokofiev
Instruments of the Orchestra (Columbia, Decca, and
Victor)

OPERAS
Overture to *The Flying Dutchman* and "Steersman's
  Song"   Wagner
"Bell Song" — *Lakmé*   Delibes
Aïda (excerpts)   Verdi

SYMPHONIES
Symphony No. 5 in E minor (*New World*)   Dvorák
Toy Symphony   Haydn

SUITES
Suite No. 2 in B minor (excerpts)   Bach
Scheherazade (Symphonic Suite)   Rimsky-Korsakov

OVERTURE
Fingal's Cave (or *Hebrides*) Overture   Mendelssohn

FUGUE
Cat's Fugue   Scarlatti

BALLET
Sleeping Beauty   Tchaikovsky

VOICE TYPES (use "live" adult performers when possible)
Sopranos: Pons   *Russian Nightingale* (Alabiev)
               Traubel   *American Songs*
Contralto: Anderson   *Spirituals*
Tenor: Melton   *Donkey Serenade* (Friml)
               Crooks   *Foster Album*
Baritone: Tibbett   *Song of the Flea* (Moussorgsky)
               Merrill   *Green-Eyed Dragon* (Newman-Charles)
Bass: Pinza   *Into the Night* (Edwards)

MARCH TYPES
"Procession of the Sardar" — *Caucasian Mountain
  Sketches*   Ippolitov-Ivanov
"Wedding March" — *Lohengrin*   Wagner
"Wedding March" — *Midsummer Night's Dream*   Mendelssohn
Pomp and Circumstance (March No. 1)   Elgar
Selected Marches   Sousa

RONDO FORM
Sonata in A major (K331) (first movement)   Mozart

THEME WITH VARIATIONS
Variations on a Theme by Tchaikovsky   Arensky
Variations on "Pop Goes the Weasel"   Calliet

EXAMPLES OF PERIODS OF MUSICAL COMPOSITION

EARLY CHURCH MUSIC
Columbia History of Music, Vol. I   Scholes
2000 Years of Music   Sachs

PRECLASSICAL MUSIC
"Hallelujah Chorus" — *Messiah*   Handel

CLASSICAL MUSIC
Symphony No. 94 in G major (*Surprise*)   Haydn

ROMANTIC MUSIC
Overture to *Rosamunde*   Schubert

ART SONGS
Das Wandern   Schubert
Der Schmied   Brahms
Der Gärtner   Wolf

IMPRESSIONISTIC MUSIC
White Peacock   Griffes

MODERN MUSIC
Fire Bird Suite   Stravinsky
Mathis der Maler   Hindemith

Example III: Basic Listening Repertoire for All Eighth-Grade Music Classes. (Developed by their teachers)

OPERAS
Carmen (excerpts)   Bizet
Das Rheingold (excerpts)   Wagner
Lohengrin (excerpts)   Wagner

SYMPHONIES
Symphony No. 3 in E flat (*Eroica*)   Beethoven
Symphony No. 5 in C minor   Beethoven

TONE POEMS
Le Chasseur Maudit   Franck
Pines of Rome   Respighi

OVERTURE
Der Freischütz   von Weber

FUGUES
Fugue in G minor (*Little*)   Bach
Fugato on a Well-Known Theme   McBride

VOICE TYPES (use adult performers when possible)
This should include records illustrating each of the following voice
types; it may be presented in conjunction with opera:
Soprano: Coloratura, Lyric, Dramatic
Mezzo-Soprano, Contralto
Tenor: Robusto, Lyric
Baritone
Bass

INSTRUMENTS OF THE ORCHESTRA

Classroom presentation of orchestral and band instruments should be
continued wherever possible, and performance on these instruments by
class members should be encouraged in the classroom situation as part
of the regular music class. Guest artists should be invited to perform
when available. In this grade much stress should be placed on instrumental tone and its use to produce orchestral color in different compositions. The emphasis is on recognition of the instrument in association
with other instruments, rather than on an isolated timbre.

MARCH TYPES
"Grand March" — *Aïda*   Verdi
"Turkish March" — *Ruins of Athens*   Beethoven
March of the Little Lead Soldiers   Pierné
Funeral March of a Marionette   Gounod
Selected Marches   Goldman

DANCE EXAMPLES
Russian Sailor's Dance   Glière
Dance of the Comedians   Smetana
Billy the Kid (Ballet)   Copland
España (Rhapsody)   Chabrier
Square Dances (Folk)

EARLY CHURCH AND PRECLASSICAL MUSIC
Examples of these will be found in the *Columbia History of Music*
Album I (Scholes) and in *2000 Years of Music* (Sachs)

CLASSICAL MUSIC
Symphony No. 41 in C major (*Jupiter*)   Mozart

ROMANTIC MUSIC

Les Préludes	Liszt
Symphony No. 8 in B minor (*Unfinished*)	Schubert
Concerto in A minor (piano and orchestra)	Schumann

ART SONGS

Der Tambour	Wolf
Der Erlkönig	Schubert
Feldeinsamkeit	Brahms

IMPRESSIONISTIC MUSIC

Prelude to The Afternoon of a Faun	Debussy
La Valse	Ravel

CONTEMPORARY MUSIC

Airborne Symphony	Blitzstein
Brigg Fair	Delius
An American in Paris	Gershwin
Schwanda the Bagpiper (Polka and Fugue)	Weinberger
Age of Gold (Polka)	Shostakovich
Ozark Set	Siegmeister

The above selections are some of many compositions which should be played and discussed in class. As many composers as possible should be included, with the emphasis on the music and on the implications of the music with regard to the progress of man and the art of music, rather than on such facts as date of the composer's birth, list of his compositions, and so forth. Above all, a real effort should be made to associate the music heard with song and other music class activities, and with the pupil's activities in and out of school.

GRADE 9 — SPECIAL PROBLEMS

No example list is included here, because in Grade 9 individual differences may make it undesirable to impose a common repertoire on all sections. A better procedure is to evaluate each class at the beginning of the year to see what achievements have been made in the past. If the class has had favorable experiences in music based upon a plan such as the preceding one, the teacher will be able to plan the final year of junior-high-school music from results of preceding years. But if an unfavorable attitude toward music exists, it is almost certain that a new approach to the pupil and music will have to be developed. In many schools this is the final year of required music — the teacher's last chance!

It is further suggested that if homogeneous grouping is to be considered, ninth grade is the level where it is probably most justified in junior-high music classes. This grouping, of course, makes necessary different course plans for various classes and rules out the common listening and song repertoires on the grade level.

Many music teachers state that ninth-grade general music classes present the most difficult problems they face in their teaching. This may be true for the following reasons:

1. When boys and girls have not found a particular interest in music by the time they enter ninth grade, they are likely to feel that "it's not for me; I'll just have to put up with it as long as I must attend class."

2. Boys and girls who have had an unhappy experience in music, such as being left out of performing groups, failing to make a musical organization, receiving low marks in music (in a traditional marking system), or failing in music for the year, are likely to be defensive and aggressive. This leads to behavior problems.

3. Pupils who come into a large consolidated, joint, or city school from a school which gave them a weak music program sometimes feel at a great disadvantage. They believe they cannot "compete" in background or experience with boys and girls who have come into ninth grade with a history of rich musical experience, so they either try to withdraw from the situation as much as possible or display undesirable overt behavior characteristics to cover up feelings of inferiority.

4. In a three-year junior high school (grades 7, 8, and 9), ninth-grade pupils who are definitely in the process of adolescence and at the same time in the top grade of the school

organization can be expected to show some signs of cockiness, restlessness, and impatience with authority. This is particularly true of a class displaying a low interest level.

5. Ninth-grade general music classes are sometimes disturbed by a small aggressive minority of pupils who are generally unhappy in school and are simply waiting until they are old enough to withdraw legally.

6. Some boys are disturbed by the unpredictability of their changing voices. When unwisely handled, they become at times extremely unhappy and resort to defensive behavior. One adult, a teacher, stated that the only time he was ever rude in class was when his teacher insisted that he sing when in ninth grade. "I didn't dare sing," he said, "because I couldn't depend on my voice, and I didn't want the others to laugh at me. The teacher kept insisting, and finally I swore at him. I was amazed to find myself doing it — it was the only time I had ever been really 'bad' in school." Extreme though this case may be, it illustrates unrecognized tensions which may exist.

7. Pupils who are below average musically may unconsciously resent and envy their more musical fellows. They may find an outlet in refusal to participate, and in an attitude of looking down on musical activities, to a point of nonparticipation. This is based, of course, on feelings of insecurity.

On the other hand, with pupils who have established themselves in an interesting musical activity, we find a peak level of musical interest, a "do-or-die" attitude and a full-spirited endeavor of co-operation and participation that is hard to match on the senior-high-school level.

Thus, it may seem that we have in some ninth-grade situations two almost distinct groups, which have been resolved into their differing attitudes as a culmination of the eight (sometimes more) preceding years of school, plus home and community environments. Instead of offering suggestions for materials to be used in this grade, we therefore include a list of suggested activities which grew out of a discussion by a graduate class of teachers[2] who felt the problem was very important in their teaching. This list of activities is intended particularly for the ninth-grade class that has had a poor musical background and displays an attitude of general disinterest in music. It will be most useful, probably, to teachers of rural and small-town pupils. At the discretion of the teacher, these suggestions may be used, of course, in other grades.

Suggestions for a Ninth-Grade Music Class with Limited Musical Background and Negative Attitude Toward Music. (Based on a class discussion of twenty classroom teachers)

I. As a starting point, use music they know and want, such as:
  A. Hill-billy music
    1. How it developed from folk music
    2. Simple chording on various instruments
    3. Phrasing
    4. Tonal quality: nasal versus "legitimate" tone, how both are produced, how good tone quality can be developed; illustrate with recordings, live performers
  B. Ballads
    1. History of balladry, discussing minstrels, bards, troubadours, ballad singers, and so forth
    2. Use of records, live performers; ballads should be carefully chosen with respect to text
  C. Cowboy songs
    1. Learning simple guitar, Autoharp, ukulele, and piano accompaniments
    2. Harmonica, ocarina, tonettes
II. Origin and arrangements of folk music; how composers use folk music; live performers
  A. Different singers, different instrumental arrangements
    1. Children sing with the records
    2. Compare different folk songs using same basic tune, such as *Camptown Races* and *Sacramento*
    3. How folk songs change slightly when passed along; (a) illustrate with records; (b) compare a folk song with its popular version, such as *Shenandoah* and *Cross the Wide Missouri*
    4. Bring in all possible live performers, even those not too advanced, from the student body; use guitar, harmonica, and ukulele players; performers on novelty instruments, such as musical saw, sometimes have great appeal for these

---

[2] Class in Music Education, Course 574b. The Pennsylvania State College, Summer Session, 1951.

classes; encourage students to listen to radio programs and to make weekly reports; some teachers have used "jug" bands successfully

III. Units used with success by members of the class
  A. Movie background music
    1. Play and discuss *Spellbound* Concerto: how does music fit mood of movie, how does it enhance and mirror moods, and so forth; follow by a recording of *A Night on Bald Mountain,* asking class to write the plot which the music represented or brought to their imaginations
  B. Radio programs; music of famous composers used as theme songs
  C. Correlate art and music — drawing and painting to express mood of music
  D. Field trips
    1. Listen to sounds in nature
    2. Science teacher explains how sounds are produced by various animals, birds, wind, and so on
    3. Relate preceding with man's voice, wind, percussion, and string instruments
  E. Popular songs that have been adapted from the classics (see list at end of chapter)
  F. Victor Herbert operettas — other current musical shows
  G. Song "plugging"; how songs become popular
  H. Films: musical subjects; to determine level of appeal, be sure to screen films before presentation
  I. American music, starting with pioneers and Indians and working up to present day; students make drums during this unit
  J. Dance bands; styles, arrangements of same tune by different arrangers
  K. History of Jazz (from Dixieland to Bop)
  L. Hit Parade: a listing of songs, sung by the class, which are best liked
IV. Guest speakers
  A. Visitors from other nations speak on music of their countries; community residents who have made trips to other countries speak on music they heard during trip
  B. Radio repairmen, or phonograph, radio and television dealers speak on buying records and music reproducing equipment and care of such equipment

Throughout the use of the above suggestions, it is important that the teacher watch the developing interests of his class, swinging the weight of the materials used to an increasing emphasis on the musical side.

MUSIC READINESS

The term "readiness" has assumed importance in educational terminology, in music education particularly with reference to the development of skills in musical performance. In music there is likely to be a great difference in the music readiness of different members of the music class because of their previous musical backgrounds. Music readiness, or the ability of the child to develop beyond the point which he has already achieved, depends upon both his innate capacity and his total

musical experience. In schools and homes there exists a wide difference in the amount and the quality of musical experience. In addition to this, as one phase of musical training made possible through the home, some children study music privately. This study, too, varies in quality and in length. Some children have had six or more years of private piano study, for example, when they enter seventh grade; others have had a few months (or even a few lessons), still others a few years, and finally, there are children who have had no private instruction. It would appear likely that in no other area of instruction does the public-school teacher face a wider range of readiness levels than he does in the music class. This in itself is a powerful argument for careful class planning, based upon thorough class evaluation and pupil participation. Such a range of readiness levels also relates to the teacher's objective of finding for each child some satisfactory musical activity. Mary, who has studied piano for six years and enjoys playing Bach, is in the class with Johnny, who has never studied an instrument and transferred into seventh grade from a school which did not offer a strong music program. Obviously, Mary is ready for more complex musical experiences than Johnny. The teacher's responsibility is to observe the class, and by means of the evaluating tools at his disposal, to determine the music readiness level of his pupils. The content of the course is then adjusted in these terms.

THE MUSIC CLASSROOM AND ITS EQUIPMENT

Everything in the music classroom should be present for the basic purpose of facilitating and enriching the musical growth of boys and girls; both room and equipment should be functional. When a new school building is constructed, not only should consideration be given to rooms for the band, choir, music library, and others, but also to the general music classroom, which is, in the junior high school, the heart of the music program. In the final analysis, however, the teacher of the general music class must accept the room assignment given to him and build an environment from there. (In using the word "environment" here, while we do not discount the human factor, we are primarily concerned with physical equipment.) The following are functional and important in the music classroom:

Movable chairs, several large worktables, bulletin board space, blackboard space, piano, three-speed phonograph, wall maps of the world, globe, tape recorder.
Percussion instruments (for rhythmic work): drums, maracas, castanets, gourds.

Autoharp, psaltery, guitar, ukulele, harmonica, ocarina (more than one each of these if possible).

File of materials for visual aids. This should include reproductions of paintings and material clipped from magazines and newspapers. From all available sources, teacher and class should accumulate and expand this file.

Library of books on music and musicians, or ready access to this material in school library. (If books are not kept in the classroom, it is convenient to have available a list of the school library's music books for ready reference.)

Record library. If library is housed outside of the classroom, list of records should be kept in the classroom. A lending library of records is highly desirable; these should be unbreakable.

Sets of songbooks, and other text materials.

Class logbook.

The use of this material will be discussed in detail in Chapters 4, 5, and 6. It may be noted, however, that the inclusion of certain "informal" instruments such as the guitar and ocarina is a reflection of the trend toward bringing out-of-school interests into the classroom. For some children, and particularly for pupils who have vocal difficulties, these instruments are informal enough in their use to be attractive; they can be learned relatively easily; and they are personal enough to represent a satisfactory outlet. In learning to play such instruments, one does not have to attempt to reach a high performance level. This erases the fear of failure, which prevents some pupils from taking up the study of band and orchestral instruments. These same instruments are useful, at times, in teaching the technical aspects of music in a practical way.

SMALL-GROUP ACTIVITY WITHIN
THE GENERAL MUSIC CLASS

One of the ways in which present-day teachers meet individual differences within the classroom is through small-group activity. This is a valuable technique to apply in the music class, although it must be admitted that, because the medium of music is aural, there are some disadvantages. Overlooking these for the time being, it should be possible in the adequately equipped classroom with a class of about thirty pupils to have five groups working on various phases of music that interest them.

For example, one group may be working out song accompaniments with the Autoharp; another group scoring a rhythmic accompaniment for a familiar song, using the instruments available in the classroom; a third group working out the steps of a square dance or play-party game; a fourth group transposing a song to be played on the psaltery without retuning; and a fifth group looking up background material on songs or records. These groups can sometimes work in adjoining rooms, the hall, auditorium, or whatever space is available. When there is a real center of interest, group self-discipline is usually at a high point in an activity of this kind; thus a minimum of teacher supervision is required. Such small-group activity should be used as a legitimate means to the end of meeting individual differences.

When a general music class has had a variety of musical experiences, a number of these experiences in terms of specific activities (such as those suggested in the above groupings) may be presented to them and each child given a choice of groups with which to work. The teacher must be prepared to make specific suggestions for the procedure of each group's activity. Perhaps part of several music periods will be devoted to the group work, after which each group will report back to the entire class on what it has accomplished. Perhaps several entire periods will be devoted to work of this nature. In any case, the teacher should realize that he must be well prepared to guide the work of these groups and to feed them materials or suggest sources of materials. Lack of thorough planning here will lead to confusion, disinterest, and general disorder. While this type of work is characterized by freedom of movement in the classroom and a variety of simultaneous musical experimentation, groups which are really interested in their work will ignore to a surprising degree the other classroom sounds, in much the way that students practicing in adjoining conservatory practice rooms do not hear each other.

GROUP PROJECTS

The general heading here may be taken to mean either projects engaging the attention of an entire class or projects upon which the previously-described small groups embark. These projects may range in subject from the production of a classroom minstrel show to developing a "unit" or creating an original song. Again, the constructive guidance of such a project calls for considerable skill from the teacher. The project is characterized by a high level of activity on the part of class members; in fact, it is necessary for each child to have some share in the project. The project topic must be chosen by the group, and should come out of discussion and as much further investigation as may be deemed necessary to insure a depth of interest sufficient to bring it to a desirable conclusion. This procedure is the opposite of verbalism; it is an example of children, whose very age is characterized by an overflow of energy, using that energy in a live and active way, working with the materials of music to achieve musical understandings.

One of the common objections to these pupil-conducted procedures is that they are inefficient and time consuming. This objection seems to be based upon the question; "Should children be allowed to make mistakes, and learn by doing so?" It seems inevitable that they will make mistakes, no matter how strenuously some adults object. In a friendly and lifelike situation they certainly should be allowed to practice until they gain sufficient skill to manage efficiently and economically. Here they are learning by doing, and here it may be that they will make mistakes. But these will not be irrevocable mistakes, so these boys and girls will not be prevented from trying to gain skill because of the fear of failure.

If democracy is to be perpetuated, the classroom teacher's willingness to help boys and girls develop in its ways is basic.

MOTIVATING FACTORS

No learning can be successful without motivation. This motivation takes many forms in music. It may be extrinsic in the shape of a teacher requiring that pupils accomplish work with the threat of failure, low grades, or other humiliations as the "whip." It may be a mother sitting by a son while he practices the piano, literally keeping him "at it." It may be based upon a competitive challenge. While these may achieve surface success with some pupils, a healthier motivation is based simply upon enjoyment of the music itself and a desire to enter more fully into many music activities. This is the motivation every music teacher would like to use as a sole factor. However, it is unlikely that in most instances the pupil's music activities will spring from a motive as simple as sheer love of beautiful music. Like everything else in the lives of junior-high-school pupils, the motives which impel them toward music may be mixed.

Practically, the teacher's problem is to secure a foothold for music in the child's life. Some boys and girls already will have established music as a source of satisfaction, whereas others will have an opposite view, and still others will be indifferent. Therefore, while the intrinsic satisfaction that the child derives from music is theoretically the ultimate goal so far as motivation is concerned, it is clearly impossible to begin with this in the face of indifferent or negative attitudes toward music. In such cases the teacher must become a salesman, using his knowledge of the prospect as a starting point for the "sales campaign." This does not mean high-pressure methods. It does mean an evaluation of the "buyer" and the "product" with relation to each other. Idealistic or not, this is psychologically sound under the circumstances. Motivation is a means to an end; if all goes well, eventually the end itself becomes motivation enough. Until that time arrives, a "sales campaign" is always underway in the junior-high-school music classroom.

Taking a case in point, we find that junior-high-school boys occasionally develop the idea that singing is "sissy stuff." Where there is a strong senior-high-school choral program, it is good policy to bring into the classroom of such boys a singing group of older boys among whom there are athletes. Usually no further argument is necessary, as one can hardly accuse the school's star fullback of being engaged in a "sissy" activity. This kind of teaching by example is particularly effective with junior-high-school pupils, who are hero worshippers. Many of the boys dream of glory on the football field, and many of the girls dream of shining in the reflected glory of such stars.

Admittedly this is a surface motivation. It is simply the spark meant to ignite the combustible material. Yet, most teachers will tell you that it is not always an easy thing to *activate* a music class and that such *activation* is the first step in the progress of the class. What happens afterwards depends upon the teacher's alertness in follow-up procedures. Procedures suggested in Chapter 4, 5, and 6 are based upon the philosophy expressed in the foregoing discussion.

CLASS SELF-EVALUATION IN TERMS OF
INTEREST LEVEL AND OBJECTIVES

At least once during the year, the teacher of the music class should, in order to measure progress in terms of objectives set for the class, take a good look at himself and the work of the class through the eyes of his students. Such a look may be obtained through pupil reaction; a good time to ask for it is at the end of a semester's work. Pupils may be asked questions concerning what they have liked *best* and *least* in music classes, what they would like to do more of in the class, what activities they would like to discontinue or add, what they feel they have accomplished, and where the strengths and weaknesses of the class lie. When they are asked to express themselves in such a manner, an attitude of confidence in the teacher must prevail; they must feel that he will not take offense at any comments that reflect a dislike of class activities. Pupils must also understand the purpose of such a procedure; it should be fully explained in class. In the case of a class that does not express itself with facility, checklists may be used on which pupils are asked to indicate by means of assigning a value (3,2,1) to lists of class activities, or simply to check those activities that they feel were interesting, double-check those they would like to continue, and so on. Provision should be made for them to add their comments. Very often when teachers receive a negative reaction to activities vital to the music program, they can explain their significance to the class, and by open discussion, work out ways of making these activities more interesting.

Planning for the remainder of the year can be done upon the results of this procedure. Since committees play a heavy role in the functioning of a democratic way of life, the classroom teacher can build a program by appointing committees, later consulting them to consider class reactions in various areas of the classroom activities. Junior-high-school boys and girls are eager to assume responsibility; they like to think their opinions are important to adults. When they have a part in planning the work of their classes, they usually assume it more willingly and wholeheartedly, for it has become, in a unique sense, something of their own. Throughout the whole process, it is the teacher's responsibility to bear in mind objectives and guide the planning in their direction.

KEEPING OBJECTIVES IN MIND

The teacher should remember that youngsters easily lose sight of objectives. They need to be reminded of them from time to time, even when they themselves have set up the objectives. For most of our children today, each twenty-four hours is full of many activities. Teachers sometimes tend to forget that life goes on for children after they leave the music class; that an interval of several days may largely distract their attention from the work they were doing at the close of a preceding class; and that such an interrupted pattern quickly serves to erase the memory of objectives, which were so clearly defined in early meetings of the new school year's classes.

Such questions as "Why are we doing this?", "What are we accomplishing?", and "How does the whole pattern of our activities fit together?" should be asked over and over in the classroom. For many children, attending a class that does not follow such a procedure must be like aimlessly driving along in an automobile; for a while it's fun, but eventually the scenery all begins to look alike, and they fervently wish the trip would end. *Knowing the destination is important.* In music classes, pupils must be conscious of objectives, or there is little motivation.

In many schools the general music class meets only once or twice a week. Maintaining a sense of continuity from one week to the next is difficult in such situations, and a "class log" may help the class keep in mind the program of the previous class meeting. The class secretary and a committee usually are in charge of the log, and in it they keep a record of the musical activities of the class. At the beginning of the class period, the secretary (or teacher) may read from the log and lead a discussion of previous activities; this refreshes the memories of the class members and bridges the lapse of time (which may be as long as a week) from one class to the next. Illustrative material furnished by members of the class can make the log an attractive as well as useful adjunct to the music program. A large scrapbook is ideal for this purpose.

PERFORMER AND CONSUMER TRAINING

Many more students will be consumers rather than performers of music. A very small per cent of the total student population will earn its living as professional musicians; a larger per cent will engage in amateur music-making. But the greatest per cent will derive most of its musical pleasure from listening to music. There is a trend in present-day music education toward recognizing this fact and gearing to it the teaching of school music. If we try to answer the question "What can a boy or girl who does not expect to perform musically take with him from his school music experiences into the out-of-school world?", we should be able to formulate a reply that has a definite influence upon the classroom teacher and the selection of materials. In this reply, the following items might be listed:

1. A song repertoire which will be permanent; for example, it should enable the individual to participate in community singing and congregational singing.
2. A useful listening repertoire and technique.
3. An intelligent attitude toward the selection of music in out-of-school music experiences (concerts, radio, church).
4. A knowledge of correct audience behavior.
5. Some knowledge upon which the purchase of musical equipment may be based.

Looking at the school music picture from the angle of consumer training, it is obvious that it means placing relatively greater emphasis on the importance of the less talented and/or interested boys and girls. Considering the fact that the public schools are equally responsible for the education of both the more and the less talented pupil, this emphasis is appropriate. It does not mean that the more talented pupil will be neglected. Music is one of the fields where those of high ability are *not* neglected to the extent that they are in certain other fields. Undue attention to these pupils in the general music class, however, tends to discourage their less talented fellows, who may despair of ever reaching the level of the former. All individuals are musical to some degree; it is the responsibility of the teacher to make this evident to the pupil in terms of his own ability.

In the case of the highly talented pupil[3] early identification is vital, for in his case specialized training must begin while he is comparatively young, if his talents are to be fully developed. This identification should be made long before the junior-high-school years; valuable time has been lost if it is delayed until then. Still, the confirmation of such talent is important, even

---

[3] See Chapter 7.

if it has been recognized earlier, and provision for its guidance and development call for co-ordinated work on the part of parent, school, and private teacher.

Once the specially talented pupil is identified, the school's responsibility lies in providing him with a "growing" environment and in furnishing outlets for the skills he is acquiring, particularly those of performance. This is commonly referred to as supplying an enriched program. The highly musical child will wish to belong to more performing organizations than the average pupil. The teacher may guide the pupil into such organizations; at times, it may be necessary to organize new groups for this purpose. The teacher also will try to fit the child's musical performing abilities into the classroom activities; for pianists and other instrumentalists, accompanying and the playing of descants, harmony parts, or special instrumental arrangements of classroom songs are natural activities. The explanation and demonstration of the instruments being studied by superior pupils is another useful activity often appropriate in the general music class. A vast quantity of reading material, which is of interest to young musicians and extends their musical horizons, is available. Special listening experiences (that is, concerts, radio, television programs) beyond the musical comprehension of the average junior-high-school pupils may be suggested for them. They may be interested in writing reviews of the concerts they hear; some of the reviews written by such pupils are surprisingly accurate and penetrating in their musical grasp. Experimenting with such classroom instruments as guitar, Autoharp, rhythm instruments, and others is often of interest to these pupils; they possess unlimited musical curiosity. Often they can be put to work on long-term projects that call for a great deal of initiative and persistence; special reports on musical compositions and composers, which require reference work, may be used here. The keeping of music notebooks is also suggested, a project which, with average pupils, is often time consuming and of only surface interest.

Such activities as the foregoing should be provided judicially but steadily in order that the musically above-average will never feel out of place in the general music class because of lack of challenging situations.

The children who are below-average musically are often a source of difficulty in the classroom planning of the teacher. These are children who usually are lacking in a satisfactory musical background and who have had inadequate musical experiences. In the music class they have a strong sense of insecurity. Frequently, they are either behavior problems or non-participants, both of which patterns reflect the lack of a sense of "belongingness." The teacher who wishes to find a foothold for music in the lives of these children must take his cue from this. He must try to find something they can do which brings them satisfaction in music class, and he must be willing at times to accept what might be considered a low musical standard where the activities of these children are concerned. For example, playing a ukulele or a harmonica may not be looked upon as a high-level music activity where a junior-high-school pupil is concerned, but it *may* bring immediate musical pleasure to the below-average pupil in the music class. The lack of interest that is displayed by these pupils is caused in part by their conviction that music is too difficult for them to understand or enjoy; in the activities the teacher provides for them, there must be a fast return in the way of musical satisfaction, or in the satisfaction of accomplishment.

What about those pupils in the general music class who are of below-average intelligence? At times, these pupils may display behavior similar to that described above, which stems from the same root. Whatever is offered them must be very specific and obvious in its implications. Most of the theoretical aspects of music are beyond them, except as a *memorized learning*, which they are unable to put to functional musical use. For them, the musical offerings of the school must be functional to the extreme, *or their musical experiences continue to thwart them.* It seems likely that the pupil of low intelligence is less able to take advantage of the musical opportunities available to him than is the pupil of higher intelligence. Nevertheless, the musical impulse can be a powerful one and at times may discount the factor of intelligence.

Suggested as a few items in the classroom experience for the low-level pupil in intelligence and/or musical ability are songs of vital rhythmic and textual content, programmatic recorded music, and music with an obvious surface appeal. Since such boys and girls are essentially *doers* in musical activities, their musical activities should involve a strong element of personal or group participation. But most of all, they must become identified with music in some rewarding way; if this happens, music takes on significance in their lives.

EVALUATING MUSICAL EXPERIENCES
IN THE GENERAL MUSIC CLASS

In designing or evolving with the junior-high-school pupils a plan for the activities of the general music class, the teacher of music is continually weighing his work and passing judgment on it in terms of its effect on classroom participants. When is the musical experience a good one and what are some of the points characterizing it? Briefly, it may be said that the teacher should be on the alert at all times to note pupil reaction in terms of the following:

1. From the musical experience the pupil should gain a sense of personal participation involving a high degree of activity. This does not necessarily mean physical activity, nor must there be immediate signs of *overt* activity. It does mean that in the classroom situation the teacher will be able to judge pupil reaction in terms of his participation. For in the final analysis, no matter how rich the classroom environment, each boy and girl learns largely on the basis of his own activity.

2. The successful or good musical experience is one which leads the pupil to identify himself with the music he hears or makes. One way of judging this is to look for the music "vitality level" in the classroom and in the individual pupil.

3. In the satisfactory musical experience the pupil will be led to identify himself with the music *and also to relate it to the world around him.* The musical experience should not be an isolated one.

4. The satisfactory musical experience carries with it in the pupil's mind an element of discovery. In a way, this is creative learning. It implies that through this experience the pupil becomes aware of something unique in *his* experience and new to his understanding.

5. The satisfactory musical experience is one which the child is able to evaluate in relation to his learning goals. It is definite and specific enough so that he can see it in perspective with his total musical experiences.

Planning with these five points in mind over a period of time can build in the classroom a unity of musical purpose which will stabilize the attitude of participants in the situation.

LET'S RELAX AND ENJOY OURSELVES WITH MUSIC

Music classes should not always be a place where boys and girls are striving mightily to reach objectives. In real life, people most often sing, play, and listen to music as a means of recreation and enjoyment. At least at times the same situation should prevail in the music class. If a class wants to sing *Darktown Strutter's Ball* or listen to the music of popular dance bands or current Broadway musicals, why not? Thousands of people have paid thousands of dollars at theater box offices to hear the music of Cole Porter, Jerome Kern, Irving Berlin, Richard Rodgers, and other composers. Or, if the same purpose is served by music of Schubert, Brahms, Beethoven and other "greats," nothing says that pupils listening to it must always be attempting to learn something. Let's relieve tension in the classroom by using some of our class time just to relax and enjoy ourselves with no aims, purposes, or objectives (except sheer enjoyment) to be fulfilled through our singing or listening.

This is as important for the teacher as for his pupils, since

his life is fraught with all kinds of responsibilities from character building to mending music, so that at times his own enjoyment of teaching and music is likely to be overshadowed by
the weight and detail of his work. Pupils need to be convinced
that their teacher really enjoys music — such enjoyment is
"catching." Let's expose them to the virus!

SUMMARY

The general music class in the junior high school is the heart
of the music program. Other activities flow from it and return
to it, if the teacher through a knowledge of his students looks
upon the class as being a central point. For example, it is
possible that the teacher of such a class may interest boys and
girls in learning to play instruments of the band and orchestra,
then use their skill in playing these instruments to add both to
the knowledge and enjoyment of the class and to develop a
sense of accomplishment and mastery in the individual instrumentalists.

The class which is too large defeats the teacher's objective of
recognizing individual differences. Two periods a week is the
minimum amount of time for carrying on a varied and stimulating program in the general music class; three periods give
the teacher an opportunity to find a place for music in the life
of each child, affording sufficient time for planning musical
activities which will offer something of interest to the widely
differing members of the class.

The objectives of the class should be planned by teacher and
pupils working together. The teacher, through the materials
and methods employed, and by constantly aiding pupils in
keeping objectives in mind, is responsible for progress in the
direction of these objectives.

In schools where each grade is divided into several sections,
planning a minimum course-content outline provides certain
musical experiences that all pupils may have in common. In
terms of its own needs, each section of the class expands materials from such a minimum. All planning of materials to be used

in common by pupils of a grade should be done by the teachers of that grade, and by other interested persons. Materials are chosen with the background, experience, ability, and interests of the pupils in mind and in their classroom use are adjusted to best serve the pupils in terms of the foregoing factors. Examples of material lists cited in this chapter were developed for one particular situation; it would be unwise to suppose they would fit the needs of another situation since no two schools are exactly alike. Such lists or plans must be custom tailored to fit the needs of each school.

Difficult classes, particularly on the ninth-grade level, call for an approach which leans heavily upon the present likes and interests of their members. Once the teacher has established a sympathetic relationship with his pupils, through developing his presentation of music activities from their level instead of from his, he is more likely to find a friendly and co-operative reception of good musical materials, provided his "upgrading" of musical activities is paced to the abilities of the boys and girls concerned.

An apparent lapse in musical performance between the elementary grades and junior high school is due to factors of change and the resulting adjustments. By explanation and group discussion teachers should help their pupils understand the reason for any lapse in musical performance.

Small-group activity and group projects help meet the interests of individuals in the class and simultaneously develop a unity of purpose.

Motivation in learning is paramount; this means the music teacher must evaluate his pupils and, by learning what appeal music is most likely to have for them, approach them through this appeal. Some boys and girls need to be offered "winning-over" approaches, which may seem quite extrinsic to music itself. Others are ready to accept music for the sake of its intrinsic beauty.

Class evaluation of objectives should take place from time to time; this gives meaning to the activities of the class.

That he may better make possible a significant musical experience for each group, the teacher must identify his pupils in terms of musical and intellectual ability.

Finally, the teacher must continually pass judgment on the values of classroom procedures in terms of their contribution to the growth of pupils. His aim must be to teach music not only as a subject but also as an avenue for producing a well-adjusted, emotionally healthy, and happy child.

4. Music: Integration and Correlation

There is considerable confusion among music teachers in regard to the organization of the subject matter in the junior-high-school classes. When one visits a number of junior-high-school music classes, variations in choices of materials used and the different psychologies underlying the curriculum organization are immediately noticeable. Beginning teachers find it difficult to decide upon a number of courses to follow. The following discussion attempts to present these curriculum problems in such a way that teachers may decide for themselves which practices they will use that will result in the greatest advantage to their pupils.

THE MEANING OF INTEGRATION

Webster's New Collegiate Dictionary defines the word "integrate" as meaning "to form a complete or perfect whole." Sometimes it is defined as meaning unification or welding into a whole. The word "integer" from which "integration" stems, means one or a unit. Thus, we say that an integrated personality, the development of which is one of the basic goals of modern education, is one that is well balanced socially, emotionally, intellectually, and physically. To become a well-balanced or an integrated personality, education must use subject matter that is rich in its very nature for developing such personality traits as co-operativeness, tolerance, intelligence in problem solving, perseverance, sincerity, and honesty, plus the many other qualities which characterize the personality of the well-integrated person. All this implies a wholeness that is in direct contrast to subject matter taught in isolation.

When the objectives of education are concerned with the well-integrated personality, the subject matter selected should aid in the development of these desirable characteristics. It is easily recognized that subject matter must have far broader implications than it does when it is taught in an isolated fashion in order to develop skills and gain factual knowledge only.

MUSIC AS AN INTEGRATIVE FACTOR

Music, because of its very structure and meaning, is rich material for integration. Since it fosters creative imagination, it may carry a pupil out of himself and identify him with far-off places, great historical events, and generous feelings for all mankind. When music is taught with such a philosophy in mind, it tends to break down the rigid departmental barriers which separate subject matter in the junior high school. If the pupil learns the human meanings of the folk and art music studied, he sees that music is a picture which reflects the significant thoughts and feelings found in literature, arts, and social studies. Thus music becomes a great integrative force in contrast to the extra-curricular place it occupies in some schools.

THE CORE CURRICULUM

Many attempts have been made to lessen subject matter isolation through curricula organization called: Broad-Fields Courses, Unified or Fused Studies, Experience Curricula, and the Core. The Core is one of the most used efforts in curriculum revision, but perhaps one of the least understood by music teachers because of the varying meanings it has in the schools which use it. The Core, which does not deal with teaching any area of subject matter, is concerned only with personal living and sociological problems based on the needs and interests of all pupils. It also emphasizes guidance of the individual in solving his personal problems as a part of the group activity. Often these problems are not recognized as curriculum studies by the teacher, although they may be common to his group of junior-high-school pupils. He feels that it is his job to teach his subject only and that the social and personal problems of his pupils are not of major concern to him.

In the Core program, the entire staff may work co-operatively with the pupils in developing this type of curriculum. This will aid teachers in seeing subject matter function with wider horizons, unlimited by area boundaries.

The music teacher should select and present materials in such a way that music contributes to the enrichment of the problem. In many problems, music has a fine contribution to make, and teachers should embrace every opportunity to co-operate in Core studies. There is no pattern to follow for work in the Core. Certainly these should be a conference with the Core teacher and the group to ascertain how much and what kinds of music (either listening or performance or both) will contribute to understanding the problem. In no case should music be used for music's sake but for enrichment and appreciation.

One school "pegs" the Core problem "Understanding My Body" to the seventh grade. Many areas contribute to this study, and music has a major contribution to make since pupils are experiencing the changing voice. Why some women are sopranos (coloraturas) and some contraltos and men are basses and tenors becomes a real personal problem at this time.

In some schools the problems are not "pegged" to a certain grade level. No subjects are fused and no curriculum structure is expected. Such problems as "Art in Public Life," "The United Nations — Its Mission," "Leisure and Recreation," and "Planning Our Education" have been used successfully in the Core program.

Some educators believe that the experience gained with music in the Core is not sufficient to meet the musical needs and interests of pupils. For this reason, classes in music other than the Core are offered. For further reading concerning the Core, the following references are suggested: *Developing the Secondary School Curriculum*[1] and *Reorganizing the High School Curriculum*.[2]

CORRELATION

Correlation was one of the early attempts to break down closely drawn divisions between subject matter fields. In fact, it may be said that it was an early evidence of dissatisfaction with isolated subject matter and was a part of the "new education" movement. It has been used to varying degrees to show relationships that exist between various subject matter fields, within a subject field (music), or between areas (music and social studies). The songs of Robin Hood become more vital to pupils when they know some of the historical background of England during the time in which Robin Hood and his followers were supposed to have lived. The pattern of living of a nation is revealed in the folk music and folk dances of that country. Existing correlations pointed out between any areas tend to enrich and enhance the subject under discussion.

These music correlations seem to thrive best between certain areas and seem to be most effective in motivating learning when used with social science, geography, art, and English. Teachers can enhance the meaning of songs by studying their backgrounds and, in this way, ensure wider and more en-

---

[1] Leonard J. Paul, *Developing the Secondary School Curriculum* (New York: Rinehart and Company, 1946), Chapter XII, "Outline of Core Units."

[2] Harold Alberty, *Reorganizing the High School Curriculum* (New York: The Macmillan Company, 1950).

thusiastic pupil participation. When correlations are pupil-teacher planned they are more effective.

In the general music class

Activities commonly found in varying degrees in the general music classes are: singing, listening, theoretical study, rhythms, playing on instruments, making class or individual scrapbooks, and discussions and reports on experiences or things studied. All of these should be interrelated. It would be unwise to be singing cowboy songs, trying to listen to Beethoven's Fifth Symphony, and constructing a notebook on the opera, all in the same lesson, if one expects growth in appreciation and knowledge of musical relationship. Substitute Ferde Grofé's "On the Trail" from his *Grand Canyon* Suite for the Beethoven and a notebook on cowboys and their customs, instruments, dances, and so on, for the opera notebook, and you will establish a relationship and coherence not to be found among cowboys, Beethoven, and the opera.

The dominant seventh chord will have very little meaning to a junior-high-school pupil when it is studied in isolation, but its beauty and use become significant if it is experienced first in a song such as Schumann's *Spring Greeting*. In fact, all activities should be related if we expect our pupils to develop a feeling for the relationship of music activities. A word of warning should be given here lest teachers run this idea into the ground and lose the interest of the class through a narrow intensive use of units. Other materials such as seasonal songs will add variety, and if a pupil asks to sing a favorite song which is outside the unit, it is a good policy to do so. Balance, plus variety in choice of materials, is an objective all successful teachers strive to obtain.

The instrumental and vocal classes can be helpful mutually when certain phases of their music are related. There should be a much closer relationship between these areas. When there is, pupils are thrilled to have teachers initiate programs uniting

pupil activities. The newer music texts have included arrangements of songs which can be played by beginning instrumental
groups. The result is that the instrumental groups have a
greater enthusiasm for their performances and see added meaning in the music. The initiative for this relationship between
vocal and instrumental music must come from teachers in both
areas. In schools where this is accomplished, the schism which
often prevails between vocal and instrumental music will dis-
appear.

With other areas

Because of its humanistic significance music has much to contribute to many other subjects in the curriculum. It is true that
it has a relationship with mathematics and the natural sciences,
but it has a great deal to contribute to the social sciences, art,
English, and physical education areas.

Some music educators look askance at these correlations.
They fear that music will lose its identity and become the
handmaid of other subjects or related fields. There seems to be
little danger that musical values will be lost and that the
beauty, which is its humanizing power will be lessened if music
joins hands with other areas in widening social and artistic
horizons. With present-day emphasis on "living today," music
has a greater contribution to make to other areas. In doing so,
music receives as much as it gives in that pupils realize more
fully that music reflects the meaning of all life.

One junior-high-school music teacher used correlation in a
school in which each subject matter area was clearly defined
and unrelated in its teaching to any other. Each teacher
prided himself on "running his own show." The principal of
that school, who is a believer in the power of music in the
school and understands the value of the interrelated program,
gave his consent for the experiment. (It is important to gain
the approval of the school administration before experimentation is started, since one needs their help and guidance in any

study.) The music teacher prepared papers, which gave brief historical and social backgrounds of the songs used in his classes. After they were discussed and approved by the social science teacher, they were read by the pupils in the music classes. The social science classes discussed these backgrounds more fully, and soon the discerning pupils remarked, "You teachers are getting your heads together."

Teachers in other areas became interested in the unit, "People Who Came to America." English classes read "The Courtship of Miles Standish," "The Legend of Sleepy Hollow," and "Rip Van Winkle." The English teacher offered suggestions for other units.

Art became involved in the study quite spontaneously. When one pupil brought his original illustration of "The Landing of the Pilgrims" to music class and requested that they be permitted to draw pictures of their songs, other pupils expressed their desire to illustrate the songs. The music teacher, very understandingly, suggested that the pupils discuss the problem with their art teacher, and because of the art teacher's and the pupils' interest, another area was added. The pupils were given a free hand in planning and executing their ideas for illustrations.

Pupils had a part in planning other units, helped plan the reports which were to be given, and brought, for class use, pictures illustrating the unit. Committees selected bulletin board materials. Recordings were used in music, social studies, and English classes. Songs were studied and sung, pictures and films were seen, stories were read in English classes, and some were assigned for outside reading. In fact, the project, like "Topsy," just grew and spread like wildfire.

As a culmination, a radio play based on the western unit was written in an English class and was presented by pupils selected from participating classes, aided by the English and music teachers. They called the show "An Original Play by Seventh-Grade Pupils in Fostoria Junior High School."

The principal of the school and the teachers of English, art, music, and social science all attest to the heightened interest displayed by pupils, the increasing co-operation between formerly unrelated areas, and the mutual understanding of the contribution each area has to make to the development of human sympathy and an integrated personality. In no way did music suffer, but instead it gained through added enthusiasm and desire to participate. This type of curriculum will flourish when there is co-operation and wholesome attitudes existing between teachers, the administration, and curriculum directors. There is no problem with the pupils since they soon see the value of the relationship and join in the project with such zeal that it is stimulating to experience it. The sum total of the related activities cannot be gained through isolated subject matter teaching, but it may be accomplished through correlation.

In accordance with the present-day movement to eliminate the high degree of specialization and overdepartmentalization in the junior high schools, the city of Columbus, Ohio, where the original junior-high-school movement was established, is organizing the "self-contained classroom" in the seventh grades. These classrooms will have a homeroom teacher who will teach English, geography, and social science. Correlations will be much easier in this type of organization, and pupil interests can be met more easily if the teacher wishes to use them in his planning. Music can function in the plan more effectively, and the subject matter can be fused into a more meaningful whole by the homeroom teacher and the music teacher.

Within the school

In the junior high school, music easily becomes a socializing force throughout the entire school. Chapter 10 is devoted to this problem, but it can be stated here that music should function whenever and wherever its power may be felt. Music is for everyone, no matter what one prefers or what one's appreciation may be.

Within the community

Chapter 10 deals with this problem at length, but it seems fitting here to mention an example of the role music can play in developing good school and community relationships. A certain community had lost confidence in its school, and the school's morale sank to a low level. An understanding superintendent felt an all-school project would aid in gaining the co-operation of the community and would develop a democratic spirit within the school. The following letter was sent to the parents by the superintendent.

Dear Parents:

The success of a democracy is largely proportional to the degree of co-operative planning and working of its citizens. The school, being the greatest single factor in democratic action, seeks constantly to promote co-operative activity. The extent to which a school can plan and co-ordinate activities often amazes the outside observer.

Last year, a group of _____ high-school students and teachers gave thought to an undertaking which would dramatize to parents and others the ability to co-operate on a large scale. No plan was entirely satisfactory. However, out of these discussions there developed a plan for an all-school performance, which crystalized this year into a production to be staged in the high-school auditorium on April 28 and 29.

From the English classes came scripts; from the art department, designs; from industrial arts, stage sets; from home economics, costumes. Combine these with talent from the dramatic and music departments, add dancing from the women's physical education department, and business management from the commercial department, and one has the ingredients for "Show Business."

The enthusiasm among students and staff for this experiment in large-scale co-operation has become contagious. The production seems to be of such merit that it would be unfortunate if a resident of _____ did not take the opportunity to see what our young local people are capable of doing. It seems as though from both an educational and an entertainment point of view, it will be worth a citizen's time to spend the evening of April 28 or 29 in the high-school auditorium.

On behalf of the two hundred students participating in "Show

Business," I should like to extend an invitation to all parents and friends to attend what may well be the first of an annual tradition.

Sincerely yours,

Superintendent of Schools

An analysis of the letter shows how thoroughly this administrator practiced democratic leadership. The result of this co-operative planning was amazing; it won the confidence of the community and restored a belief in itself to the student body. Music played an important part in this highly successful school project and demonstrated its power to unite a strife-torn community into a loyal constituency. Although this plan was worked out on the high-school level, it could be equally successful in a junior high school if the same co-operative planning was practiced.

Modern educational philosophy has attempted to overcome the traditional organization of subject matter into highly specialized subjects, which are learned by a *memoriter* process by setting up experiential "centers of interest." These centers have been labelled under a number of titles, such as units of work, work-units, topics, activity units, and experience units. The modern concept of an interest center should not be considered a topical organization of subject matter but as experiencing activities centered around pupil-interests. This means that all the music activities such as singing, listening, rhythms, and so forth should be interrelated as to content, feeling, and idea.

SOURCES AND CHOICE OF INTEREST CENTERS

The best source for centers of interest comes from the pupil's experience. To start with his experience, deepen it, and guide it into some new channel is one of the important principles of modern education. This experience should be pupil-teacher planned. This planning develops co-operation of the highest type and requires that the teacher prepare for the pupil-teacher planning session. Pupils who have never participated in this type of planning need careful guidance in order that musical growth may take place. Teachers should never face their classes without definite preparation but should veer from that plan as soon as the pupils are ready for the problem.

Interest centers cannot be identical for all grades in each community. Communities near large urban centers where opera is given are more receptive to a study of opera than rural schools far removed from opera performances. What interests one seventh grade may have little appeal for the next class, and what arouses keen interest in one section of a city may fail in another. Music heard on television and the radio or in the movie, the church, and the concert furnishes sources for interest centers.

Study the pupils and the community carefully, considering the human factor, the personality background of the pupils, and community attitudes before the choice of the interest center is made. Also, the materials and equipment available will help the teacher decide what study is feasible. Thus, it can be seen that there can be no prescribed course of study which will be universally effective.

The following list of interest centers, which often appeal to junior-high-school pupils, can be used as suggestions for consideration in the pupil-teacher planning sessions:

America's Contribution to Music
Bands on Parade
Christmas in Many Lands
Come to the Fair
Countries of the North (Norway, Finland, and so on)
Great Americans (true and legendary)
In the Days of "Abe" Lincoln
Mountain Folk and Their Music
Music of Grandmother's Time
Music for and about the Sea
On Plain and Prairie
Rivers and the Sea
South of the Border
Vacation Time Travels
Work and Play in Pioneer Days

CONTENT

As previously mentioned, the center of interest should contain all the activities in which pupils may participate, all of which should be related to the central theme selected by the pupils and the teacher. Not all pupils will be interested in all the activities; neither can participation of all pupils be expected in each activity, since individual differences must be recog-

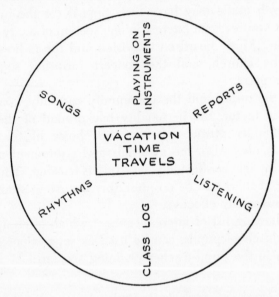

nized. In contrast to the usual singing class, the following diagram of the center of interest will show the interrelationship of these activities.

Pupils enjoy "doing something" with their study, and it is often expedient to culminate these activities in a program given in the assembly for an invited class or for the PTA. Music needs a social outlet. Educational outcomes, concerned with appreciation, knowledge, skills, and creative activities, should be kept in mind constantly in order to avoid those materials which "fit in" but do not contribute to the desired educational results.

The center of interest "Vacation Time Travels," used in one class, is included here since it has an almost universal appeal to pupils when they return to school in the autumn, eager to share their summer experiences. Oftentimes, they have heard

music characteristic of the section of the country where they have vacationed, and they are willing to report on it to the class. With that as motivation, the group will soon be off to a good start. The geographical direction studied should follow the pupils' vacation experiences rather than a formal sequence. The following musical trip started at home, in Ohio, and went down the Ohio River to the Mississippi (Father of Waters). Then it turned to the Great Southwest, California, the Northwest, Minnesota and Wisconsin (where there is much Scandinavian influence), the Northeastern Section, and finally to the Southern Appalachian Mountain region. All these vacation sections of our country offer fine opportunities for musical studies. It is impossible to include sources for all these sections, but sources for one section will be given to show how to organize the center of interest unit.

VACATION TIME TRAVELS — THE OHIO AND MISSISSIPPI RIVER AREA

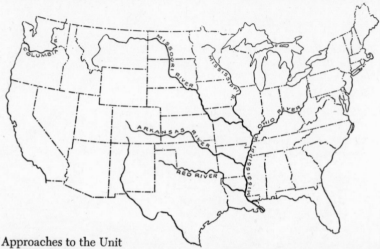

Approaches to the Unit

This unit as a whole may be approached as an imaginary journey throughout the United States, such as one might experience in vacation travels. In traveling throughout the different parts of the country, there will be characteristics peculiar to each section.

Such maps as the Folklore Music Map of the United States by Dorothea Dix Lawrence, from the *Primer of American Music* published by the Hagstrom Company, Inc., New York, might, and should be used to follow the journey. The route that we have chosen to take begins with the Ohio River and follows down the Mississippi River. The following films might be used to introduce this section: *Mississippi River*, 1948 (color), Academy Films, P. O. Box 3088, Hollywood, California; *Old South*, Slide and Film Exchange, Columbus, Ohio; *New Orleans Mardi Gras*, Wurtile Film Production, P. O. Box 504, Orlando, Florida. Pictures may be found in the *National Geographic Magazine* for April 1930, December 1931, September 1937, February 1941, and December 1947; in *Holiday* for February 1948 and October 1949; and in *Life* for January 1947. A movie that has appeared recently is the Metro-Goldwyn-Mayer production of *Show Boat*. All or any of these materials may be used to motivate interest in this unit.

1. Song Material:

SONGS OF THE SOUTH LAND

Unit, "Sunny South" — *Music Americans Sing*, pp. 60-73

Mardi Gras — *Sing Out*, p. 61
Levee Song — *Adventure*, p. 41
Ol' Man River (Kern) (sheet music)

MINSTREL SHOW

Unit, "Bones, Banjo and Burnt Cork" — *Music Americans Sing*, pp. 42-59
Darling Nelly Gray — *Twice Fifty-Five Brown Book*, p. 96
Silver Threads Among the Gold (Danks) — *Sing*, p. 46

SHOW BOAT

Down the River — *Music Americans Sing*, p. 78
Clementine — *Music Americans Sing*, p. 82
Ol' Man River (Kern) (sheet music)
Songs of Stephen Foster — University of Pittsburgh edition (free)

RIVERS AND CANALS

Ol' Man River (Kern) (sheet music)
Beautiful Ohio (Earle) (sheet music)
Sweet Betsy from Pike — *Music Americans Sing*, p. 81
Canal Songs: Captain Pearl Nye, Archaeological Museum, Ohio
                State University, Columbus, Ohio
Sailing Song — *Sing Out!*, p. 156
Lazy River — *Sing Out!*, p. 186
Boatman's Dance — *Sing Out!*, p. 81

2. Listening Material (Recordings):
    Mississippi Suite (Grofé)
    New Orleans Jazz — Creole Jazz Band
    Largo from Symphony in E minor (*New World*) (Dvořák)
    Juba Dance (Dett)
    Show Boat Album (Kern)
    Ol' Man River (Kern) (sung by John Charles Thomas)
    I Got Plenty of Nuttin' and *Summertime* from *Porgy and Bess*
        (Gershwin)
    Stephen Foster Album
    Rhapsody in Blue (Gershwin)
    Walk Together Chillun — Hall Johnson Choir
    Mah Lindy Lou (Strickland) (sung by John Charles Thomas)
    Music of George Gershwin — Paul Whiteman Orchestra

3. Rhythmic Activities:
    Old Dan Tucker — *Sing and Dance* (Hunt and Wilson), p. 70
    Good Morning (Old Southern Schottische) (Mr. and Mrs. Henry
        Ford), p. 99.

4. Pupil Activities in Class:

  (*a*) Reports

     (1) Folk Music — *Keyboard Junior*, January 1952

     (2) *The Story of the Mississippi* (McClintock)

     (3) Characteristics of Negro Music
        How Music Grew (Bauer and Peyser), pp. 17-19
        Music and Romance (Kinscella), pp. 317-320
        Log for Music Americans Sing, pp. 36-45

     (4) Minstrel Shows
        Gentlemen, Be Seated (Paskman and Spaeth)
        Log for Music Americans Sing, pp. 28-35
        Ohio Elementary Music Guide, pp. 85-87
        Mr. Tambo and Mr. Bones (Carl Wittke)

     (5) Ohio Rivers and Canals
        Ohio Elementary Music Guide, pp. 81-82

     (6) The Showboat
        Dramatics Magazine: G. Harry Wright, "Heyday and De-
        cline of Showboat Theaters," April 1949; "Theater is
        Born," November 1948
        Ohio Elementary Music Guide, pp. 82-85

     (7) Famous Composers and Singers
        Dvořák — *Keyboard Junior*, November 1948
                  Log for Music Americans Sing, p. 42
        Burl Ives — "Wayfaring Stranger," *Keyboard Junior*, Feb-
        ruary 1950
        Gershwin — *Keyboard Junior*, October 1945; April 1949;
        January 1952

     (8) Famous Songs
        Joshua Fit de Battle — *Keyboard Junior*, May 1948; *Log for
        Music Americans Sing*, p. 37
        Go Down, Moses — *Log for Music Americans Sing*, p. 37

  (*b*) Films
     Beautiful Dreamer — Library Films, 1948 (25 min., sd., b&w)
     De Camptown Races — Admiral, 1948 (18 min., sd., b&w)
     Come Where My Love Lies Dreaming — Admiral, 1947 (18 min.,
     sd., b&w)

5. Instrumental Experiences:

Songs of the minstrel show and the Southland lend themselves ad-
mirably to the use of such "social" instruments as the guitar, the banjo,
harmonica, ukulele, and the Autoharp. The "bones" (*Music Americans
Sing*, see p. 55) make excellent rhythmic accompaniments for *Buffalo
Gals* (Louisiana) and *Polly Wolly Doodle*. The guitar, Autoharp, ukulele, and banjo are effective with *In the Gloaming* and *Swing Low, Sweet
Chariot*.

For the songs that are within their ability to perform, use class members who play orchestral instruments for these accompaniments.

Another center of interest unit, which was made and enjoyed by a committee of pupils and their teacher, is included here to show that a great variation in organization of the unit is possible. No class will care to learn all the materials listed, but it will serve as a resource unit for teachers.

WORK AND SING

Contents

   I. Approaches to the Unit
  II. Activities of the Unit
      1. Song Material
      2. Listening Material
      3. Rhythmic Activities
      4. Pupil Activities in Class
 III. Associated Interests of Pupils
 IV. Correlation Possibilities with Other Subjects
  V. Culmination
 VI. Desired Educational Results
VII. Purposes of the Work — Song Unit

 I. Approaches to the Unit
    1. Correlation with:
       (*a*) A study of occupations conducted in the social studies class
       (*b*) American history

(c) A historical American movie or with current trends in radio, television, and movies

2. Visual Aids:

  (a) The following films were selected from the *Educational Film Guide*, published by H. W. Wilson Company, New York

    (1) *To Hear Your Banjo Play*, Brandon, 1948 (20 min., sd., b&w). Peter Seeger plays his banjo and narrates the story which traces folk music on the banjo in America from the first such instrument constructed by a Negro slave. Includes ballad singing and square dancing.

    (2) *American Square Dance*, Coronet, 1947 (10 min., sd., b&w). Relates square dancing to social dancing; teaches positions of dancers in relation to calls and demonstrates calls.

    (3) *Cowboy Squares and American Indians* (2 parts) Perry-Mansfield, 1946 (30 min., si., b&w). Part 1 — cowboy dances.

    (4) *Promenade All — Western Square Dancing*, Gateway, 1947 (11 min., sd., b&w). Includes 18 or more different figures of square dancing.

    (5) *Textile Worker*, Livingston (4 min., sd., b&w). A modern dance performed in the Hindu-Mongolian folk style by a girl who dances the motions of textile machinery, sewing, weaving, and so forth.

    (6) *Atlantic Coast*, Filmsets, 1942 (8 min., si., b&w). Surveys topography, resources, and industries of New England, Middle Atlantic, and South Atlantic States.

    (7) *Cattle and the Corn Belt*, UW-Educ., 1949 (20 min., sd., b&w). How the people who live and work on the vast areas of level land, which constitutes our midwestern plains, produce large quantities of food for the peoples of the world and feed for livestock.

    (8) *The Changing Cotton Land*, UW-Educ., 1949 (20 min., sd., b&w). Although much of the land in the South has been destroyed through wasteful farming practices, this film shows that the area has the resources for large-scale agricultural and industrial production.

    (9) *Ohio River* (upper valley), Academy, 1949 (11 min., sd., b&w). Upper half of Ohio River featuring cities of Pittsburgh and Cincinnati and their principal industries.

  (b) The following magazines contain pictures pertaining to this unit:

    (1) Chuck Wagon — *Colliers*, February 9, 1952, pp. 30-31

    (2) California Cowboy — *Holiday*, September 1951, pp. 26-31

(3) Rodeo — *Life,* November 1, 1948, pp. 22-24
(4) Cowboy — *Life,* August 22, 1949, pp. 63-73
(5) Rodeo — *Life,* March 6, 1950, pp. 14-16
(6) Oldtime Cowboys — *Life,* July 30, 1951, pp. 84-85
(7) Champ Rider — *Life,* October 22, 1951, pp. 123-129
(8) Reunion in Texas — *The Saturday Evening Post,* July 2, 1949, pp. 36-37
(9) Rodeo — *The Saturday Evening Post,* January 28, 1950, p. 10
(10) St. Louis Museum shows art of the Mississippi's great past — *Life,* March 6, 1950, pp. 73-78
(11) Spring on the Mississippi — *Life,* April 11, 1949, pp. 80-89
(12) Great Blue River — *Holiday,* January 1950, pp. 30-31
(13) Bold Skippers of the Lakes — *The Saturday Evening Post,* August 19, 1950, pp. 34-35
(14) Wonderful Arks of the Great Lakes — *The Saturday Evening Post,* May 27, 1950, pp. 34-35
(15) Pittsburgh — *Holiday,* October 1949, pp. 34-51
(16) Men and Mines — *New York Times Magazine,* January 29, 1950, pp. 8-9
(17) Tracks West — *The Saturday Evening Post,* November 5, 1949, pp. 22-23
(18) Super Chief — *Holiday,* October 1949, pp. 88-89
(19) West Wind Express — *Holiday,* January 1950, pp. 72-74
(20) Trouble Shooters of the River — *The Saturday Evening Post,* September 10, 1949, pp. 20-21

II. Activities of the Units
   1. Song Material:

Folk Songs

Title	Source [3]	Page	Title	Source [3]	Page
Cowboy			Railroader		
Goodbye Ol' Paint	A.S. 7	11	Levee Song	Discov.	41
The Cowboy's Meditation	A.S. 8	11	I've Been Workin' on the Railroad	S.O.	151
The Old Chisholm Trail	A.S. 8	134	Drill, Ye Tarriers, Drill	S.O.	153
Oh Saddle the Roan	Treas.	126	Pat on the Railway	O.W.S.	151
Home on the Range	Adven.	18	I've Been Workin' on the Railroad	M.A.S.	5
The Lone Prairie	Adven.	41	John Henry	M.A.S.	64
The Cowboy	Adven.	140			

[3] *Key to Source of Songs:* Adven., *Adventure;* Discov., *Discovery;* A.S. 7, *American Singer* 7; A.S. 8, *American Singer* 8; O.W.S., *On Wings of Song;* M.A.S., *Music Americans Sing;* S.A., *Sing Along — The World of Music;* S.D.R., *Singing Down the Road;* S.O., *Sing Out!;* S.P., *Song Parade;* Treas., *Treasure.*

Folk Songs (cont.)

Title	Source [4]	Page	Title	Source [4]	Page
Cowboy (cont.)			**Sailor**		
Whoopie Ti-Yi-Yo	S.D.R.	8	Away for Rio	A.S. 8	156
I Ride on Ol' Paint	S.D.R.	50	Blow the Man Down	Adven.	40
Goodbye Ol' Paint	S.O.	148	Cape Cod Girls	S.D.R.	10
Home on the Range	S.O.	148	Shenandoah	S.D.R.	79
Dogie Song	S.O.	150	Blow, Ye Winds	O.W.S.	123
The Roving Cowboy	O.W.S.	152	Blow the Man Down	M.A.S.	30
The Old Chisholm Trail	S.P.	214	Shenandoah	M.A.S.	79
Wandering Cowboy	S.P.	55			
Night Herding Song	M.A.S	. 83	**Boatman**		
Lumberjack			The Erie Canal	O.W.S.	91
The Shantyman's Life	A.S. 8	111	The Erie Canal	M.A.S.	86
Driving Saw Logs on the Plover	S.O.	146	Down the River	M.A.S.	78
The Shanty Boy and the Pine	S.O.	147	**Farmer**		
Miner			The Farmer Comes to Town	A.S. 8	152
Down in a Coal Mine	S.O.	151	Sandy Land	S.O.	52
			Pick a Bale of Cotton	S.D.R.	5
			Shuckin' of the Corn	O.W.S.	15

Art Songs

Title	Composed	Source [4]	Page	Title	Composed	Source [4]	Page
Farmer				**Fisherman**			
The Farmer's Breakfast	McKay	S.O.	56	Fisherman	Kramer	Adven.	12
Yankee Hill	Stroughton	S.O.	58	Pull in Your Nets	Strickland	S.A.	71
Harvest Song	Wentworth	S.O.	58	**Boatman** The Boatman's Dance	Emmet	S.O.	8
I Will Go with My Father Aplowing	Freeman	S.A.	66	**Longshoreman** Roll Out, Heave That Cotton	Hayes	S.O.	10

2. Listening Material:

The principle of "music while you work" was discovered long ago when men first saw that rhythm and unity of action helped

---

[4] *Key to Source of Songs:* Adven., *Adventure;* Discov., *Discovery;* A.S. 7, *American Singer* 7; A.S. 8, *American Singer* 8; O.W.S., *On Wings of Song;* M.A.S., *Music Americans Sing;* S.A., *Sing Along — The World of Music;* S.D.R., *Singing Down the Road;* S.O., *Sing Out!;* S.P., *Song Parade;* Treas., *Treasure.*

to perform a task with greater swiftness and efficiency. Music, more than anything else, gave their actions the joint effect that was needed. The rhythms of the shanty expedited work on sailing ships — the hauling of ropes, the turning of wrenches, the heaving of the anchor. The railroad man drove his spikes, laid his ties, and dragged his rails to tunes whose music and words grew out of the work itself. The principle still exists. The sailing ships are gone, and the era of laying new rail lines has come to a halt. During World War II, however, factory workers in many countries found their speed increased, their nerves quieted, and their efficiency heightened, if they worked to music which was rhythmically stimulating.

The sea chanty illustrates most clearly how the old songs were specifically tailored for a job; sea chanties are divided into four categories — halyard chanties, windlass or capstan chanties, short drag chanties, and forecastle chanties. In the singing of the old chanties, one man was a leader, and traditionally he improvised new lines for the solo parts which he sang. Most of them are a conglomeration of English ballads, American yarns, and the rhythmical melodies of American Negro dockworkers and stevedores.

The railroad song which is another type of work song grew up in America during the great era of expansion when shining roads of rails were being laid across the continent. Men of every nation and race took part in the work; the musical record of it we owe largely to bands of Irishmen who were imported as cheap labor. The swinging, swaying, chopping rhythms of the railroad songs are less easily categorized than those of the chanties, but they were a great stimulus to work.

The cowboy song is strictly a ballad and not a work tune. If the cowboy songs served any working purpose to the cowboy, it was probably, as one old timer remarked, "to keep himself awake." The songs were heard mainly around the campfires at night in company with guitar and accordion, and a chorus of lusty voices, or were sung alone on the solitary night watches when even the most robustious, tuneless cowboy singer had the courage to shout the familiar melody at the stars.

Although not strictly a work song, the cowboy ballad has many of the qualities of a work song. Countless singers have added to and improved the words and tunes and succeeding generations of Americans have remembered the more popular versions to give them a kind of national fame.

Patriotic (Military Songs as an Occupation)

When Johnny Comes Marching Home Again
 (Gould Arrangement) ....Victor

This is the Army (Album) ....Decca
This is My Country (Waring Album) ....Decca
Yankee Doodle Went to Town
    (Gould Arrangement) ....Victor
Stouthearted Men (Romberg-Eddy) ....Columbia

Mining Songs

Days of Forty Nine (Allen) ....Victor
Songs of Old California (Luther) ....Decca

Railroad Songs

American Folk Song Album ....Decca
    New River Train
    East Bound Train
Midnight Special ....Victor
One Hundred Miles ....Asch
Pat Works on the Railway (Seigmeister) ....Victor
John Henry ....Columbia
Coming Round the Mountain (Album P-155) ....Victor

Sea and River Songs

Roustabout Songs (Collection of Ohio River Songs)....Decca
    Valley Songs
    I'm Workin' My Way Back Home
    Ain't Got No Place to Hang My Head
Sea Chanties (Leonard Warren) ....Victor
    Blow the Man Down
    Rio Grande
    Shenandoah
Songs of American Sailormen (Bauman) ....Musicraft
Barnacle Bill the Sailor (Costello) ....Decca
Erie (Luther) ....Decca
The Erie Canal ....Columbia

Southland Songs (Spirituals and other composed music)

Jack O'Diamonds (Niles) ....Victor
Hard Times (Joshua White) ....Musicraft
Shortenin' Bread (Andrew Sisters) ....Decca
Mississippi Suite (Grofé) ....Columbia
Minstrel Show (Gould) ....Columbia
Ol' Man River ....Victor
Music by Stephen Foster ....Columbia
Kentucky Babe (Crosby) ....Decca

Deep River ....Victor
Oh! Susanna (Boston Pops Orchestra) ....Victor
On Springfield Mountain ....Musicraft

Western Work Songs and Composed Music

On the Trail (Grofé) ....Victor
Grand Canyon Suite
Jessie James (Plunket) ....Columbia
Tabloid Suite (Grofé) ....Victor
Rodeo Suite (Copland) ....Columbia
Cowboy Rhapsody (Copland) ....Columbia
Sante Fe Symphony (McDonald) ....Victor
Cowboy Camp Meetings (Spenser) ....Victor
Columbia Square Dance Album (with calls) ....Columbia
Home on the Range (Merrill) ....Victor
Round the Campfire (Famous American Cowboy
  Songs) ....Victor
Oklahoma (Rodgers and Hart) ....Decca
Down in the Valley (Ives) ....Decca
Carry Me Back to the Lone Prairie (Melton) ....Victor
A Cowboy's Lament (Ives) ....Decca
Sweet Betsy from Pike ....Okeh
Ballad for Americans (Robinson) ....Victor

Note: Many of the above selections are recorded by more than one artist and more than one company. The teacher should check new releases and make the selection accordingly.

3. Rhythmic Activities:
   (*a*) The various square dances were very popular among the pioneers of our country. Many of the song books for junior-high-school students contain very good opportunities for such rhythmic activities. Three outstanding examples of this are:
      (1) *Let Music Ring,* A Singing School, C. C. Birchard Co., Boston.
         Bow Belinda (Southern Dance Song), p. 21
         Barn Dance (American Tune), p. 25
         A Life on the Ocean Wave (Old American Song), p. 44
         Nelly Bly (Foster), p. 46
         Lady Walpole's Reel (Old American Tune), p. 47
      (2) *Sing Out!* A Singing School, C. C. Birchard Co., Boston.
         Pioneer Song, p. 30
         Captain Jinks (Old American Song), p. 32
         Red River Valley (American Song), p. 34
      (3) *Music Americans Sing,* Silver Burdett Co., New York.
         Yankee Doodle (British and American Soldiers' Song),
            p. 41

   Shoo Fly, Don't Bother Me (American Popular Song), p. 57

   She'll Be Comin' Round the Mountain (Southern Mountain Song), p. 77

   Hornpipe (Sailors' Dance), p. 34

(b) The following books were written for the sole purpose of presenting the different types of square dances:

  (1) *Dances of Our Pioneers*, Ryan, Benford, and Emerson, A. S. Barnes & Co., New York

  (2) *Old Square Dances of America*, Dunlavy and Boyd, Recreation Training School of Chicago

  (3) *Cowboy Dances*, Shaw, The Caxton Printers, Ltd., Caldwell, Idaho

  (4) *The American Square Dance*, Marzo, Sentinel Books, New York

  (5) *Sing and Dance* (folk songs and dances including American Play Party Games), Hunt and Wilson, Hall and McCreary, Chicago

  (6) *American Country Dances*, Burchenal, G. Schirmer, Inc., New York

(c) Other Dances:

  (1) *Old Brass Wagon* (singing game settlers used after picking apples). *America Sings*, Carmer, p. 98

  (2) *Goin' to Boston* (after corn-shuckin' in Kentucky). *Singing America*, Zanzig, No. 15

  (3) *Traditional Music of America*, Ford (contains complete section of "Old Time Play Party Songs with Dancing Games"), p. 237

  (4) *Skip to My Lou. Folk Songs and Dances of the Americas*, Pan American Union, Washington, D. C., p. 15

4. Pupil Activities in Class:

 (a) Bulletin boards showing current magazine pictures appropriate to unit; concert programs featuring folk music

 (b) Displays of historical period

  (1) Costumes

  (2) Pictures

  (3) Types of work and tools used

 (c) Notebooks

 (d) Book reports on fiction, and historical books about the periods pertaining to work songs

 (e) Maps showing origins of songs

III. Associated Interests of Pupils

 Television

 Radio

 Movie (historical, and so forth)

 Historical pageants

Interviews
Folk instruments
Square dancing

IV. Correlation Possibilities with Other Subjects
American History
Art
Social Studies
American Literature
Science (the technical development of America)
Home Economics (through the making of period costumes)

V. Culmination
1. Program for:
(a) Parents and PTA
(b) Other classes
(c) Community meetings

Suggested Script for Medley of Work Songs

Did you ever wash dishes or mow a lawn, and find yourself humming as you did so? If so, you were doing what Americans have done ever since the land was young — singing at their work. Clearing the land, putting up houses, churches, and schools, making railways, digging canals, loading boats and sailing them — in short, making America the land where millions could live and prosper was a man-sized job. It could not have been done without music.

Music? But how? Does playing a fiddle sail a boat, or singing a pretty tune pick a field of cotton? Well, not altogether, but it helps.

If it didn't, you certainly would not find the rawboned Yankee captains of old, hiring and giving extra pay to men whose main job was to bawl out chanties all day. The sailor's songs, which were called sea chanties, reflect the rhythmic movement of the sea and the bobbing of the ship. In the early days, when all ships were driven across the water by means of oarsmen, or the wind, the sailor brightened his work and kept up his spirit by singing. The verse of the song was usually sung by one sailor, who was called the chanty man, and then the others joined in on the chorus. Some of their songs were sad tales of sailors being lost at sea; some were tales of adventure; and still others were about the sailors coming home after a long voyage.

The American sailor was a tough and hardy fellow. Without his strong muscles, the frail ships would have been helpless. The sailor was also a lonely man because he had to leave his family at home while he sailed across the sea. Next to sailing, he loved to sing, and his songs show it. One of his favorites was *Blow the Man Down*.

This is a halyard or "long-drag" chanty. It was used for long tasks such as hoisting sails, pumping ship, or catting the anchor. The mate chosen to sing the solo line had to have either a big voice or the ability

to make up, on the spur of the moment, new and amusing verses. The chorus was half sung, half grunted by the crew as they pulled in rhythm.
— Sing *Blow the Man Down* from *Music Americans Sing*, p. 30

Just as there were sailors of the sea, so were there sailors on the inland rivers and lakes. The boatmen of the Ohio were a glorious and uproarious tribe. Old pictures show them singing as they poled their craft upstream or steered it downstream, very often with a fiddler sitting on the cabin, scraping away to make the time pass and the work less tedious. Canallers on the Erie cried out, "Low bridge" or "Giddap, there, mule" so many times that eventually they took to singing it, and one of the grandest songs of all was born: *The Erie Canal.*
— Sing *The Erie Canal* from *Music Americans Sing*, p. 86

The music of labor is the music of America. But while workingmen in all parts of the country have told of their joys and sorrows in song, there are none who have done this more powerfully or more beautifully than the Negroes. In the days of slavery, and today as well, the Negro was accustomed to moving, working, living in time to music. Some of their songs were joyful spirituals like the one *Goin' to Shout.* But many of them were sad, and they showed the Negro's longing for home and freedom. Quite often, they used the banjo or the mouth harp to accompany these songs, but, at other times, they used only the clapping of hands to keep the time. I wonder if you will get that same lonesome feeling that the Negroes had, when you sing this song.
— Sing *Nobody Knows the Trouble I've Seen* from *Fireside Book of Folk Songs*, p. 302

One of the oldest occupations in America is farming. From the beginning, American farmers worked their own private pieces of ground, and did it alone or with a few members of their families. If they sang, it was not usually at work, but in the evening among a group of friends, or on Saturday nights at a "play-party" or square dance. One of these singing games they often sang after harvesting their crops was *Old Brass Wagon.* The accompaniment was played on either a mouth harp or a fiddle.
— Sing and dance *Old Brass Wagon* from *Kit P* (Lynn Rohrbough), p. 23

No doubt the work songs you know best are those of the cowboy. The first cowboys were Mexicans. When Americans came to the cow country, they took over the Mexican ways of branding. They wore the same chaps, and used lariats or lassos, high saddles and high-heeled boots. In the old days when ranch life was of a most primitive type, the cowboys gathered in the big ranch house on the long evenings. There they entertained themselves and each other by singing of their life and past experiences. Sometimes they sang tunes they knew, changing them to suit the words which they improvised.

When cowboys drove their herds on the long trails to the north in the summer and to the south in the winter, they sang as they drove their cattle on the trail. And when they rested for the night, the cowboys on guard sang as they rode around the herd in order to quiet the "dogies" or yearlings and to avert a stampede.

Perhaps some of the cowboy songs you know are *Git Along Little Dogies, Goodbye Ol' Paint, The Streets of Laredo* and others. Now as you listen to Harl MacDonald's *Cowboy Rhapsody* see if you don't recognize some of the tunes which you know.

— Play recording of *Cowboy Rhapsody*

So far our music has come mostly from the wide, open spaces. By now you are no doubt wondering what kind of work music can be found in a big city. Or has our work today been made so automatic by various machines that we don't even think of singing to make it less strenuous. Perhaps many of us don't, but if you have ears to listen you can hear music despite the roar and clang of the city. Listen to the fascinating sing-song of the newsboy, or to the bell of the vendors, the roar of the fire engine, the wail of the siren or the cries of the fruit peddlers and you'll get some ideas of the city and the people who work in it.

Probably the work songs of the future will be more general than those of the past. But it will be a long time before we forget those that are so much a part of our history and the men who have made them. They are remarkable men, and perhaps you are wondering who they are. Listen as the *Ballad for Americans* tells you.

— Hear *Ballad for Americans*

    2. Radio or Television Program on:
       (*a*) School's public address system
       (*b*) Tape recorder
       (*c*) Local radio station
    3. Student Reports
    4. Original Operetta

 VI. Desired Educational Results
    1. Appreciation of:
       (*a*) American history
       (*b*) Amount of American folk music developed through work
       (*c*) Kinds of people who make up America and their work
    2. Skills:
       (*a*) Further development of reading and singing ability
       (*b*) Increased rhythmic co-ordination through square dancing
       (*c*) Ability to distinguish between music which comes "from the people" and music composed "for the people"
       (*d*) Acquisition of a deeper sensitivity toward listening
    3. Knowledge of:
       (*a*) Native American folk and composed music
       (*b*) Folklore and legends of our country
       (*c*) Our American history and geography

VII. Purposes of the Work-Song Unit
1. To show that music originates from "people," and that it can be a vital, functional part of living
2. To show that music relaxes people and provides a means of "letting off steam"
3. To show that music "unites people both physically and mentally" in developing the spirit of co-operation
4. In general, to show that there are many kinds of music for all types of people, and to acquaint pupils with a variety of these types

MUSIC TAUGHT AS ISOLATED SUBJECT MATTER

Teachers with a good musical background often wish to teach their pupils what they consider is excellent music. With love of fine music in their hearts, they offer "pearls of beauty," whether or not the class is ready to accept them. For example, one teacher who prided himself on having had the "very best musical training" began his groups with "tuning up exercises," which ended in disinterest and negative attitudes, and then chose the following songs for his series of eighth-grade classes.

The first song was Mozart's *Ave Verum,* a four-part song arranged for adult voices. Each part was drilled separately at the beginning of the lesson, with no attempt made to imbue the pupils with the inherent beauty and majesty of the song, the meaning of *Ave Verum,* the mass as a church service, and the glory and power of the organ when accompanying a choir. The song, beyond the music ability of the pupils and their understanding, was soon given up, much to the disgust of the teacher and to the relief of the pupils.

Next, the teacher suggested *Madame Jeannette,* a beautiful song arranged in four parts. This song is lovely in sentiment and rich in harmonic structure but is much too difficult for the untrained ears of most general music classes. After struggling with the difficult parts for fifteen minutes and becoming utterly confused, the pupils left *Madame Jeannette* when they were two-thirds through the song.

This was followed by a four-part arrangement of *Dry Bones,* a composition which the pupils loved. But again they were unequal to its vocal demands. As before, they were drilled on each part separately with the same frustrating results.

The next class was another eighth grade, which was given the same unrelated difficult songs, and received the same results. What do you think the Boys' Chorus, which followed, sang? You guessed it — *Ave Verum, Madame Jeannette,* and *Dry Bones* — all with the same chaotic and disheartening results. The pupils had no interest in the music, and the teacher was becoming a neurotic wreck due to "combat fatigue."

Often we find that songs are selected according to a sequence based on the degree of difficulty of certain rhythmic or tonal patterns. This is a fatal mistake since adolescents have little sympathy with this idea, and they are unwilling to fit into a curriculum based on logical, step-wise, or chronological procedures. We can no longer justify teaching the bass clef to a group of girls or to a group of unchanged voices simply because they are in the eighth grade and knowledge of the bass clef is required in this grade.

Those classes organized only to acquire skill and knowledge through isolated drill, using an atomistic psychology, are rarely successful. Teachers may well question the value of vocalizes and sequential singing since psychologists tell us there is little or no transfer of training. Trying to "pour in" music which appeals to the teacher but has no attraction for the pupil is fatal to the development of sensitivity to the engaging qualities of music. We must learn to apply the meaning of "readiness" in teaching junior-high-school pupils. Then those methods which advocate a page-by-page procedure will be avoided since *memoriter learning* (prescribed, dictated, and controlled by a logically organized text) may result in disinterest.

MUSIC TAUGHT AS RELATED TO PRESENT-DAY LIVING

In direct contrast to the method previously described, many educators believe that since music plays such a large part in the culture of today the classroom should reflect the life interests of the pupils. Music, developed from people through the folk song and dance, the universality of music, and its appeal, strengthens the brotherhood of mankind. American life is filled with music, because the phonograph, radio, television, films, and concerts of many types of music are available to the pupils in our classes. Being unwilling to be told what they should or should not like, children bring with them a great variety of preferences and dislikes for music. They need to be led to evaluate what they prefer and know why they prefer it.

The newer concept of education envisions the school as a social group and as a part of the community. This means that the subject matter used in the classroom should attempt to aid the pupil in enjoying and understanding his environment and that community resources should furnish a part of the curriculum. The local concert, the nearby violin factory, the local pipe organ, and the coming television and radio programs given by the Firestone Orchestra and discussed in *Keyboard Junior* make worthy community sources for subject matter. This type of teaching requires ingenuity, which many beginning teachers possess, but have not been encouraged to use. Pupils, seeing the reasons for music when it functions for them, no longer embarrass the teacher by the unanswerable question, "Why do we have to learn this?"

One teacher, knowing that the film *Rhapsody in Blue* (on Gershwin's life) was being shown in the local theater, decided to play a recording of the Rhapsody for a seventh-grade class, which was lethargic and antagonistic both toward music and school in general. He knew, also, that these pupils were ardent movie-goers. Their response to the recording was astonishing, for they had an experience to share with other class members. They brought records of other artists, conductors, and orchestras performing the Rhapsody, and the discussions revealing their preferences were so stimulating that they decided to study other contemporary composers. Irving Berlin was suggested by the pupils because they knew *White Christmas* and loved it. A committee was selected to bring in the names of other composers, while other committees were to choose the songs, decide on the music to be heard, and find sources in the library telling about the music and the composers studied. This study, lifted from community life, and making use of the pupils' interest and environmental conditions, resulted in a change from negative attitudes to positive enthusiasm for music. One pupil's interest in Indian lore led to a class-planned unit on Indian music.

How different these results are from those gained with subject matter isolated from pupil-interest and experiences! The former type of teaching is governed by the maturation of the pupils, which is a developmental, continuous growth process, rather than a belief that there is a prescribed time for the mastery of skills and the memorizing of facts.

SUMMARY

Because of different psychologies used in music education, teachers of music are often confused when they plan the curriculum. There are those who believe that the development of a well-integrated personality is a vital purpose of education and use music as an important factor in promoting the growth of desirable personality traits.

Many attempts have been made to break down rigid area barriers and use subject matter for solving the social and personal problems of pupils. The Core curriculum attempts to do this. It needs the co-operation of the staff and pupils in the selection and solving of the chosen problems.

Correlation may be used in the general music class to relate various music activities, which are selected in regard to pupil interests and needs. It also lends itself well in developing relationships with other subject matter areas such as social science, art, and English.

Music should be used as a socializing force throughout the school, and it has been used to foster desirable school and public connections in a community that has lost confidence in its schools.

Teachers have been successful in organizing music activities around some central idea based on pupil interests. These units are sometimes called "centers of interest." They may vary with each class in a school and reflect environmental and personal experiences of the pupils with music. These units may be organized in various ways by pupils and teachers and presented as a culmination for their own class, in the assembly, or as a public performance.

The music class should aid pupils in understanding the culture of our day and should interpret the meaning of television and radio programs and some movies. Using these sources as subject matter promotes enriched living and advances understanding of, and sensitivity to, the problems of present-day living.

In direct contrast we find music taught as isolated subject matter, using a page-by-page procedure to gain factual knowledge of music. Little attention is given to art values, and music is considered a science. The humanistic values of music and pupil-interest are sacrificed for memorizing notational facts; in fact, music for music's sake sometimes becomes the main purpose of the program. It is hoped that teachers will use music selected and presented in terms of pupils as consumers, for their enjoyment, rather than as a chore to be done or a lesson learned.

5. Junior-High-School Singers

THE CHANGING VOICE

In Chapter 1, we learned that pupils of junior-high-school age are individualistic, meaning that there is a great difference in their physical, emotional, intellectual, and social characteristics. Likewise, it is true that there is just as much variation in the pupils' singing voices. Some pupils have a speaking voice with a high, piping quality; some possess a fuller, rounder quality; others, a husky, reedy, and uncertain quality; still others, a deep, full, and lower voice. These same qualities are often found in the singing voices of the pupils in a class. Voices follow the physical development of the body; so, the music teacher faces a vocal problem about which, unfortunately, few scientific studies have been made.

Two theories concerning adolescent voices seem to be foremost in the thinking of junior-high-school teachers, but, regardless of any theory, American schools advocate that all pupils should sing through the period of voice change (mutation). One theory advanced is that there is a gradual lowering of the voice and that the boys' voices, called *alto-tenor* during mutation, have very small range. It is believed that girls' voices change also, but mostly in quality. There may be somewhat of a change in range, though not to the extent of lowering an octave as is characteristic of boys' voices.

The second theory, concerning the boy's changing voice, is propounded by Dr. Irwin Cooper of Florida State University, and has been demonstrated by him to many music teachers. He believes that this voice, which he calls the *cambiata* (an Italian term meaning *changing*) has a range extending from

to , and if it is handled correctly, there need be no break in the voices as believed by the exponents of the alto-tenor theory. This means that the changing voice retains some of the alto quality and range and does not shift into a range limited to tones between the staves. If this theory proves correct, we may be able to find the reason for the paucity of tenors found in many high-school music classes.

KINDS OF VOICES AND RANGES

Nearly every general music class will contain some boys who have high, unchanged voices. They can sing exactly the same part as girls with soprano voices. So as to avoid any possible suggestion of femininity, the clever teacher will not call these boys *sopranos* but, instead, *high voices*. They often

have a two-octave range, , but it would be unwise to use the two extremes of their range very often. This range,

, is the most comfortable for the high voices, and will sound light and clear if the voices are not forced. Boys should be encouraged to sing with this "flute-like" voice as long as it is not difficult for them to do so.

There are few real alto voices in the junior high school, and since many children come to the seventh grade with a negative

attitude toward singing alto because of an unhappy experience
with the part, it may be better to call these voices *low voices*.
Boys whose voices are unchanged, but who sing with girls, have
voices which are fuller, rounder, and mellower in the lower part

of their range, which is . Many of these voices

can sing the two-octave range illustrated previously, but it is
unwise for them to sing songs that continuously use the extremes of their range. Teachers should avoid materials that
force these low voices into the adult alto range and should
encourage unison-singing that requires the use of the upper
part of their range. Some unchanged voices do not have the
lower pitches of the low voices, and they do not sing the upper
pitches of the high voices easily, although they have much of
the same light quality. These voices have been called *second
soprano*, and again we often meet negative attitudes toward
singing this part, although it, like the meat in the sandwich, is
most important.

The junior-high-school pupil loves to feel important, and he feels that being called a *second* implies inferiority or playing "second fiddle" to some more important part. Consequently, it seems wiser to avoid classifications which have unpleasant connotations for the pupils. Here is a typical range for these voices, , which we can label as the *middle* part. In a group of unchanged voices, they are most valuable for harmonic reasons.

In many general music classes we find boys with changing voices, previously referred to as alto-tenor, or *cambiata*. Why not call them what they are, changing voices? There are as many ranges in this group as the well-known "57 varieties."

Their range lies somewhere between and . Some boys will have lost their upper range because of lack of use of this part of the voice; other boys will not have many tones left, and are limited to a few pitches for a short time. We need to use music that has enough range in it to stimulate singing a melody rather than teeter-tottering on a few pitches to complete chords. In some changing voices the tone is rich and full, while in others it may be coarse, uncertain, and reedy. The most important thing is to keep the boys singing throughout this changing period. A boy needs encouragement from the teacher, and it is at this time many boys are lost to music because of a popular fallacy that changing voices are not pleasing in quality. These voices may find it difficult to match pitches since they are not sure how to use this new voice, and as a result they are called *monotones* by teachers who do not understand their problem. This feeling of inability may cause boys to become social problems in their group. During this period many uncertain boys become excellent singers when the teacher understands and shows confidence in the pupil's ability to learn.

The boy bass should not be confused with the adult bass. It is generally accepted that the range of the young bass should not be too low, but often boys can sing lower than the range which is indicated 🎼 . They may sing a first line G, but it is unwise to choose songs that use this pitch to a great extent. Since this voice is on its way down, it may lose some of its top pitches. Occasionally, in the junior high school, some of these voices become tenors. Many boys in this group have deep, full, and heavy voices, especially those of certain racial backgrounds. They should not sing only the low tones of chords, but should have unison experience in songs that uses the upper part of their voices.

VOICE TESTING AND CLASSIFICATION

Testing voices is a most important activity, and must be handled carefully lest the pupils become frightened, and re-

luctant to sing. Keep it foremost in mind that the teacher needs to win his class first of all. Perhaps it would be wise to start the classes singing unison songs, which appeal to boys, for if you win them, and they leave the class thinking music is fun (not chaos), the girls will come along with you.

The unison songs must not only be virile and typically boyish, but they must be in a range which most of your class can sing with ease and pleasure. The following range,

, is a safe one for unison-singing, and the less

deviation there is from this range, the more successful the song will be. Be sure to transpose the songs to fit this range. Do not take a soprano-range song to your group and expect participation from the changing voices and boy basses.

After you have established good class morale, begin testing voices quietly. We have been told that each pupil alone should sing scales down and up from G second line treble, or a familiar song transposed to his range. This procedure will work very well in classes where the pupils have been taught to sing alone in the elementary grades and know no fear in individual or solo singing. In schools where individual try-outs are an accepted pattern and winning pupils to music is not paramount, the individual tests will be satisfactory. One young teacher lost her class because she insisted on individual tests before the boys were ready for such procedures. The boys refused to sing alone, and she was forced to learn that in many cases group testing can be used quickly and effectively, followed by individual tests done in private when a need for it is felt by both pupil and teacher.

If you wish to classify the voices by using a group procedure, choose a unison song such as *Dear Evalina* (G), *Down in the Valley* (E flat), *Home on the Range* (E flat), or *I've Been Workin' on the Railroad* (F). Ask both boys and girls to sing the song, then girls alone, then boys alone. Among the boys you will hear some who sing in the treble, above middle C.

Silence the voices that sing an octave below the trebles and call this group the *boy basses*.

Use the same song, but transpose it a perfect fifth higher, asking the remainder of the boys to sing the song in the higher key. The high voices (soprano) will sing easily in the new key. The boys who sing below the trebles are the changing voices (alto-tenor). If there are boys who sing in the treble range but who do not sing the upper tones easily in the new key, they are the low voices (unchanged).

Use the same procedure with the girls. Those who sing easily in the newly transposed key are the high (soprano) voices, and those who sing easier in the originally used key, are low (alto) voices. Those who do not sing the top tones easily with the high voices are the middle voices. Making no previous announcement and saying little about it, use this procedure rapidly to avoid any tension in the pupils and your class from becoming a social problem. You will thus have high, middle, and low boy and girl unchanged voices and boy bass and changing voices segregated in short order.

No doubt some errors will be made in such quick checking of voices; so, teachers should watch for physical evidences that indicate the part assigned is incorrect. Scowling, a protruding lower jaw, and strained neck tendons are all signals that the pupil should be changed. Individual tests with no other pupils present may settle this problem if the pupil is interested. In no case should pupils who can carry a part be forced to sing out of range in order to insure balance of parts.

SEATING PLANS AND PART-SINGING

In some seventh, and occasionally in some eighth grades, all the voices will be unchanged. None of the voices have mutated or have started on their downward path. The voices are called high, middle, and low. If the group has not had much part-singing experience in the elementary school, it is wise to start with unison and two-part song. The unison songs should be of

medium range, as illustrated: 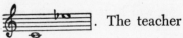. The teacher

must remember that there are groups which have not developed a readiness for part-singing, and to coerce these groups into difficult part-singing brings negative attitudes. To keep musical interests alive is the paramount objective in the general music class; so, isolated drills should be avoided. Singing descants and rounds are most valuable in developing readiness for part-singing. Rounds learned first in unison and then in two and three parts are pleasurable and helpful.

With such inexperienced groups the lower part may carry the melody. The pupils call this kind of singing "harmonizing"; they love to do it on hayrides, bus trips to athletic events, and in camp. This is the most natural way to learn to sing in parts. Often the high voices sing a melody, with the lower voices singing thirds and sixths below "to make harmony." The following seating plan aids in developing a feeling for part-singing:

HIGH	LOW

It is very easy to move into three-part singing after the class has enjoyed two-part songs. Those songs which do not move too fast and have the melody in the middle part are valuable for developing three-part work. Here is a seating plan that adjusts easily from two- to three-part singing:

HIGH	MIDDLE	LOW

Those classes which have changing voices should use a seating plan, which will group these voices strategically near the teacher. You may like this plan:

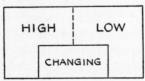

The tempi of the songs suitable for this group should be slow. The changing voices should have the melody often, for interest is soon lost when the part for changing voices furnishes only a harmonic support for the melody given to the high voices.

There are groups which have four kinds of voices, and for them this plan is useful:

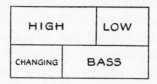

The basses should have a slow moving part which uses I, IV, and V of the harmonic structure. Simple scale passages can be used, but it must be remembered that these boys are learning to manage a new voice, sing a harmonic part, and read in a new clef simultaneously. After interest is gained and kept alive by the use of some songs which have the melody in the bass, chords may be used to develop skill in part-singing. They are more functional if they are taken from a song that is studied. The following chords taken from *In the Evening by the Moonlight* will be helpful in developing a feeling for I, IV, and V chords when one is teaching a song.

Put such chordal progressions from your song on the blackboard. Or, if possible, dictate them to increase both interest and skill in singing songs in tune.

There are other groups in which there are too few changing voices to carry a part. If there are only one or two, they may be placed with the bass part and encouraged to sing what they can. Be doubly careful that the range is not too low. The whole problem of changing voices and boy basses requires a teacher who not only has musical ability but tact and understanding, and that understanding must be conveyed to the pupil — through a frank discussion, if need be.

SELECTING SONGS

1. First of all, keeping the boys uppermost in mind, select songs which will interest the class. Girls will sing what boys enjoy, but the reverse is not true. Teachers teach best the music they prefer, but the pupils may not accept the teacher's choice wholeheartedly, and this may create a difficult classroom situation.

2. After several songs have been heard and discussed, afford the class the opportunity to aid in choosing a new one. When a class has never had this opportunity, the students may not have a good standard of evaluation. So, the teacher should have some "sure-fire" songs, such as *Home on the Range*, ready for use. A combination of the teacher's choice and group decision makes better participation and class morale.

3. Consider carefully what the text has to say, remembering that many junior-high-school pupils desire sensations rather than ideas.

4. The range and arrangements are all important. The ranges for various kinds of voices have been given previously, and arrangements to fit the voices in the groups are a prime necessity. It is wiser to select songs which fit the voices than to try to fit the voices to the arrangements we have.

5. An especial warning should be given not to select materials which are too difficult. Many songs simple in musical structure are among the most beautiful and heart-warming. Avoid music that is either too adult or too juvenile.

6. Pupils like the music which they hear outside of school. The teacher should be willing to sacrifice some musical standards occasionally and permit the pupils to sing some of these songs in order that they will not always be required to sing what the teacher prefers. Developing musical taste requires a give-and-take attitude on the part of both teacher and pupil.

7. Remember that unison songs have a place in all junior-

high-school classes, but when they are used they should be within the ranges previously discussed under voice testing and classification. These unison songs should be balanced with part songs since the various kinds of voices need part-singing, and future participation requires it.

8. The *tessitura* of the song should be considered when a song is chosen. All music teachers need to understand the meaning of the term *tessitura* in addition to knowing the ranges of the voices. Grove's Dictionary [1] defines it as a "Term used to indicate how the music of a piece lies"; that is to say, the prevailing or average position of a composition's tones in relation to the compass of a voice or instrument is high, medium, or low. The range of the voice should not be confused with the *tessitura*. The range may be wide, but the continued use of a too high or too low *tessitura* may be injurious to voices.

The American Academy of Teachers of Singing has issued a chart, relative to this problem, called "Problems of *Tessitura* in Relation to Choral Music." This chart fixes the range of the adult soprano from D or E to G or A, and the *tessitura* from A to D, . Songs that use the full range of the soprano voice, but whose *tessitura* is confined to the above chart, will be right for the soprano. The *tessitura* for all voices should be considered when music texts or octavo arrangements are selected.

MUSIC TEXTS

There are many texts available for use in the general music classes. Since classes are so varied, no one book is adequate to meet the interests, abilities, and ranges of all the pupils. Instead of assigning one book to each grade, it gives much more variety to the program to make several books available to

---

[1] *Grove's Dictionary of Music and Musicians* (New York: The Macmillan Company, 1935), V, 310.

seventh, eighth, and ninth grades. This way the correlated program as opposed to a page-wise procedure is possible. Teachers will need to be careful to select songs which are suitable in voice arrangements, since some texts are designed especially for seventh grades and some for the eighth and ninth grades. A music book cannot fit the vocal needs of every grade because no two sections of a grade are alike vocally; there are boy basses in some seventh-grade classes, for example, while in others the voices are all unchanged. Some texts listed at the close of this chapter are suited best for assembly singing, but are included, because in some instances they are suitable and enrich the general music class materials.

TEACHING THE NEW SONG

Of course there is no one way to teach a new song, but procedures which are based on sound educational principles are effective in the classroom. Educational leaders tell us that we learn easiest what we desire to know. For this reason, there may be a short period of time devoted to interesting the pupils in what the music has to say, the length of this motivation to be determined by the type of song and the interest of the class. This development of readiness may be called the *preparation*.

Preparation

1. You may wish to use a visual aid, a film, or a picture, which contains the identical mood of the song.

2. The scene might be set by using a recording of the song and by giving a brief background of the performer, the composer, or the composition.

3. A poem or a story may be used in connection with the song, in order to enhance the beauty and mood of the song.

4. Try reading as expressively as possible the music text for your class, or ask a pupil to read it. A group cannot express well what they do not understand. Discuss the meaning of the words, and, if possible, connect the song with everyday living.

5. Assign the parts carefully, and have those pupils who have had little experience with music point to the place on the page where their part is located. Take nothing for granted.

6. Discuss repeated phrases, melodic patterns, and recurring rhythms briefly.

7. Unless you desire a pure sight reading activity, play the song as artistically as you can, using the same dynamics you wish your class to use. Play the voice parts, leaving out the accompaniment until the song is learned. The first hearing sets the stage for artistic singing. In case you have a group that reads music well, it would stimulate their interest if they were asked to hum along as the accompaniment is played. In this way they can get an over-all idea of the song, the procedure being psychologically from the whole to the parts.

Participation

The preparation should take a very short time, because pupils can be bored easily with details. Now we are ready to sing.

1. Tune all parts from the root of the beginning chord, using the vowel found in the first word, unless it is a closed vowel ("ē" or "ī"). Then use some open vowel such as "ä" or "ō." Tuning is most important, since there are pupils who cannot find the beginning pitch unless it is sounded for them and they hear it sung by others on their own part.

2. It is important to set the tempo so that all class members will begin together. There is no one way to do this. Saying the word "sing" on the pulse before the one on which the song begins will aid in securing a good attack. The teacher may need to give more than the initial measure to insure feeling for the tempo. Beginning teachers will need to practice in order that the class will understand when to start singing. If you feel that the use of "sing" is too mechanical and dictatorial, you may prefer to ask the pupils to count to themselves while the introduction is being played.

3. Sing the first stanza and possibly the chorus in all parts, using the words while the piano plays the voice parts. As pre-

viously stated, the accompaniment should not be played, unless it includes the voice parts, until the song is learned. If the words are too difficult for the class, use a neutral syllable such as "ah" or "lah."

Drill

The best choirs work hard to make their performance good, and certainly music cannot be sung well by amateurs unless they work to correct their errors. Junior-high-school pupils will feel the need of this if the drill is motivated and done in short spans on materials they wish to perform. The following suggestions for effective drill may be useful to beginning teachers.

1. Ask your class to suggest where help is needed. Some classes will find this a new experience, since they have been taught to do what the teacher demands. To develop a sense of evaluation and judgment encourage your class to be self-critical. This may be a slow process, but it is a valuable one; take their suggestions and use them before you offer your criticisms.

2. Select what you consider the most glaring error and start at once to correct it. Isolate the error and work fast with the part concerned.

3. Have the part sing the corrected error with another harmonic part or have the whole class sing the phrase containing the newly learned spot. This should be done rapidly.

4. To repeat singing the song incorrectly makes it more difficult to learn it correctly. One cannot hope to have the song sung perfectly during the first experience with it; so, it is wise to leave the song with a feeling of accomplishment and a liking for it. Overdrill kills interest and "interest is paramount." Knowing how long to stay on a song is one of the marks of a good teacher. This timing can be learned through developing a sensitivity to class response.

Resinging the song

Favorite songs will be requested many times by the class and will need to be reworked with every repetition if there is to be growth. Some songs become favorites after they have been reworked although they may not have caught fire at first. These recall lessons should be handled carefully, since in some classes the songs are not sung any better than during the first attempt.

1. Recall quickly the most appealing qualities the song has, but not in such detail as in the first preparation.

2. Remind the class, or have them remind you, of what was learned previously and suggest the things for which they are to listen.

3. Play the song, bringing out the parts which need to be strengthened.

4. Correct errors which were not corrected previously.

5. Stress dynamic and tempo changes.

6. Select a single or double trio or quartet to sing the song, if the class does not respond first to a call for volunteers.

7. Again, ask for suggestions from the class.

8. Occasionally, bring in some technical aspects found in the song similar to the following:

(a) Is the song in the major or the minor mode?

(b) Locate 1-3-5 (tonic triad).

(c) Which phrases are alike? Which are unlike?

(d) Which rhythm patterns are repeated?

(e) In which direction does your part go — up or down?

(f) Does your part progress in steps or skips (narrow or wide)?

The above mentioned factual knowledge is important, and should be taught as incidental rather than accidental learning. To begin a lesson with a battery of questions based on the so-called "fundamentals" is a fatal mistake and a good way to divorce pupils from music.

MUSIC READING

The problem

Many teachers are perplexed, confused, and frustrated by the problem of music reading in junior-high-school classes. It appears that there is no more an easy solution to this than there is to the problem of teaching all children to read language. Some teachers believe they are realistically facing the issue by admitting that not all pupils can learn to read music independently and that, furthermore, not all pupils will find a functional use in life for music reading. Others believe that an attempt should be made to develop music reading ability in all children through formal classroom procedures; they make reading music the all-important classroom activity. They assume that children fail in their musical experience when they do not achieve success in this area. Still others have reached no conclusions. However, it is evident in any discussion of this controversial issue that music educators are having difficulty in attempting to adjust their ideas about music reading to the newer educational philosophy.

When pupils enter the junior-high-school grades, usually they have either decided or begun to wonder whether or not music reading serves any real purpose in their lives. Both the extent and quality of previous musical experiences, as well as musical capacity and intelligence, enter into this attitude, encouraging some and discouraging others in the music reading process. Since motivation is a key to learning, teachers who meet negative attitudes toward music reading evident from their initial contacts with some pupils are baffled and discouraged. Having done nothing to bring about such attitudes, they feel powerless to remedy them. Fortunately, many teachers are alert to the factors which produce such negative attitudes and do not expect the impossible. A teacher may say, "Sam can't yet read the directions for doing an arithmetic problem; how can I expect him to read a page of music symbols plus the words of a song?"

The crux of the problem seems to lie here: Proponents of an older philosophy are still bent upon making all children into performers of music, thus justifying the need of reading skills. Proponents of the newer philosophy are more concerned with encouraging all children to be participants in musical activities, with the emphasis upon music for serving the needs of the individual rather than upon the future needs of a band, choir, orchestra, or audience. We may say, in defense of the first group, that this is true: Some pupils will find their greatest satisfaction in performing music. On the other hand, the majority will become consumers rather than performers. The difference is much the same as that between a sports spectator and a participant — the former can recognize and applaud a forward pass without possessing the ability to play on the team.

From the viewpoint of life adjustment, it seems better to be an interested but unskilled spectator (or consumer) than either a disillusioned and frustrated performer or one who rejects any interest in music. We cannot force a child to attempt the acquisition of a skill beyond his maturity level or ability without expecting a loss of security and interest to result.

A realistic approach

Junior-high-school pupils, beginning the long struggle to establish themselves as independent individuals, are particularly sensitive to what is and what is not useful in their lives. They are likely to rebel against the music reading process if it appears to be nonfunctional. "We want to sing songs," they say, "we don't want to read notes. Do, re, mi and 1-3-5 we don't need. We can learn to sing the songs we like by listening to them on the radio, television, or a jukebox." Implied in such statements is the attitude that they will not readily accept reading music simply as a drill process; they want it to produce evident results in their musical lives. Embarrassing as this may be to some teachers, it is probably the best thing that could happen to the music program. It forces teachers to use all skill-building procedures as an end to immediate musical enjoyment. The desire to make music is present in the majority of boys and girls, although the way they want to make it differs. One boy wants to sing, another to play the harmonica. A girl may have a concealed ambition to sing a solo in her church choir; another has wanted to belong to the high-school choir ever since the time she heard them sing at a spring concert. A shy, indifferent boy sees and hears the school male quartet clowning and singing at a school assembly, applauded vigorously by the audience. Needing an outlet for self-expression he says to himself, "That's for me." Whether the urge is intrinsically musical, or whether it is basically social, it is a beginning point for the teacher. We can sing more music and in a more interesting way (harmonizing in class or in small ensembles), if we can read music.

The changing voice, which places the male voice in a new clef, is an excellent starting point for the teacher. Singing music written in the bass clef is a male perogative; this appeals to the boy's need to establish himself in a manly activity. Girls are interested in the new combinations of voices and singing parts, which begin in the junior high school when voices change.

We can learn a simple unison song quite easily by rote procedures. When we come to learn a three- or four-part song for mixed voices, however, it takes so long if we do it by rote that it often becomes tedious and boring. This problem can be solved by learning to read music.

Recognizing and discussing such reasons for the reading program will stimulate interest and bring about a co-operative attitude in music classes, whereas an imposed drill procedure often results in the loss of interest and even active resistance. Teachers should take their cue from this.

Implementing the music reading program

First, think about the terms *rote* and *note* as they apply here. Are you one of those teachers who believe that note reading must be strictly interpreted, that is, the pupils are given the pitch, and then must sing a new song with no other assistance? If so, ask yourself: How many adults can do this? Can *you?* The authors believe that many music educators as well as many lay people cannot. If you are still unconvinced, ask the directors of church choirs, college choirs, and community choirs how many members of these organizations can do so. If this is our goal, it appears to be an academic one.

Rote singing, generally defined, means singing by imitation. But an important implication here is that the singer manages to imitate by means of his aural experience.

As he accumulates experiences of this sort in singing, listening, and playing on simple instruments, he eventually comes to relate to the musical score what he hears, thus associating the written notes with their actual rhythmic pattern and pitches. This is a development of the so-called "inner ear." The goal is that the notes are translated into and signify these musical sounds directly as the pupils looks at them. Thus the process seems to unfold somewhat in this manner:

1. We hear, then sing.
2. We hear and see, then sing.
3. We see, hear (inner ear), and sing almost simultaneously.

This last step is what we call reading music, or singing by note. Unfortunately, some teachers forget that it does not necessarily mean singing musically, which includes not only a total interpretation of the score, but also that elusive factor, the expression of the singers' feeling for the music.

Since the rate of speed at which a child develops skill in this process depends not only upon his musical capacity but also upon his intelligence, we cannot expect all pupils to show evidence of the same gains. Indeed, we cannot expect all pupils to *make* significant gain.

Needless to say, the attention of the pupil must be directed to the score. Simply because a music book is in the hands of a pupil does not mean that he is following the notes. For one thing, he may be watching the text alone instead of text and music, or he may present the appearance of looking at the music without really doing so. This is particularly likely to be true of those pupils who have had very little in the way of musical experience preceding junior high school and who are so overwhelmed by the immensity and perplexity of the task that they simply withdraw mentally from it. Teachers must not assume that because a child is in seventh grade, for example, he understands the significance of the score and its use; such an assumption itself may throw the uncertain pupil into great confusion. Having established in the minds of the class reasons for reading music, the teacher should next explain clearly and simply the significance and use of the score. Next, through the use of many songs and thematic materials from listening activities, he should begin the gradual process of helping pupils understand and use the musical score. Specific ways of doing this (however not to be followed sequentially), which have been used by many teachers, include:

1. Understanding the form, or construction, of a song.
2. Recognizing the outline of phrases.
3. Recognizing like and unlike phrases.
4. Orienting the voice range to the range of the staff.
5. Locating own vocal line.
6. Following progression of notes up or down on the staff.
7. Understanding the meaning of scale-wise and skipping intervals.
8. Recognizing specific groups of notes, such as 1-3-5.
9. Using tonic and tonic triad as orientation points.
10. Finding intervals which are associated with familiar songs and already well known.
11. Trying to make a part sound right in association with the notes on the staff and the sound of a harmonizing part.
12. Interpreting tempi, dynamics, accents, and phrasing as indicated in the score.
13. Verbal chanting.

The child's understanding and application of such techniques progresses from the general to the particular, from the crude to the refined. Most important, progress is made through the use of many materials and varied procedures. Instruction should be given a little at a time, so that from each short lesson some mastery will be achieved with resulting satisfaction.

Teachers often ask, "Shall we use syllables, numbers, pitch names, or position recognition in order to develop music reading?" Again, there is no one answer. If the class has a good attitude toward any one of these, it certainly makes sense to continue its use. If there is a negative attitude toward any one procedure, however, it should be discontinued. At times, a class which has been discouraged by failure to grasp the significance of syllables can be interested by throwing open to their consideration the problem of evolving ways of reading music. In one class where this was done, an apparently disinterested boy, challenged by the discussion, said, "It seems to me that if we gave each note of the scale a number instead of a crazy syllable, it would make more sense." Instead of telling him this was far from an original idea (it *was* original for him) the teacher said, "That sounds good; let's try it." Reading in this class then proceeded with numbers.

Sometimes a teacher who has despaired of interesting a class or a particular individual in the reading process finds that suddenly, and seemingly for the most unlikely reasons, interest is aroused. A struggling teacher, who felt he was getting nowhere in this process with one particular group, was suddenly interrupted by a boy who rarely bothered even to look at the music book. "What's that there sign that looks like two golf clubs, one right side up and one upside down?" he asked. "Show me," said the teacher, somewhat bewildered by the description. At this the boy came forward and pointed to a natural, which occured in the song. "Put it on the blackboard, please," said the teacher. He then explained its meaning to the class and its particular effect on the melody of the song. The class looked for other naturals in songs they knew and sang them as demonstrations of the symbol. "Now be sure," the teacher said, "to ask me about other signs you don't understand, because that was an excellent question and helped us all to learn." In the meantime, he had realized that the boy asking the question had spent the preceding summer caddying and playing golf whenever he could — he interpreted the musical score in terms of his greatest interest. Strange as it may seem, this was the beginning of a real interest for the boy in learning to read music and seemed to bring about a different attitude toward the process on the part of other class members.

From such simple and unexpected incidents does learning begin, and in this case, from interest in an activity quite extraneous to the subject at hand. Incidents such as this certainly tell us, "*Never* give up and never stop looking for ways to develop music reading interest that make sense to the boys and girls we teach."

On the whole, however, the best stimulus for helping boys and girls to want to read music is a vital musical environment with many activities functioning constantly. When this exists, it provides obvious reasons for learning to read music. No teacher should feel that he fails if every child does not become an independent reader of music, because this is no more possible than making every child a first-string basketball player. Nevertheless, it is the teacher's responsibility to give every pupil an opportunity to learn music reading as a functional part of the enjoyment of *making* music.

CHOIRS

The choir, sometimes called the mixed chorus, has been in existence in the church for many centuries, but it is a recent addition to the junior-high-school curriculum. Choirs seem to be increasing in numbers since many administrators and music educators realize the educational significance of these select groups. Most junior high schools schedule general music classes, but only recently has it been realized that boys and girls can sing fine music beautifully in spite of the problems of mutation.

The purpose of this organization is to provide the musically talented pupils with a means of expression of strong emotional and social feeling. The choir affords an opportunity to acquire skills according to their ability and provides for greater appreciation of fine music through richer experiences. The choir may be used to stimulate interest in music in the less talented pupils; some teachers have been able to help boys and girls develop good singing voices when they are placed with pupils who could sing well, and were encouraged to "keep on trying" because of the teacher's faith in their ability to learn.

Most administrators and teachers accept the principle of individual differences, and the choir is organized as a means of meeting these varied, individual, musical differences. The general music class must function in such a way that all levels of ability will have an opportunity for growth, but it is most difficult to use music which is challenging for the talented pupils in this class. The choir meets the needs of talented singers. This holds true equally for the boys' and girls' glee clubs.

The choir furnishes music for the entire student body and may stimulate the less gifted to participate according to their ability in music classes. It raises the level of appreciation throughout the entire school and makes good music available to pupils who otherwise would have little opportunity to hear music other than that performed in the classroom.

Choirs have a direct influence on the community and gain communal support for the schools and the music department. Parents become interested in the fine performance of their children, and often their taste is improved as a result. These organizations may wield a powerful influence by keeping pupils interested in school and by offering a fine social atmosphere for their members. Glee clubs offer the same values and function in the same manner within the school and community as do choirs.

Organization

If the teacher feels there is enough interest among the pupils, he should gain permission from the principal to organize a select group. In case there is doubt about gaining enough members for an organization, it may be wise to organize a quartet, a double quartet, or an ensemble selected from the general music classes and use this group as a nucleus for the larger organizations.

The choir and glee clubs should be selective as well as elective. If it is possible, select in May the members for the coming year. These organizations should be scheduled during the school day, two — five periods a week. If it is necessary, it may be that the groups will have to meet outside of school hours to get started, but this situation should not be encouraged. It is unfair to students and teachers.

These organizations should be accredited on a laboratory basis, the ninth-grade pupils receiving credit toward high-school graduation. The seventh and eighth grades should receive credit, and their work should not be considered as extra-curricular.

Invite singers in the general music classes to try out for the selected groups. Pupils from grades 7, 8, and 9 should be selected in order that the younger pupils will form the nucleus for the next year's choir. In some schools, the ninth-grade pupils refuse to belong to organizations which include seventh graders, and in such cases it may be necessary to have a choral organization which enrolls only the younger pupils. Sometimes boys prefer all-male groups, and it is for this reason some schools offer glee clubs. Some larger schools support both choirs and glee clubs. The try-outs should be conducted individually since only those who are willing to sing before others and are vitally interested in singing will want to belong.

Some consideration must be given to balance, but it is impossible to secure balance by choosing a certain number of pupils for each part. We can go on the assumption that it takes more high and low unchanged voices to balance changing and bass voices. In some schools, choir members serve as a committee to aid the teacher in selecting new members.

Having student officers is an excellent means of developing democratic ideas and ideals in choral groups. Junior-high-school pupils enjoy having responsibility for the success of their organization and are highly co-operative in aiding the teacher when they feel they have a part in the planning. The teacher should be a leader and not a dictator and should seek the advice of the elected officers. In the book, *Glee Club and Chorus*,[2] there are many suggestions, which with modifications made to fit the junior high school, would be most helpful to the choral director.

Kinds of voices, ranges, testing, and seating plans

Some of the most talented musical pupils are boys with unchanged voices. They should be members of the choir, since they have a fine contribution to make and will become excellent tenors, baritones, and basses later. These voices are found in grades 7 and 8 generally, but occasionally in the ninth grade. When they are not encouraged to sing, they often are lost to music and never join any singing groups. These boys should sing with girls on the so-called soprano and alto parts, but for strategic reasons, as mentioned previously, it is better to call them high and low voices. They work better when they are grouped together and are not interspersed among the girls.

Of course, we have the changing voices, which sometimes are in the minority. To secure balance, it may be necessary to ask girls with low voices to aid this part, but under no circumstances should they be assigned definitely to the part since it might be too low and ruin their voices. There are certain physical characteristics, which are clues to the changing voice and are used by teachers along with the speaking voice timbre in order to separate the changing from the unchanged voices. They are a large Adam's apple, an appearance of a beard, big feet, and large wrist and ankle bones.

The bass voices are most important, since they do much for the success of the whole group being in tune. They often are sluggish in tempo and indistinct in diction. Thus, they need much help in learning to manage their new voices.

2 Van A. Christy, *Glee Club and Chorus* (New York: G. Schirmer, 1940), pp. 17-20.

For the most part, the ranges are the same as those listed before for the various voices found in general music classes. However, the ranges may be a little wider since these voices are selected. We always should avoid the continued use of the extreme parts of the range and avoid those songs the *tessitura* of which is not suitable for the voices.

The testing of the voices should be done carefully, remembering to do it individually. Often, pupils prefer to sing a familiar song, the teacher transposing it to fit the range of the voice. The speaking voice is a clue to the pitch of the singing voice; if the boy's speaking voice sounds light and piping, you may expect that his voice is unchanged. For this voice it would be wise to pitch the song high enough so that the teacher may hear the high part of the range. Then, transpose it to a lower key, which will use the lower range. In case this is not satisfactory, start on G second line treble and ask the pupil to sing up the scale as far as it is comfortable, and then sing down. If the pupil is afraid to sing high pitches it is wiser not to permit him to see the keyboard as you play, for he may be frightened at seeing the hands move up the keyboard. Those pupils who have less tension when singing alone often are interested in finding out how high and how low they can sing. For them, following the movement of the hands at the keyboard is an incentive. Teachers become expert in recognizing the characteristics of the pupils they are testing and use the methods best suited to each individual.

For the changing voice, use the pitches suggested earlier in the general music class discussion. The ranges will be about the same, but the voice may be more pleasant in quality because its owner is not the run-of-the-mine pupil. Because some will become basses and others will become tenors, it is wise to use these voices.

The basses may have several pitches higher or lower than those discussed under the general music classes, but for the most part they are the same. Reliable basses are essential to a successful choir, and should be given every consideration to insure proper development of their voices.

The kinds of voices which are used in choirs depends largely upon what is available. Some schools have had unison choirs composed of unchanged voices or young basses. No matter what kinds of voices are available it is a good thing to have a choir. In some large schools two choirs are organized, one with unchanged voices (acting as a feeder), and a second choir composed of unchanged, changing, and bass voices.

The following seating plans will be useful in some situations.

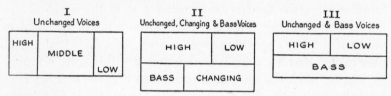

Materials

Many types of materials should be used to insure the interest of both pupils and audience. The repertoire should include folk and art songs, composed songs, operetta selections, and contemporary and classical music. Both sacred and secular songs have a place in the program, some with accompaniment and some *a cappella*.

This is a good age to start unaccompanied singing, but to use it exclusively and make it a shibboleth is the lesser part of wisdom. Musicians know that the accompaniment may add much to the beauty of the song and that, if it is omitted, the composition may lose some of its vitality and striking tonal effects. No one would think of presenting a Gilbert and Sullivan operetta without the traditional rhythmical and tonal effects the accompaniment offers. When the accompaniment is but a duplication of the voice parts, it is unnecessary, and should not be used unless the group is very inexperienced. *A cappella* singing requires much patience and careful preparation. Teachers should encourage *a cappella* singing whenever possible, but exercise discretion in its use.

A list of selections recommended by successful junior-high-school teachers may be found at the close of this chapter.

BOYS' GLEE CLUB

In some schools the boys' glee club is a very important activity. In American life there is a decided increase in the number of male groups who enjoy singing together. Barbershop quartets sponsored by their national organization have developed artistic performance to a degree never expected from lay groups. They became the envy of women to the extent that women have applied for membership in the all-male Society for the Preservation and Encouragement of Barber Shop Quartet Singing in America. Male groups always win favor in a community, and in many locales the public-school music teacher directs or sponsors adult barber shop quartets.

Singing by male adult groups has a great influence on junior-high-school boys, and because of these adults, it is an easy thing to interest boys and the community in a boys' glee club. Bringing an adult or high-school male group to perform in the school assembly is a good way to stimulate interest within the school. Boys enjoy music as much as girls, but not always the same kind. They require a teacher with humanistic qualities, patience, persistence, and the ability to select music to their liking.

Organization

The boys' glee club should have the same objectives and values as listed for choirs. Also, the suggestions given for the organization of the choir will function equally well for glee clubs. The clubs thrive in schools in which the administrators believe in the power of music as a wholesome, emotional, and social influence. In many schools the arts are an accepted part of the pupil load, and are not considered an extra.

The selection of the boys should be made from grades 7, 8, and 9. Voices from the three grades are needed in order to provide the various ranges required for harmonic singing. The club should be organized to use every kind of good voices the boys in the school possess.

Kinds of voices, ranges, testing,
   and seating plans

All boys with good voices should be used in this club. The prime requisite is a liking for music and a willingness to co-operate and take responsibility. The voice may be unstable and ready to change, but this voice can be taken care of (if the teacher is willing to sacrifice balance of parts) by transferring the pupil to a lower part. Since the changing of the boys' voices demands shifting to different parts, this group may not be so satisfying musically to the teacher, but the enthusiasm of the boys will compensate for any musical lacks.

If the club is inexperienced and the ability to carry a part has not been developed, it is unwise to attempt four-part singing at the beginning. With these groups, virile unison and two- and three-part songs may be used. There is very little material available for such groups, but one inexpensive book called *Songs for Young Gleemen*[3] is most effective for use in building a boys' glee club.

There are four kinds of boys' voices in the junior high school, namely, high and low unchanged (trebles), changing, and changed voices. There is considerable disagreement over what they should be called. It is most unsatisfactory to the boys to be called sopranos and altos. Since they desire to be treated as men, and to emulate masculinity, it seems preferable to call them what they will become in adulthood, thereby putting them on a par with their barber-shopping male relatives.

Two seating plans are suggested and can be used according to the type of group available. For a group which has had little experience and whose inner voices have trouble carrying parts, the first chart on page 167 is recommended.

You will notice that both labels are used, indicating what they are and what they are called. The second chart suggests an arrangement which may prove more satisfactory to experienced groups.

---

[3] Haydn Morgan, *Songs for Young Gleemen* (Chicago: Hall & McCreary Company, 1948).

Every care should be given to voice testing. It should be done individually, avoiding any feeling of embarrassment. If a boy fears singing before the group, he should be permitted to

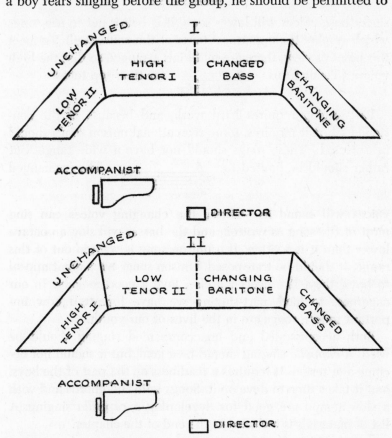

sing in private for the teacher. If the teacher creates a favorable attitude before testing is begun, most boys are willing to sing before others. (See suggestions for testing on pages 139-141.)

Materials

Concerning the ranges of high voices there are two points of view, which are reflected in the arrangements of the songs. Some teachers believe that the arrangements should use the upper part of the range as long as the boy is able to sing the tones. As a result, the *tessitura* of the score is very high in pitch and hovers about ⟨music⟩ . Others believe that since these voices will lower soon, it is better not to use songs which employ the uppermost tones of the voice at all. To meet this point of view, there are materials arranged so that the high voices (Tenor I) use ⟨music⟩ for their top tones.

Part-singing requires hard work, and because of the continued effort it requires, some recreational unison songs should be selected. These songs should not have a wide range, but rather should be limited to ⟨music⟩ . The unchanged voices will sound as written, the changing voices can sing most of the song as written, and the basses will sing an octave lower than it is written. If a unison song is written out of this range, it should be transposed. Unison songs have great appeal to boys; they, like everyone else, love a good melody. In our eagerness to have part-singing we have forgotten how important unison songs are in the lives of our youth.

Both accompanied and unaccompanied singing should be used. A *cappella* singing should be a goal, but it should not become a criterion. It requires a readiness on the part of the boys, and it takes time to develop it. Songs with full chords and with a slow tempo are good for developing *a cappella* singing. A list of materials is included at the end of the chapter.

GIRLS' GLEE CLUB

The girls' glee club offers rich musical and social rewards to its members and is most gratifying to the teacher. Girls, by their very nature, love the dramatic and are so social minded that it is easy to organize the club. They are great "joiners," and if an announcement is made in the general music classes that a glee club will be formed, plenty of girls will want to belong. They are willing to work hard for the finesse which good public performances require, and will give unlimited co-operation and loyalty to their organization. Girls' voices change in quality and range, but they do not offer the mutation prob-lem associated with boys' voices. This is one of the reasons why we find the girls' glee club flourishing in the junior high school while the same school boasts no similar group for boys.

Organization

The same suggestions for organizing the choir and the boys' glee club are applicable to the girls' club. (See pages 160-161, 165 for procedures in organization, accrediting, and selection of membership.)

Kinds of voices, ranges, testing, and seating plans

There are three classifications of girls' voices, and although the same labels are used for their identification as for adult groups, their connotation is different. There are very few real altos in the junior high school; they often have a two-octave range, and for this reason should not be forced to sing an alto part arranged for women's voices. This range is comfortable for alto (low) voices. The occasional use of tones a third lower is not damaging to low voices, but music having whole phrases which hover about low G should be avoided. The rich, mellow quality of a girl's low voice is most welcome in a glee club.

Soprano voices, which are lighter and thinner in quality, are plentiful. They should be lyrical in quality, devoid of heavy, forced tone. At this age, voices must be preserved, and the de-velopment of the voice should be left to a later time. This is a good range for the soprano (high) voice although many have a full two-octave range. Since they produce their top tones more easily, they should sing the soprano part. Remember, it is not range but quality which decides which part a girl should sing.

Some sopranos find the top tones of the range difficult to sing, and their voices are fuller on the lower pitches. These voices are called second sopranos (middle). Many girls feel the term second means inferior in importance; so, when this idea is prevalent, it might be better policy to call them middle voices. The teacher will need much patience and persuasive power to convince the group that it is the filling in the sandwich that counts. The following is a good range for the middle part

 .

There should be two-part singing by the girls' club since there is much fine music, including descants, written for two voices. The range of these songs is suitable for the girls' voices. The following plan will be useful for groups which do much two-part and some three-part music. Put the lower soprano voices with the higher alto voices to form the middle part.

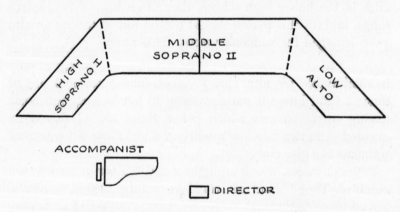

You may have groups, which have had very little experience in part-singing, resulting in a struggle for the middle group to keep on its own part when they sit between the melody and alto parts. For this situation try this seating arrangement.

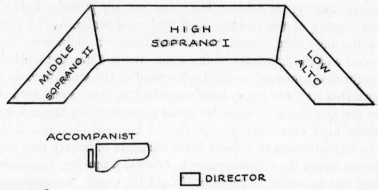

Materials

There is an unlimited amount of material available for the girls' club, including music written for adult female voices and music arranged for them. It should be borne in mind that songs which require a great amount of tone should not be selected for adolescent voices. Songs that are emotional, dramatic, tender, graceful, and delicate in nature are suitable for girls' groups. Folk, art, composed, sacred, and secular songs and selections from cantatas and light operettas should be used and organized into programs in which the club will participate.

Unison, two-part (descants), and three-part songs should be used according to the ability of the group. Care should be exercised to avoid arrangements suitable for adult groups. It is often a temptation to use arrangements which are popular with older groups, but a wise teacher will always keep his group up to their challenging best, yet will not try to emulate the vocal performance of older groups. For specific compositions consult the materials listed at the conclusion of this chapter.

SUGGESTIONS FOR CHORAL REHEARSALS

The teacher should have each rehearsal planned well, and the music, preferably in folders, should be passed out by librarians in the least possible time.

It is best to start the rehearsals promptly with a well-known song, insisting on relaxed but good singing posture. Follow the singing of the familiar song with new material. The text of the new song should be studied briefly to determine the mood and the character of the song. At this time, the teacher might also comment on the background of the song. Boys and girls sing well when they have something to express and are led in the expression of some beautiful message. Only songs with some high emotional appeal should be used, because it is through attempts to express these elements of beauty that the music leaves the commonplace to become a moving, exhilarating, and beautiful experience. To aid the pupils in expressing these ideas is the rehearsal problem.

The teacher or the accompanist should play the voice parts as artistically as possible; this facilitates expressive singing. To do this, the teacher and the accompanist should know the music before rehearsal. After the voices are tuned carefully (see pages 150-151) and the tempo is set, the first stanza of the song should be sung by all parts. Then errors should be corrected. Keep things moving, waste no time, and have no lulls if you do not want problems in social control. Some directors give "breaks" in the rehearsal so that pupils may talk and relax for a short time. This is an excellent plan, and it is in keeping with the old adage, "Work while you work and play while you play."

Partially learned songs should be rehearsed (see pages 151-152) with emphasis on improving intonation, diction, tone, phrasing, dynamics, and memorization. Sometimes it is expedient to close the lesson with a familiar song.

Directors have found risers or collapsible platforms most helpful at rehearsals and programs. Some schools build the risers in the rear of the room and make them wide enough so that chairs placed on them may be used by instrumental as well as by choral groups. The risers enable the pupils to see the director more easily and to hear better what others are singing. There are many risers made by commercial firms, but when it is impossible to finance their purchase, they may be made in the school. (See pages 411-412 in *Music in the High School,* by Wilson.)

There are many available sources concerning rehearsal techniques. Excellent suggestions for rehearsals will be found in Christy, *Glee Club and Chorus,* pages 37-50; Dykema and Gehrkens, *High School Music,* page 121; and Wilson, *Music in the High School,* pages 129-132, 144.

PROGRAMS

Choirs and glee clubs soon find that there are many programs within the school and community for which they will be required to furnish music. Teachers have an obligation to furnish music for school assemblies, festivals, pageants, and for programs integrated with other areas, such as the art and the physical education departments.

Some schools expect the choral groups to give programs for Armistice Day, Thanksgiving, Christmas, and Easter, and each club is busy at every rehearsal preparing for the programs. Consequently, the teacher must find out just what programs he must furnish and lose no time in selecting and teaching the music, if he expects his group to be accepted well by pupils and the community. Folk programs featuring the songs and the dances of America and other nations are always received well. Whenever it is possible, it is a good idea to include whole school participation in the program so that the entire student body may become music minded and have an opportunity for participation in music.

Music clubs often are asked to furnish music for so many community groups that administrators and teachers feel that the pupils are exploited. This situation should be guarded against carefully. In every instance only the educative effects and the influence upon pupils and the school should have uppermost consideration. On the other hand, public performances can sell the music program to the community and become a significant part of the public relations program of the school.

Activities vary in each community, but only such community activities that are altruistic, achieve the greatest good for the largest number, and are interdenominational, civic, patriotic, and nonpolitical in character deserve the support of these choral groups. Those activities which do not fall into these categories should not be considered obligatory. Further discussion of these problems will be found in Chapter 10.

Since it is often impossible to use the clubs en masse, it is expedient to organize selected ensembles which can represent the school in the community. These smaller groups should contain the best performers and be ready to meet emergency engagements which are bound to arise. Double trios, double quartets of boys, and mixed voices are good groups to develop. They may sing music other than their large groups sing if there is rehearsal time, or they may sing the identical materials if the music does not demand too much tone, thereby forcing the voices to produce it.

Programs should be planned carefully. Elements in planning a good program are:

1. The program should have unity and variety in many styles of music; it should represent several schools of composition.
2. The complete program should seldom be over an hour and fifteen minutes in length.
3. Use especially effective and well-rendered numbers at the beginning and end of the program.
4. Introduce new numbers occasionally; use some good contemporary music.
5. Introduce solos or small ensembles between numbers.
6. Place music most difficult to appreciate toward the beginning of the program.[4]

Hints on performance

Keep in mind that performances are given to please the audience and for the benefit of the performers, and not to

---

[4] Ohio High School Standards, *Music Education for Junior and Senior High Schools* (Columbus, Ohio: State Department of Education, 1946), p. 29.

glorify the director. Keep unobtrusive, well poised, and pleasant! Every detail should be planned carefully in advance so that each member of the group, the accompanist included, knows exactly what to do. The director should know the music well and be able to reflect the mood of the music as he conducts.

Placement on the stage is important. Compactness and more lines are preferable since long lines are conducive to out-of-tune singing. If it is possible, have the group stand in a semicircle, since this aids intonation. Risers or movable platforms are most helpful, and when they are used, the performers should know how to get on and off them with ease. Place the shorter pupils in front so that they can see the director, and can be seen by the audience. The accompanist should be placed so that he, too, can see the director and the pupils can hear the piano, which should support but not overbalance the singing.

Be sure that the group is tuned carefully before the song is started; excitement causes pupils to fail to hear pitches sometimes, and disaster is the result. Use the same tempi and dynamics employed in rehearsal and radiate confidence in the group's ability to perform well.

SUMMARY

Music teachers in the junior high school need to understand the changing voices (mutation) of their pupils, for both girls' and boys' voices change, but in different ways. At this time pupils are most sensitive to the quality of their voices, and utmost consideration needs to be given to help them through this ofttimes embarrassing period.

Voice testing and classification in the general music class should be done rapidly, with as little attention paid to any individual as possible. Making no previous announcement of the plan, start while the group is singing. A procedure which will not frighten the timid or embarrass the insecure is recommended. A seating plan arranged according to the kinds of voices should be used; no two classes are alike, so identical seating plans are inadvisable.

Great care in the selection of songs should be exercised. A variety of songs to meet varied pupil interests should be used. Lists of music texts for the general music class will be found at the close of the chapter.

A varied procedure in the presentation of songs is suggested and is included. There is no one way to teach a song, but some presentations secure better results because they are psychologically sound.

The place of music reading in music education (plus *how* to teach pupils to read) is one of the most controversial problems teachers face. The reading of music has its place, but in terms of a newer educational philosophy, all pupils cannot be expected to see the use of reading music or to possess the identical ability to read it. A background of pleasurable musical experiences, which may be imitative, is necessary for keeping alive a desire to read and to keep from divorcing a pupil from music. Suggestions for carrying on a reading program are included.

Choirs and glee clubs serve pupils well in the junior high school. They may be organized to serve both the musically talented and those with the desire to sing but who are limited in good vocal production. Testing these voices and grouping them can be carried on individually with less fear of embarrassment than in the general music class, because these singers elect to belong. Excellent music is available; compositions suggested by successful junior-high-school teachers are listed at the close of the chapter.

Directors of choral groups need to learn how to conduct rehearsals effectively in order that musical results may be gained quickly. Most of these groups will appear within the school and in the community. For this reason, music materials need to be chosen with good programming and audience appeal in mind. Hints on how to make a performance good are included to aid teachers in making the best of their opportunity to bring good music to their groups, the student body, and the community.

Music Books for the General Music Class

AMERICAN BOOK COMPANY
American Singer — Book VII
American Singer — Book VIII

C. C. BIRCHARD AND COMPANY
Adventures in Singing
Let Music Ring
Sing Out!
Singing Youth
Twice Fifty Five — New Brown Book
Twice Fifty Five — New Green Book

GINN AND COMPANY
Adventure
Discovery
Latin American Song Book
Sing Along
Song Parade
Treasure
Singing Juniors — Book VII (Our Singing World Series)

HALL & MC CREARY
Chorus and Assembly

Golden Book of Favorite Songs
Gray Book of Favorite Songs
Songs of the Hills and Plains
Songs We Sing

NEIL A. KJOS MUSIC COMPANY
Book I — *From Descant to Trios*
Book II — *Great Songs of Faith*
Book IV — *Songs of Many Nations*
Book VI — *Our Third Book of Descants*
Book X — *Descants and Easy Basses*
Songs of Norway and Denmark
Songs of Sweden and Finland
Teen-Age Singer

SILVER BURDETT COMPANY
American Music Horizons
Music Americans Sing; Log for Music Americans Sing
Music the World Sings
The Singin' Gatherin'
World Music Horizons

Choir

SELECTIONS RECOMMENDED BY JUNIOR-HIGH-SCHOOL TEACHERS

Title	Composer or Source	Vocal Arr.	Book	Number	Publisher
Alleluia	German	S-B	Choral Hour	312	Hall & McCreary
Ash Grove, The	Welsh	SATB		2109	Row
America My Own	Cain	SAB			Flammer
Battle Hymn of the Republic	Olds (arr.)	SSATB		1561	Birchard
Beautiful Savior	Wilson (arr.)	SAB	Choral Programs (IV)		Silver Burdett
Carol of the Bells	Wilhousky	SAB		4747	C. Fischer
Christmas Bells	Elliott	SAB		46101	Hoffman
Cindy	Wilson	SAB		5012	Hall & McCreary
Cindy	Wilson	SATB		1098	Hall & McCreary
Climbin' Up the Mountain	Spiritual	SATB		1001	Kjos
Country Gardens	English Folk	SAB		88010	Flammer
Crusader's Hymn	Hymn	SAB		222	Wick
Go Down, Moses	Spiritual	SATB	Music Many Lands		Silver Burdett
God Bless Our Land	Kountz	SAB		8849	G. Schirmer
Holy, Holy, Holy	Ringwald (arr.)	SATB		141	Words and Music
I Got Shoes	Spiritual	SATB		81172	Flammer
I Passed by Your Window	Brahe-Taylor	SATB		2301	Boosey & Hawkes
Jesus, Son of God	Mozart	SAB	Choral Hour		Hall & McCreary
Lead Me, Lord	Wesley	SAB		8700	G. Schirmer
Listen to the Lambs	Dett	SAB		537	Gray

Title	Composer	Series	Voicing	No.	Publisher
March of the Peers	Gilbert-Sullivan		SAB	2018	Boston Music
Memories	Van Alstyne		SATB	5R.3034	Remick
Moonlight Bay	Wenrich		SAB		Harms
My Homeland	Speaks	*Music of Today*	SAB	7361	G. Schirmer
On This Good Christmas Morn	Cain	*Choral Hour*	SATB	84177	Flammer
O Praise Ye the Lord	Franck		SAB	219	Wood
Over the Rainbow	Harburg		SATB	F7167	Feist
O Western Wind	Clokey		SAB	153	Birchard
Panis Angelicus	Franck		SAAT	cm6452	Hall & McCreary
Pines of Home	Luvaas		SAB	261	C. Fischer
Prayer (God Ever Glorious)	Lwoff		SAB		Wick
"Prayer" — Hansel and Gretel	Humperdinck		SAB	88019	Flammer
Remember Thy Creator	De Paul		SATB	1229	Pro Art
Ride the Chariot	Smith (arr.)		SATB	1015	Kjos
Song of the Night	Verdi	*Choral Hour*	SAAT	654	Hall & McCreary
Sons and Daughters	O'Hara		SATB	9293	Bourne
Spring Song	Rosenberg		SATB		G. Schirmer
Teach Me, O Lord	Scholin-Watson		SATB	831	Belwin
This Is My Country	Jacobs-Scott		SATB		Shawnee
'Twas the Night Before Christmas	Darby		SATB		Shawnee
Twelve Days of Christmas	Heller		SATB	1129	Hall & McCreary
While by Our Sleeping Flocks	Gloser		SAB	2235	E. C. Schirmer
You'll Never Walk Alone	Waring		SAB		Shawnee

179

Boys' Glee Club

SELECTIONS RECOMMENDED BY JUNIOR-HIGH-SCHOOL TEACHERS

Title	Composer or Source	Vocal Arr.	Book	Number	Publisher
Beautiful Savior	Riegger (arr.)	TTB		82532	Flammer
Bells of the Sea	Lamb-Solmon	SA		504	Fox
Carol of the Bells	Wilhousky	SAB		CM4747	C. Fischer
Chiapanecas	Mexican	TB		6009	Willis
Christmas Hymn	Jungst	SATB	Music the World Sings		Silver Burdett
Down the Open Road	Haney	TTBB		560	Wood
Drink to Me Only	English	TBB		192	Birchard
Dry Bones	Gearhart (arr.)	SATB			Shawnee
Goodbye Ol' Paint	Cowboy	TBB		3018	Hall & McCreary
Hiking Song	Krones (arr.)	SATB		4000	Kjos
Kentucky Babe	Geibel	SATB		5250	Morris
Moonlight Bay	Wenrich-Madden	SAB	Music of Today		Harms
Old Man Noah		SAB	Music Americans Sing		Silver Burdett
Ol' Man River	Kern	TTB			Harms
On the Mall	Goldman	Uni	Music Highways & Byways		Silver Burdett
On the Road to Mandalay	Speaks	SA		7962	G. Schirmer
Pirates' Song	High	2-part		82601	Flammer
Recessional	DeKoven	SAB		2822	Church
Rock A My Soul	Spiritual	Harm.	Buckeye Ballads		Rohrbough
Roger Young	Loesser	Uni	Sheet Music		Frank Music
Songs for Young Gleemen	Morgan	Various Arr.			Hall & McCreary

Title	Composer or Source	Vocal Arr.	Book	Number	Publisher
Stouthearted Men	Romberg		*Music of Today*		Harms
Vagabond, The	Cain	Uni	*Music of Many Lands*		Silver Burdett
We Sail the Ocean Blue	Gilbert-Sullivan	TB	*Singing Down the Road*	41101	Hoffman
When I Was Single		ATTB			Ginn
Where In the World	Powell-Waring	SATB			Shawnee
Your Land and My Land	Romberg	TBB		538	Harms

Books

Title	Composer or Source	Vocal Arr.	Book	Number	Publisher
Songs from Many Lands for Junior High School Boys	The Krones				Kjos
Tune Time for Teen Time	Cooper				C. Fischer
Unison Songs for Boys	Cooper				G. Thompson

181

Girls' Glee Club

Title	Composer or Source	Vocal Arr.	Book	Number	Publisher
All For You	Brown	SA		8788	G. Schirmer
Alleluia, Christ is Born		SSA		1543	Birchard
Boats of Mine	Miller	SSA		3008	Flammer
Brother James Air	Jacob	Descant			Oxford
Cantique Noël	Adam	SSA			Birchard
Chiapanecas	Mexican	SA	*Rose Twice 55*	6009	Willis
China Figure	Flemm	SSA		83176	Flammer

GIRLS' GLEE CLUB (Cont.)

SELECTIONS RECOMMENDED BY JUNIOR-HIGH-SCHOOL TEACHERS

Title	Composer or Source	Vocal Arr.	Book	Number	Publisher
Come Down to Kew	Deis	SA		6569	G. Schirmer
Come Holy Spirit				1546	Birchard
Come Unto Him	Handel	SA			Hall & McCreary
Gay Fiesta	Mexican	SSA		2214	Flammer
Gesu Bambino	Yon	SA		4656	J. Fischer
Grandma's Thankgiving	Simeone	SSA			Shawnee
Green Cathedral	Hahn	SSA		2682	Church
I Wonder As I Wander	Horton	SSA		9360	G. Schirmer
In Spain	di Chiara	SSA		231	Birchard
Indian Love Call	Friml	SA	Music of Today		Silver Burdett
Jesus Is Born	Bohemian	SSA	Choral Hour		Hall & McCreary
Jesus, Jesus Rest Your Head	Kentucky Mt.	SSA		552	C. Fischer
Kentucky Babe	Heibel	SA		1026	White-Smith
Let My Song Fill Your Heart	Charles	SSA		8579	G. Schirmer
Lord's Prayer	Mallotte	SA		8788	G. Schirmer
Lullaby	Brahms	SSA		420	

182

Title	Composer	Voicing	Collection	No.	Publisher
Man I Love	Gershwin	SA	*Music of Today*	4872	Harms
May Day Carol	Taylor (arr.)	SSA		7656	J. Fischer
Morning	Speaks	SA		9595	G. Schirmer
My Johann	Grieg	SA			G. Schirmer
Night and Day	Porter	SA	*Music of Today*	1001	Harms
Night Song	Clokey	SSA			Birchard
Quest, The	Gibb	SSA		54	Birchard
Rapid Stream, The	Elgar	SA		7722	G. Schirmer
Skip to My Lou	American	SSA	*Way Up On Old Smoky*	117	Ginn
Snow White Fantasie	Don Wilson (arr.)	SSA	*With Flute and Violin*	1414	Bourne
Somewhere a Child is Singing	Dykema	SSA			Birchard
Song of Joy	Edwards	SSA		8439	G. Schirmer
Spring Heralds	Daniels	SSA		8072	G. Schirmer
Spring Idyl	English	SA		6801	J. Fischer
Spring Rain		SSA		2-G1008	Remick
Star, The	Clokey	SSA		7364	Birchard
Summertime	Gershwin	SSA			Chappell
Swiss Skiing Song	Krones (arr.)	SSA		1200	Kjos
Tea for Two	Youmans	SA		4011	Harms
Thanks Be to God	Dickson	SA		2111	Boosey & Hawkes
Think on Me	Scott	SA		2682	Church
Welcome, Sweet Pleasure		SSA		8470	G. Schirmer

6. The Listening Experience

WHAT IS THE LISTENING EXPERIENCE?

First, it should be understood that the term *listening experience* is used here to describe an activity in which the pupil himself is listening to music performed by others, rather than playing or singing himself. This is a loose expression of the meaning, but not as loose as the term *appreciation*. Although teachers have expected pupils to exhibit a somewhat passive demeanor while listening to music, at times there are physical reactions, some of which are involuntary, such as changes in blood pressure. To say that *listening* implies inactivity, even physical, is inaccurate. If by physical activity, such as muscular response, the student finds himself enjoying and expressing the meaning of the music he hears, he should be left reasonably free to engage in such activity. The term means that the emphasis in the experience is aural, supplemented by whatever other response seems natural and appropriate in the minds of pupil and teacher. (The term *appreciation* in this connection seems narrow because it suggests that appreciation does not apply to

184

performance activities. We know that appreciation develops through all musical experiences.)

Actually, the material of music appreciation is the substance of the world around us, *since the response of the listener to music depends upon his total previous experience as a whole.* To say that the experience should focus chiefly upon any single phase of experience, such as the memorization of musical themes or the identification of instrumental timbre, is to say in such an activity as riding a bicycle the rider should concentrate chiefly upon pedalling, steering, or balancing. The experienced rider, attempting to develop a high degree of skill, may concentrate upon one of these factors in an effort to improve his technique as a whole, but the inexperienced rider must have the "feeling" of the whole experience before he concentrates upon the parts. Furthermore, in view of the fact that in individuals musicality varies in regard to sense of pitch, rhythm, timbre, and so on, expectation of the same response from each is impossible. Therefore listeners must be allowed freedom in individual response to their musical experiences.

Some teachers presenting the listening experience may be misled in expecting an immediate overt response. Others may fail to realize that, beneath the surface of an apparently passive listening attitude, there may be a definite reaction to music heard. An immediate, overt reaction — such as a rhythmic response, a comment, or a question about the music — is not necessarily the only indication of a good listening experience. Surface response and inner response vary to such an extent with different individuals that patient and watchful observance of the listener over a period of time is probably the most satisfactory means of judging his growth in this phase of appreciation. Definite measurement, in terms other than those of factual information, is a difficult task, and should not be considered a primary objective.

The pupil who enjoys the music he hears in the classroom is at least going through the process of "soaking it up"; in time, he may translate the experience (at least in part) and react in some overt way. Such reactions may not always come to the teacher's attention. In a seventh-grade class, when music with a strong rhythmic content is presented, Peter captures the pulse immediately, conducting with emphatic gestures. Mary's foot taps almost imperceptibly. John's eyes shine, and he leans forward in his chair, resting his chin in his hand. Each of these children is reacting in an individual pattern; how shall we say which one is getting the most from the music? We must conclude that there is no accurate means of measuring the inner response of these three individuals or of larger groups of children who listen to music.

To summarize, then, the listening experience may appear to be a passive one compared to the singing or performing experiences, which obviously require physical activity. In listening, however, the participant cannot be wholly passive unless he resists altogether any reaction to the music to which he is exposed. The degree of passivity varies, as the same factor varies in spectators at a football game. The situation in which the music is presented also makes for the degree of overt response; for example, the audience at a symphony concert is not expected to manifest a high degree of overt response to the music itself, except conventional applause. In the classroom, however, freedom of the pupils to respond to the music in many ways is a desirable situation.

THE OBJECTIVES OF THE LISTENING EXPERIENCE

The over-all objective is musical enjoyment. Ideally, it should be *immediate* enjoyment in some way for each child. In other words, the music should reach each child. This objective includes:

1. Emotional satisfaction.
2. Musical learnings.
3. Imaginative response.

WAYS OF RESPONDING TO MUSIC

There are certain ways in which we can expect boys and girls to respond to the music they hear. Some of them are:

1. An emotional response, often brought about through the

establishment of a mood. Boys and girls react, with appropriate comments, to certain obvious characteristics of music such as "sad" music. Children, and adults too, are more deeply affected by music at various times of stress or again, may associate certain experiences with particular musical compositions, thus giving the experiences an emotional color. An example of this is noted in the first line of Conrad Aiken's poem "Music I Heard (with You)":

Music I heard with you was more than music,[1]

Again, the power of music to serve as an emotional release is expressed in Edna St. Vincent Millay's "On Hearing a Symphony of Beethoven":

Sweet sounds, oh, beautiful music, do not cease!
Reject me not into the world again.
With you alone is excellence and peace,
Mankind made plausible, his purpose plain.[2]

No pupil should be required to analyze such response; in any case, probably the junior-high-school pupil's feelings are often beyond his ability to express in words. But the heightened emotions of early adolescence find a satisfying outlet in listening to music. An eighth-grade girl wrote that when she listened to music, the world seemed happier for a little while, although she did not exactly know why. Another said simply, "My troubles go away." Release from the tensions of everyday living must be considered a desirable response in today's troubled world.

2. A physical response through the listener's reaction in terms of bodily movement. Foot-tapping to strongly rhythmic music is an example of this, as is the dance response, seen through the ages from "jungle to jive."

---

[1] Conrad Aiken, *The Second Book of Modern Verse*, ed. Jessie B. Rittenhouse (Boston: Houghton Mifflin Company, 1919), p. 50. Reprinted by permission of the author.

[2] "On Hearing a Symphony of Beethoven" from *The Buck in the Snow* published by Harper & Brothers. Copyright, 1928, by Edna St. Vincent Millay. P. 69. Reprinted by permission of the estate of Edna St. Vincent Millay.

3. An intellectual response (musical and related learnings) through the ability of the listener to analyze the component parts of the music and develop his knowledge of such technical matters as tone quality, dynamics, tempo, form, techniques of the performing media, individual characteristics of the composer's style, characteristics of the style of the performing artist, and others. (This is closely associated with the emotional response and cannot be separated altogether from it.)

A further phase of the intellectual response is the listener's understanding of the music as an expression of the composer's sociological background. Music is not composed in isolation from the social pressures of the composer's period. It grows from a period of history as part of the social scene, and, whether as affirmation or denial of this scene, it is a reaction to the social situations of the period in which it was composed. Included in this phase of the listener's response are a recognition of the composer as an individual and an awareness of his particular contribution to the development of music as an art. In this entire phase, a knowledge of the composer as an individual human being may serve to color the listener's attitude toward his music. This is especially true of young listeners.

4. An imaginative response through the ability of the listener to project himself into the music, making it in terms of his total background a unique experience, and even in the broad sense of the term, *a creative one*. A program-note reaction to the music is certainly no criterion of musical sensitivity: Music suggests, and may set off, a chain reaction of association in the mind and emotions of the listener, but only the most obvious of musical compositions dictate a channelled reaction. Carl Seashore has written:

> The hearing of music is a response to a stimulus. It has been said that what a man shall see in a landscape depends on what he is; so in music. The ideas and feelings which constitute the response are the creation of the listener in his own image.[3]

---

[3] By permission from *Psychology of Music*, by Carl E. Seashore. Copyright, 1938. McGraw-Hill Book Company, Inc. P. 382.

These four main classifications of the listener's response may be broken down into innumerable subdivisions. However, since individual response to music is highly unpredictable, little purpose would be served by attempting to categorize in particular detail the musical reactions of boys and girls.

However, it *is* important that the teacher develop sensitivity to the reactions of each boy and girl who hears music in the classroom and that musical compositions are chosen for the class with these individual sensitivities and needs in mind. For those pupils who seem most indifferent, even hardened, to the music they hear are often those who are in the greatest need of the "food" of music. Both the emotional and the imaginative response may touch, at times, upon the spiritual.

BASIS FOR CHOOSING LISTENING MATERIALS

The teacher's first function as a guide in the development of the foregoing phases of the listening experience in the classroom is to choose, with the direct or indirect aid of his pupils,[4] materials which may best serve as a basis for such development. Several points must be considered in the choice of materials.[5]

1. The maturity and ability of the listeners. This involves consideration of both mental and emotional maturity. The superior child, with an abundance of intelligence, must be challenged by musical presentations which will bring into play his mental gifts; selections which are below his level will bore him and cause him to withdraw from the situation. One such child in an eighth grade appeared completely indifferent to the listening activities in the classroom until he was released from the class to read several books on music; instead of remaining in the classroom, he went to the library. Among the books given to him by the librarian at the teacher's suggestion were nicely illustrated stories of Wagner's *Ring*. Soon he asked to hear some of the recordings of *Das Rheingold*, which were in the

---

[4] For means of evaluating the individual student, see Chapters 2 and 7.

[5] The reader is asked to review the general discussion of these points in Chapters 1 and 3.

school record library. Eventually he presented a report in class, played some of the records he liked, and led a class discussion centered around his readings and record presentations.

Other children sometimes become interested in the actual mechanics of how music is made by listening for various instruments, recognizing thematic material which reminds them of music they have already heard, following the music with a score in hand, noting dynamics, comparing the timbre of different instruments, in fact, in analyzing the materials of the music rather than in listening to the music as a whole. Such activities, of course, are encouraged by the teacher chiefly as a means of fostering the growth of a larger appreciation in the child, namely, his response to music as a satisfying total experience. Perhaps such an approach may be defended by reminding the reader that many a boy takes the clock apart long before he learns to put it together as a functioning whole. In line with this, the pupil must not be thrown into a musical sea where the waves are so high they will drown him before he learns to swim.

An important psychological principle holds true in bringing about a good listening reaction; each pupil should proceed at his own pace in musical experiences. Here, as in all other areas of learning, the teacher's knowledge of the pupil is crucial. Underestimating or overestimating a pupil's ability to grasp musical experiences and to absorb them is a sure path to boredom in the classroom. Faced with a class of children, the teacher must choose a listening program with a view to nourishing all of them. But for those who have special needs, particular materials must be selected and offered whenever possible. By assisting a child until he is ready to reach out for music independently, the teacher has fulfilled a vital function.

Emotional maturity of each pupil is of great concern to the music teacher because music is chiefly an emotional art. If a pupil is immature emotionally the impact of the music upon him will be less than might be expected were he average or superior in this respect. He may be unable to respond to the more subtle moods of a musical composition — perhaps he is only able to react to the obvious rhythm of a march, the foot-tapping swing of a popular tune, or the imperative demands of a jive trumpet in a dance band. The child who has been over-protected and kept by his home situation from experiencing the flow of everyday living among many different people has a limited apperceptive background against which to interpret music. Again, it is the teacher who must weigh this side of the child's nature in relation to the music he hears and to his grasp of it.

We do not mean to rule out in this discussion the fact that musical capacity itself is a prime factor in a child's enjoyment of his listening experiences. Native musical capacity, coupled with native intelligence, probably places a ceiling of some sort on the level of enjoyment any child obtains from his listening experiences. The good teacher is wary, however, of limiting in his mind a child's future musical development on the basis of these factors.

2. The musical background of the listeners, including home, community, school, and church. This has, obviously, a direct connection with native musical capacity and native intelligence. The range of musical background which exists in a single junior-high-school music class may be illustrated by a class one of the authors taught in which one boy knew all the major symphonies by composer, title, and *opus number;* in the same class there was a girl whose musical background was close to zero. There was not even a radio in her home. To expect very much in the way of response from a child of such limited musical back-ground would result, surely, in making her highly insecure. Possibly it might make her defensive to the point of adopting a "don't-care" attitude in order to justify her shortcomings to the teacher and to her fellow classmates. On the other hand, expecting too little of the boy who knew symphonies by their opus numbers would cheat him of his rightful place in the music class. The teacher must ask himself such questions as those on page 192 in evaluating musical background.

(*a*) What music does the child have in his home?

(*b*) Are his parents interested in music; what experiences or training have they had, musically?

(*c*) Does the service of his church afford an opportunity to participate in group singing, or is its music good enough to help him develop a sense of musical values?

(*d*) Is the community in which he lives musically inclined; are musical activities looked upon as worthwhile and respected?

(*e*) What kind of previous school music experiences has he had?

Whatever the native capacity of a child, it cannot flourish unless it finds fertile soil and climate in the way of environment, any more than the finest seeds can germinate and mature in poor soil and unfavorable climate. One of the most useful things a music teacher can do, however, is to discover the gifted child who has had an impoverished musical background and furnish the necessary environment and encouragement for the child's development. At times, the speed with which such children grow musically is almost miraculous. This may be especially true of junior-high-school pupils who, once they have found an avenue of expression, throw themselves into it with unreserved enthusiasm.

Limited time and limited resources often work against the teacher's desire to equalize the musical experiences of boys and girls, but in no case should the teacher surrender to such obstacles before the battle has begun. More than we realize, children appreciate a teacher who makes the most of the resources at his command, and it is still true that the teacher, rather than the books, building, or time schedule, is the pivotal factor in a good educational situation. He is the equalizing force where the question of background is concerned.

3. Interests of the listeners — musical and others. This factor is closely related to the discussion of musical background and is important in the same way. Teachers in today's schools realize that a child does not sever his connections with the rest of his classes when he enters the music class, nor does he suddenly become separated from his out-of-school life. Since these are

part of the child, the music listening experiences must be presented against a background of his total personality and against the more comprehensive personality of the entire class.

Perhaps there are readers who will stand and die on the grounds that music is music and needs no particular approach, that its inherent beauty and appeal will suffice as a basis of presentation. This may be the case for the teacher who is working with a highly select group of musically talented children. *For the many who are honestly trying to educate all the children,* it often does not hold true.

In any event, the listening experience is not solely a skill-building experience in intent or purpose for the majority of children in the junior high school. It is *extensive* in its musical purpose rather than *intensive;* that is, its aim is more to broaden musical horizons than to penetrate deeply into any particular area of music. (Few junior high schools operate on a time schedule which would permit teaching an intensive course in listening to musical literature.)

Obviously, it is easier to open any door by grasping the handle, and the handle which opens the door to music for many children is the interests that they have already developed. Shy and insecure children need to be stimulated into active participation with their classmates; probably the use of their interests best expedites such a procedure, as with the case of a seventh-grade boy who appeared to be remote from any interest in the listening activities of the class. The teacher learned that his absorbing interest was horses and found a way to have the class listen to a musical composition in which horses had a prominent part.[6] Through his interest the boy had built up a fund of information concerning horses, and when the teacher, as a part of the class discussion of the music presented, put to the class several questions involving a knowledge of horses, the boy who had seemed so remote found himself participating as the only pupil who could answer certain of the teacher's questions. He gained in prestige and self-con-

---

[6] *The Ride of the Valkyries* (*Die Walküre*), Wagner.

fidence through this single incident, and through an approach which definitely capitalized upon an extrinsic feature of the music, he eventually became interested in the music itself.

Given enough time and materials, it is probable that no teacher would have to resort to such an oblique approach. But in the junior high school, lack of interest and withdrawal from the situation sometimes results in unfortunate and annoying classroom behavior, which interferes with the learning and enjoyment of the rest of the class. It would be misleading to tell teachers that they must be at all times "purists" in their approach to the teaching of music; if the process of a boy's learning to enjoy music (and thus that of the entire class) can be hastened by appealing to his interest in something outside of the music itself, it is common sense to do so. Music speaks directly in its own language to many children. For those who do not grasp this language immediately or easily, we must use what they already know as a bridge to build understanding.

It should not be assumed, however, that in the listening experience emphasis should be primarily upon anything but the music itself. All such extrinsic approaches are justified only when they serve the purpose of bringing the child closer to the music. Where such an approach becomes so involved or laborious that it takes more time and assumes more importance than does the music, the situation is out of balance, and to a large extent the teacher has lost the main objective. (The last statement is qualified because no procedure is altogether useless when it enables a teacher to reach a pupil and help him gain stature, in the classroom or outside of it.)

4. Amount of time available for the listening experience in the classroom. This factor varies widely in different schools. Where the general music class meets but once a week, it may be limited to fifteen or twenty minutes per week, which creates a very restricted situation. If the end of our listening experiences is immediate musical pleasure, the teacher must carefully select recordings or performances which will be well within the compass of the children's understanding, and which will make an impression deep enough to be retained for the intervening week. Nevertheless, in a school year of 180 to 200 days, the class should hear about twenty-five musical compositions. Breadth of musical experience is more desirable than is detailed analysis of a few presentations, although the teacher may wish to present a few compositions in considerable detail. By careful planning in which the class participates, emphasis may be placed on different musical features in successive lessons.

From this minimum amount of class time, schedules vary all the way to the class which meets every day for a period of from forty to fifty minutes. Here a superb musical experience should be possible for the class. The teacher may wish to follow a plan *similar* to that suggested in Chapter 3 as a basic minimum listening repertoire and expand it in the direction of class needs and interests. (Again we note that no list of materials should be adopted unless it is planned for the particular situation in which the teacher is involved.)

5. Availability of such supplementary musical experiences as

radio, television, recordings, concerts, performing experiences. The reinforcement and expansion of classroom listening experiences is made possible through such channels. The teacher constantly should point out to his pupils the musical activities which are available to them outside of the classroom and which have a direct or indirect bearing upon classroom experiences. The majority of children have access to radios, and an increasing number are watching television. Sometimes only a word or two of comment is needed from the teacher to turn the attention of boys and girls to worthwhile musical programs available through such media. A music bulletin board which displays concert programs, the week's radio and television offerings in advance with worthwhile items marked, photographs of today's outstanding artists in the world of music, articles clipped from newspapers and magazines — all such material is valuable because it may reach individuals and motivate out-of-school activities.

In addition, the teacher can stimulate interest in forthcoming concerts and radio programs by playing compositions which have been announced as part of such programs. Many teachers today take carloads, even busloads, of children to nearby communities to hear performers and organizations, which they otherwise would not have an opportunity to hear. When motion pictures with unusually beautiful musical scores are in town, the teacher should not fail to mention these; at a slight cost, information about the musical scores of current motion pictures can be obtained. In this connection, it seems possible that the musical tastes of children are influenced to some extent by the musical background of the many motion pictures they see. So concentrated is their attention on the picture itself, however, that most movie-goers are not actively conscious of the fact that they are hearing music while watching the picture. Without announcing the identity, many radio and television programs use as "theme songs" excerpts from well-known compositions; children are interested and usually surprised to learn that such themes are parts of famous music masterpieces.

When a child says in music class, "On the radio last night I heard the record you played for us in class last week," the teacher knows that his work has not stopped at the door of the classroom but has made an effective connection with the child's life in the community.

THE PART PLAYED BY THE TEACHER
IN MAKING MUSIC LIVE

How do you, the teacher, visualize your class in its response to hearing music? Do you see a friendly, receptive attitude, pupils engrossed in what they hear, hands waving in the air after the music is played, with many boys and girls eager to ask questions and make comments on what they have heard? Or have you had the unhappy experience of having the records you play fall upon seemingly deaf ears, and do you see the faces of bored and indifferent children as you think back over your experiences in playing music in general music classes? Why does one teacher seemingly "spark" his class in the listening experience so that children come to life, while another succeeds only in setting up a tense, unhappy situation in which children must be ordered to be quiet so that the music may be heard at all?

Perhaps some teachers expect the mere process of placing the needle upon the revolving record to cause a hush in the classroom, with all pupils automatically drinking in the music in an atmosphere of reverent attention, simply because so-called "great" music is being reproduced. These teachers forget that music on a record is still "canned" music, and to many children, the emphasis is on the word "canned." For there is no longer any miracle about music, invisible and unseen, pouring from a phonograph, radio, or television set. Such music has become a background of everyday living; dishes are washed to it, babies fed, children scolded, and homework done. Much of the time the music goes unheard as well as unseen.

Suppose we have a fine recording of Heifetz performing on

his violin. We play it for our eighth-grade class and it does not receive an enthusiastic hearing. But suppose by some miracle we were able to produce Heifetz in the flesh in our music class; what then? *Then* we would have the atmosphere of absorbed interest, which is lacking when we play some of our most treasured records. The things which most attract children's interest today are things they both see and hear, or which combine *two* or more attractive features, such as comics (highly colored and showing characters in high-geared action), mystery and western radio programs (rapid-paced action, violent sound effects, dynamic characters, terse dialogue), or television, which offers both aural and visual appeal. Should Heifetz, as well as his music, be present in the classroom the situation would come to life. Wherever, in fact, a performer of even limited skill steps before the class and makes music, attention is freely given. The word *live* seems to be a key word here.

In the listening situation, the teacher is about to give, and the pupils are about to receive. Therefore, we can assume that the teacher must supply the *live* element which is otherwise lacking. *He must exert himself to do so.* By his presentation he must make the music come to life; he must deliberately set out to capture the attention of his audience. In a way which does not detract from the music itself, the teacher becomes the performer, or at least sets the stage for the music.

This may seem unnecessary to some readers, who are considering the matter more from a theoretical viewpoint than from a basis of actual experience with junior-high-school children. Not all these children have the ability to project themselves imaginatively into the music; not all of them possess enough musical background to enjoy the music for its inherent beauty. Many of them are distracted from the situation by extraneous matters; they have what might be called either a "low distraction" or a "high resistance" level which prevents their giving complete attention to the music.

We do not advocate "high-pressuring" children into giving their attention to a musical performance, but we are convinced

that the teacher must find, with the average heterogeneous
class, a focal point of attention which is potent enough to capture the listening of the class until the music itself takes over.
For example, in an eighth-grade music class a young teacher
that the teacher must find, with the average heterogeneous
was using records of the opera *Carmen*. He knew the story

thoroughly and felt that the class should find it interesting, but
he was baffled by their indifferent attitude. After a conference
with a more experienced teacher, he entered the classroom one
morning prepared to present the Card Scene. When the time
arrived for the presentation of listening materials, he took a
deck of cards from his pocket, stood in front of the class, and
without saying a word, began shuffling them and laying them
out on a nearby desk. Activity in the classroom ceased as every
boy and girl stared, fascinated, at what was going on before
their eyes. Having completely won the attention of the class,
he then told them the story of the music they were about to
hear and played it for them. Needless to say, the level of interest in the music itself was much higher than it had been in
preceding class sessions.

Actually, the business of getting the attention of the class with the cards took no more than a minute or two. Then the teacher skilfully shifted the emphasis from the extrinsic "attention-getting" device to the music itself. As long as the result in like situations is an increased emphasis on the music, the use of such an approach is justified. In fact, it may be that teachers are guilty of too little use of "razzle-dazzle" techniques in the classroom. Because the learning process in the hands of some teachers has been dull, even painful, does not prove that this makes it more effective.

Children sometimes get the idea that music, other than the popular tunes they hear plugged assiduously on the air, belongs to a bygone era and has no place in their "modern" lives. One such child had a stock question he put to his music teacher whenever he played a record, to wit, "Is the composer alive or dead?" If the teacher, cornered, had to reply that he was dead, the child apparently went through a process of shutting off his listening apparatus for the duration of the record. The ways in which we talk to children about composers, emphasizing dates of birth, death, and nationality, and the pictures we show children of composers do not always help us bridge the gap between the dead composers, their living music, and our young listeners. For usually we are speaking of men born many years ago (while to our junior-high-school children anyone over twenty is ancient) in a place far removed from our country and known only in geography. The pictures we show of these men from their style of dress certainly place them in an era belonging to the past. In helping children to realize that the music they hear was written by real, living men, who still *live* in their music, here are a few procedures we can follow which may help us:

1. Know some interesting details about the composer, for example: "He liked children; in his pockets he kept candy to give to his young friends. He had a dog whom he dearly loved . . . ," and so on. Find common bonds between the composer and his listeners. Children have at times a composite

mental image of all great composers as strange beings who sat in garrets all night copying music, or doing nothing but practicing away on an instrument.

2. Let the children tell you what *they* think the composer was like from hearing his music. Play it for them, then with your help let them evolve a picture of him.

3. Stress action, situations, and feelings of the composers rather than dates and places. "His mother hid him in the belfry of a church when an invading army came so he would not be harmed." Here is a graphic example of an incident in a composer's life.

4. Include music of living composers. This is part of the heritage of today's children, and even though a teacher may not prefer it, part of his job is to understand it and give his pupils the opportunity of making its acquaintance. Children hear music in this idiom in various motion picture scores and as background music for radio and television shows. In some cases they find it more interesting than do their teachers.

5. Use *graphic* language when talking about composers. While we respect great composers for their contribution to our culture, it is not necessary to adopt an attitude of figurative obeisance when we mention their names. This at times can border on the ridiculous, as with a young teacher who insisted upon referring to *Mr.* Beethoven and *Mr.* Bach.

6. Don't insist that junior-high-school pupils spell correctly the names of all the great composers. In the case of Russian composers, there are variants in the spelling of the same name, and even without these, "Tchaikovsky" and "Rimsky-Korsakov" are a sizable piece of spelling for an eleven- or twelve-year-old. Children worry about such matters and usually inquire, when written work or tests in music are announced, whether "spelling will count." However, the names of composers should be written on the board so that children will see them and have a *chance* to learn to spell them correctly, if they are capable of doing so. Again, the music is the important thing; it would be possible to spend so much time teaching a class the correct

spelling of names of composers and compositions that they
would never get around to hearing the music itself. First the
emphasis should be *on* the music, not on information *about* the
music.

Teachers often ask, "Just *how* shall I begin a record presentation? Shall I play the record with no comment, or shall I tell
the class something about the music and then play the record?
How shall I begin?"

If there were one direct answer to these questions, the whole
matter would be simple indeed! But part of the business of
holding the interest of junior-high-school boys and girls lies
in avoiding routine; therefore, use different approaches to the
music they hear. At times, a class is so receptive to music that a
whole composition may be played through with little or no
comment; at other times, classes must be almost startled into
giving their attention to the music they are about to hear, just
as good public speakers sometimes secure the attention of their
audiences by beginning with a startling statement. As is the
class, so does the teacher temper his approach. The fact that
teachers are uncertain about just how to present the listening
experience is a healthy sign; it means they must look for the
right technique for each class, even for each lesson; and it
also tends to keep them from settling into a well-worn, com-
placent groove which each year finds "this" being presented
"this" way and "that" being presented "that" way.

A characteristic of the junior-high-school student is his
tendency to rebel against authority. In listening to music, this
trait is evidenced by his occasional unwillingness to accept
what is put before him in the way of a musical diet selected by
the teacher. One solution is, of course, to make as much use as
possible of student co-operation in planning. But even with this
safeguard, the wide range of differences in classes makes it
difficult to hit upon musical offerings which will instantly ap-

peal to all members of a class. Too often, unhappily, teachers find the attitude of "Show me!" or "*Make* me like it — just make me!" Making an issue of such attitudes only serves to intensify them; children who display them should, rather, be disarmed, and if possible, taken into camp without their ever realizing that the weapons of antagonism and bravado have been painlessly removed.

This is one reason why the growing teacher is ever on the alert for new and better ways of presenting his music in the classroom; it is certainly a reason why no simple answer can be made when teachers ask, "Just exactly *how* shall I do it?" It is possible to suggest a number of ways in which the situation may be handled at various times, but the teacher's sensitivity to the needs and attitudes of the individuals who make up each class is still the most important factor in the situation. He must be an expert diagnostician before he decides which approach to use or works out particular methods of his own, just as a physician must treat each patient individually and prescribe treatment with the whole picture of the patient's needs in mind. The following general suggestions are not, then, cure-alls, and should not be regarded as such:

1. Avoid having in mind any set opinion as to how a class will receive a particular musical experience. Try to sense the moods, the in- and out-of-school attitudes, and previous reactions of the class to music, then be prepared to adjust your opinions about and comments on the music to meet whatever may be forthcoming in the way of reaction from each particular class. This does not mean adopting a wishy-washy attitude that lists with each gust of wind. It *does* mean treating the opinions and values of the children with respect and tolerance. A sense of values does not develop overnight; the teacher must work patiently in the right direction, watching for growth, spotting and encouraging its gradual development in individual members of the class.

2. Have a flexible plan, including the use of supplementary and alternative materials. This is largely dependent upon the

teacher's musical background; he should constantly expand his familiarity with musical compositions and available recordings. In addition to building up a school library of recorded materials, the teacher should build up his personal record library to as large an extent as is financially possible. With the advent of long-playing records, small as well as large record companies are producing a steady stream of new releases and re-releases. Musical materials are related to each other in many ways; it is the teacher's responsibility to point out such relationships. The limits of the teacher's understanding determine the limits of the pupil's opportunity to understand.

3. In presenting listening experiences, it is best to use materials which have to do with a sequence or "parcel" of learnings, rather than presenting each musical composition as a separate entity unrelated to the rest of the activities of the class (song materials, creative activities, reading, and so on). Moreover, try to relate the listening lesson to something with which the pupils are familiar; current events, school, community or world, subject areas (such as assigned reading in English classes — the Deems Taylor *Through the Looking Glass* is an example), or even personal problems in the lives of boys and girls (great love stories in music, or examples of filial rebellion against parents, such as Brünnhilde's, in *Die Walküre*). It has been said that adolescents sometimes believe the problems they face are unique, lonely experiences; it helps to know that they are universal, and have been made the subject of books, paintings, and musical compositions.

4. With regard to the question "Shall I play the music first or discuss it first?" the only possible answer is that either may be done successfully. If the class has an established and stable attitude toward listening to music, part of the time they may enjoy hearing music with no verbal introduction; sometimes it is not even necessary to identify the composition and composer, since hearing the music stimulates the class to a point of curiosity about its identity. Again, teachers come into contact with classes which need "hooks" upon which to "hang" the music

they hear — focal points of attention. Frequently used ways of providing focal points or "stimulators" follow:

(*a*) Encourage the class members to project themselves imaginatively into the music. One teacher may say, "Can you listen carefully enough to tell me what your hear happening in the music?" while another may go so far as to say "If this were the musical score for a motion picture, what would you imagine the plot to be?" A young teacher, eager to have his class feel the mood of Debussy's *Afternoon of a Faun,* found a hand-wound victrola and took them into a park near the school on a spring day. There they sat on the grass, and, sprawling full-length or leaning against trees, recreated in their own imaginations the story of Debussy's music. The teacher thus provided an outlet for the daydreaming of early adolescence, in a setting as nearly suited to the music as he could find.

(*b*) A list of key words placed on the board before a record is played serves to stimulate imaginative or constructive listening. Some of these words will be "clues" to the music while others will be "false leads." Perhaps this might be called a "Treasure Hunt." In listening to the music, the children try to select the words, usually descriptive, which best suit the music. As an example of this, a few key words selected for the Debussy *Golliwog's Cakewalk* might be: humorous, serious, important, whimsical, funny, clumsy. Although no two people hear exactly the same things in music, the discussion of which words best describe a piece of music is stimulating, and consideration of the various words sometimes gives self-confidence to pupils who participate reluctantly or with little initiative. At times, the list is made up after the children have heard the music, and various words (or descriptive phrases and sentences) are volunteered by members of the class.

(*c*) Stress the musical content of the composition by asking pupils to identify in it the musical learning they have already acquired, for example: form, dynamics, tonality, or medium.

(*d*) Visual aids of various kinds are often effective. A simple device consists of displaying a number of strips of colored

206 THE LISTENING EXPERIENCE

drawing paper and asking the pupils to consider which colors
most nearly reflect the mood of the music they are hearing.
More elaborate devices consist of showing several prints of
paintings all concerned with the subject of the music (for example, the sea) and asking the pupils to react to the suitability
of these paintings with reference to the music. The technique
of having pupils draw freely, using paints, chalk, or crayon,
while they listen to music is not only a visual reinforcement
of the listening experience, but also a correlation with art
experiences.

Every music classroom should have large maps of various
parts of the world. This is a source of correlation between social
science or current events and music, since in listening to music
we cross many national frontiers.

The following approach has never failed to stimulate the
interest of seventh-grade classes in which it has been used. The
teacher says, "Today let's imagine we are all going on a trip.
We are allowed to choose any means of transportation we wish,
so we decide we will go on a huge air liner. Along the way we
will make several stops, and the only "catch" in our free ticket
for this trip is that when we land, we must all try to decide
where we are by listening to the music which will be played for
us at the airport. If we come up with the correct answer, our
trip will continue, but if we miss twice in succession, we must
all fly back home." For classes which have members who are
lovers of adventure and mystery stories or radio programs,
sometimes the teacher says, "In this part of the trip, we are
going to have an adventure. During a storm, our plane will be
forced down, and, when we climb out, the pilot will tell us that
he has been blown off his course and the radio is not working.
It is dark. We have only the vaguest idea where we are. Looking around, we see that we have landed in mountainous terrain,
and although no one has been hurt, we must try to decide in
which direction to proceed for food and shelter. Then, coming
through the darkness, we hear strains of music a long way off.
This is the music we hear. (Teacher plays record.[7]) Where do

---

[7] For example, *Caucasian Mountain Sketches* by Ippolitov-Ivanov.

you think we are? Who can show us on the map? Trace the route over which our pilot flew."

Some classes keep a world map displayed on the bulletin board and mark with map pins the countries whose music and composers they have heard. Whether the approaches mentioned, or others, are used, maps not only serve as "stimulators" but also correlate music with the world around us.

(e) Games such as "Twenty Questions" can be used in classes where the interest level is low. After hearing the music played, pupils attempt to identify its composer and/or title by asking a limited number of questions. A small group of students may take the place of the teacher by playing the record and answering the questions of the class.

For a second hearing of the same composition, or a review before a test, the teacher may write on slips of paper answers to various questions he intends to ask and distribute them to the class. As questions are asked orally, the pupil who thinks he has the correct answer responds. Questions may be written on one set of papers with answers on another, shuffled and distributed so that each child has both a question and an answer. As each child asks his question, the child who believes he has the correct answer replies.

(f) Current events often furnish the teacher with an opportunity to show students that music is related to happenings in the world around them. The death of a king suggests particular music, perhaps a well-known funeral march. Ships in trouble as a result of storms on the high seas suggest the use of such musical compositions as the Overture to *The Flying Dutchman*. Much suggested material for use in this manner will be found listed under "Suggested Musical Materials Grouped Around Topics of Interest" at the end of the chapter.

(g) Classroom demonstrations by pupils should be used whenever they will add to the interest and understanding of music heard in the classroom. For example, in a unit of dance music, the possibilities vary from ballet demonstrators (in many schools there are girls who have taken ballet lessons for several years and have acquired enough technique and poise to explain and dance ballet) to dance band record collectors who are eager to explain what makes the style of one dance band differ from that of another. A fine opportunity to relate the school instrumental program to the classroom listening program develops through inviting pupils to demonstrate instruments they are learning to play. By making a careful analysis of each class, the teacher will find such sources of pupil demonstrations.

(h) A widely-used approach to certain musical compositions is through "popular" song arrangements. Often, boys and girls are unaware of the original sources of such songs and find it interesting to compare the adaptation or arrangement with the original. With classes of high-level musical ability this can be a real means of developing musical learnings through comparison of rhythms, instrumentation, harmonization, and melody.

(i) One teacher capitalized on the children's interest in Valentine's Day and approached his record presentation through it. When the children came into the room, he had drawn on the board a large red heart, complete with piercing arrow. In this heart he had printed: "Hercules loves Omphale!" [8] Questions flew thick and fast, and the youngsters waited impatiently through class preliminaries to hear the music and its story.

(j) When the teacher has any gift for drawing, a few illustrative sketches of the composer or the story of the music, even in the form of stick drawings, act to focalize the interest of the less musical members of the class. This is, in a way, a type of chalk talk.

To be worthwhile, all of the preceding activities must have a direct basis of musical experience. They appear in practice to be of particular use to the average and below-average child in stimulating interest, as well as to act in the direction of unifying class interest. Many failures in the presentation of listening experience seem to stem from the short attention span of junior-high-school boys and girls, particularly in the seventh

---

[8] *The Spinning Wheel of Omphale* by Saint-Saëns.

grade.[9] It cannot be repeated too often that such devices as the ones mentioned are intended only to breach the gap existing between child and music. If such a gap does not exist it is unnecessary, even foolish, to use them.

If the pupils do not have in their hands books which contain the musical themes of records they hear, such themes should be placed on the board as often as possible. Even if the teacher cannot find time to do this, often there are children in the class who find it interesting and instructive to undertake the task. Such themes not only lead to a better understanding of the musical composition involved, but also help with the process of developing reading skills when pupils identify and follow the musical line as it is played.

When the teacher finds a class which is ready to hear music with no extrinsic approach, or when a class has grown beyond such an approach, increased emphasis can be placed upon developing understanding of the music itself. Here the limit of musical exploration is determined only by the teacher's knowledge of the music; such classes often exceed the widest boundaries tentatively set for them. They may be interested in form, instrumentation, comparison of performer's styles, interpretation; in fact, usually the musical curiosity of such a class leads naturally from one topic to another. The teacher's most important function in such a class is to provide and know thoroughly a wealth of musical materials to feed such musical interest and curiosity.

----

[9] Relative to this, teachers often ask whether or not a record may be stopped before it has been played in its entirety, or whether they may stop sometime during the playing for comment and explanation. This is somewhat like asking whether one must read through a book without stopping. If the interest of the class is so great that they can hear an entire musical composition without any break, by all means play it through. But as with a book, we often read a chapter or two, or even a few pages, then stop to discuss or think about what has been read. The factor which determines the procedure to be used is the attention span and degree of interest of the listeners. It is better to stop a record and recapture the interest of the class than to continue the record for a restless and inattentive class. Nevertheless, it is certainly best to try to create a situation which will keep the class listening through at least one complete portion of a composition. Where this is not possible, we must remember that the child is the most important factor in the classroom and that there is nothing sacred about a phonograph needle and a revolving record; they *can* be separated.

But if the musical interest and curiosity of the teacher does not equal that of the class, a "dead-end" situation results. However small or isolated the community, musical experiences and sources of information about them are available if the teacher seeks them out. However meagre the musical background of the teacher, he can extend it; in fact, he is cheating his pupils if he fails to do so. The bibliography provided at the end of this chapter suggests sources of musical information for the teacher who wishes to provide richer musical experiences for his pupils; in doing so, he will grow with them. Unevenness of opportunity and education create a wide difference in teachers as well as in pupils, but the only teacher who can be blamed for inferior professional preparation is the one who does not try to remedy the situation; he is deliberately robbing his pupils of their birthright in a country where educational opportunities are available to all.

KEEPING A RECORD OF MUSICAL LISTENING EXPERIENCES

A music notebook may be a record of meaningful listening experiences, or a collection of facts about music. Today's teacher is not interested in the latter. If there is time enough in the music class program to keep a music notebook which has real significance to its owner, it is a worthwhile activity. If time is limited, the teacher should weigh the advantages of such a written record against those of spending the same amount of time in added listening experiences. Notebooks, if kept, should be a true reaction of the child to the music he hears and should be correlated with other areas of school life and out-of-school activities. They should not be a mere compilation of facts about composers, performers, and records.

Notebooks have a special value for pupils with a particular or above-average interest in music, as they may be assigned to develop them as special projects. Clippings from magazines and newspapers, in the form of articles or illustrations, special reports relating to musical events or reading, pupil "reviews" of concerts, all may find a place in such a notebook. Once pupils begin to add to them on their own initiative, more and more musical interests and information are located.

When the teacher feels that a written reaction of some sort will aid the pupil in his listening growth, a summary form may be given each child so that he may write in information concerning music he hears as well as his own reaction to it. Such a form might be called a "Listening Guide." It may cover only one composition, or may include a comparison of two or three by way of review. In classes where books containing information about the music heard are not placed in the hands of the pupils, such guides are valuable in that they afford an opportunity for pupils to write down names of composers and compositions plus other pertinent information and reactions. This serves as a reinforcement of the aural experience, and may be kept as a cumulative record. Because such activity tends to be time consuming, however, teachers should be careful that it does not degenerate into "busy work."

The following is an example of a guide sheet used in a seventh-grade general music class:

LISTENING GUIDE   GRADE 7

A comparison of a musical composition we know with a new one
   Directions: Select the completion you think right and write it out in the correct blank. (You will not need all of the completions given.) Or, you may try to complete some of the blanks in your own words.

I

An Old Friend — the record of *The Little Shepherd.*

1. This piece of music is part of a group of pieces called_____
   written by the _____ composer _____
                        (nationality)   (name)

2. This shepherd is in _____ Europe.

3. The little shepherd is playing on his instrument, the _____.
   During the day, he plays on his instrument to _____
   _____.

4. Of the themes on the board, which is the skipping theme? _____
   Which theme seems to express a feeling of loneliness? _____

Listening Guide (continued):

II

A New Friend — another shepherd, playing while he waits for a ship to come in; Prelude to Act III of *Tristan and Isolde.*

1. The mood of this shepherd is _____.

2. This shepherd is playing _____.
                                            (where)

3. The orchestral instrument which plays this melody is the _____.

4. The melody is played as part of a large musical work called an _____.

5. This music was written by the composer _____.

Completions to use in the blank spaces:

A. English horn   G. opera   L. watching the sheep
B. Richard Wagner   H. sad, melancholy   M. at a castle on the
C. Claude Debussy   I. *Tristan and Isolde*   coast of Brittany
D. French   J. *Children's Corner*   N. flute
E. entertain himself   Suite   O. northwestern
F. shepherd's pipe   K. southern   P. improve his playing

6. On the other side of the paper, try to explain the way the music makes you feel. Both records will be played again while you write. Can you tell how the music of the two players is different? Do you think their music is alike in any way?

LISTENING TO ART SONGS IN
THE JUNIOR HIGH SCHOOL

Perhaps a special discussion concerning the presentation of vocal selections in the junior high school should be included. Pupils should hear a fair proportion of such materials, but in the past it is possible that in some schools most of the listening materials presented have been instrumental or orchestral numbers. Yet each pupil possesses a developing voice, and should become acquainted with the sound of mature voices and their musical possibilities.

The difference in the sound of the adult voice and the adolescent voice should be explained carefully, because, as one alto-tenor pupil said, after hearing a recording of a tenor solo, "It sounds so different from *our* voices!" The use of adult performers from the community or even older pupils will aid in developing a concept of mature voice quality.

A natural barrier in the way of using song materials is that many of the most beautiful songs for solo voice are sung in foreign languages. In illustrating various voice types teachers must either present understandable translations or seek song recordings in the English language. Included in a list at the end of this chapter are English songs on the junior-high-school list of records, and a more inclusive list of art songs which are certainly too beautiful to be neglected in the musical education of our children. Each is a work of art, a composite of words and music so perfect that the message of the song is often understood by the listening children despite language barrier.

Many of the songs selected for the list given here are easily understood by boys and girls because they deal with situations which are universal in occurrence. *The Trout* (*Die Forelle*) by Schubert, for example, tells of a fisherman who employs tactics which, to the onlooker, seem unfair . . . the listener, like the onlooker who sings the song, is completely on the side of the merry little trout! Every boy or girl who has ever gone fishing, or who has watched fish swimming in a sunny pond or in an aquarium, will be interested in its story and the way the music, as well as the words, tells it.

OPERA IN THE JUNIOR HIGH SCHOOL

Opera, like art songs, contains much beautiful music to which children should be introduced. Again, foreign language is a barrier. More than language, however, children who are plunged into the hearing of opera without a thoughtful introduction are likely to find the vocal style, in its bravura passages, beyond their understanding, and at times, simply funny. One class which thought a certain coloratura aria quite hilarious was won over when the teacher explained that the ability to sing such an aria represented great skill and long hours of training and practice; that the skill could be compared to the performance of a top athlete — for example, a gymnastic performer, since its performance required much control as well as outstanding natural ability.

Increasing attention has been given during recent years to

ways of making opera interesting to youngsters. Among procedures which have been developed are classroom dramatizations of skeleton opera plots (using improvised costumes), radio-type scripts with classroom singing of more famous selections of the opera or interpolations of recorded musical portions, bringing the story of the opera up-to-date by a popular translation of the plot into present-day speech and situations, and all-school assembly programs with scenery designed by the art department, costumes by the home economics department, narration of plot by speech classes, soloists from the music department, and assembly singing of familiar songs from the opera. Since opera is likely to seem farfetched and even ludicrous to many an uninitiated adult, thorough preparation by the teacher is necessary to make it understandable to, and appreciated by, children.

Perhaps one of the greatest difficulties here is that many teachers of music have not had time to explore the great operas and thus have failed to become aware of the musical satisfaction to be gained therefrom.

At times every teacher is amazed at what may develop from a listening experience. Sometimes this is a direct musical reaction, as with the case of the eighth-grade boy who liked the "Flower Song" from *Carmen* so much that he wanted to hear it over and over again. Other times it is a reaction to the social situation which develops in the plot of, for instance, an opera. One eighth-grade girl protested mightily because of the situation in *The Bartered Bride* whereby a girl might be affianced to a man she did not love. This led to a discussion of marriage customs of other times and other countries. The maturity of a similar discussion, which arose spontaneously in a class hearing portions of *Madame Butterfly*, surprised the teacher. The whole class was indignant at Pinkerton's treatment of Butterfly and her child. On the surface, the latter two reactions may seem primarily verbal, a type of intellectual response. But since both occurred after the class had heard the music, it seems possible that at least the *Madame Butterfly* discussion was influenced by the mood of the music. The attitude of these thirteen- and fourteen-year-olds is not always as "hard-boiled" as they would like us to think. Sometimes, through music, they stand revealed to us as possessing an understanding and a sensitivity which we hope they will retain as adults.

THE DIFFICULT CLASS

Occasionally a teacher meets a class which, in spite of his best efforts, insists that it "does not like to listen to *records*." Many of the suggestions in this chapter will aid in working out a solution to such a problem, particularly the discussion which refers to "canned" music. For it is significant that classes rarely say "We do not like to listen to *music*." Generally, however, it is the attitude of the teacher which has the most to do with resolving such a situation; children are bored by recordings which do not reach them musically.

Each child has a right to his own opinions and values with respect to music. Furthermore, children are as sensitive as adults and as likely to take offense where an attack on their sense of values is concerned. Musicians, even when their chief role is that of the teacher, all too often develop fixed standards with regard to what is and is not "good" music. They forget that children do not mature in this respect just because an adult tells them certain things are good or bad: Maturity, in the sense of developing musical values, is a deliberate process. It has to do not only with the musical environment provided by the teacher, but also with the child's innate growth processes, and it cannot be rushed. Hymes has this to say about the process of maturing:

If someone is urging you to do something that isn't yet in your power, it doesn't make much difference whether they are nice or mean about it. If you haven't grown enough to do the job, you feel defeat. An emptiness inside yourself, an anger at the people pressing you, a giving up, an urge to hit out — just what you feel will depend on you. But it isn't an inspiring feeling. And you can't do better for having it, now or the next time.

Grown-ups don't have to shove children. You can be humble. You can know that growth has the controlling power, growth calls the turns, growth sets the pace. But instead of making you weak, knowing this can make you creative.

You can see your job as setting the stage. You fix the environment. You work so that when a child is ready to grow, you have made it possible and easy and simple for him. This is where your adult strength comes in. This is where you become powerful.

Concentrate on the child's surroundings. Fix them so that he can glide into the next move of his development when he has grown enough to do the gliding. The child still throws the switch, but he does it IF you have opened up the track ahead. The two of you work together as a smooth-running team.[10]

Since individual children differ, we know they cannot be poured into any sense-of-values mold and expected to take on its form. We would not want them to be fixed in such a form at any point in their development, since we want them to continue to grow. A sense of values with respect to music stems from the child's reactions to music, and whether his experiences have been similar or dissimilar to those of his classmates, a healthy variance in opinions as to just what is "good" music will always exist. Stokowski, in discussing whether or not there is a fixed standard for music, says:

Fortunately there is no such norm or standard, because if there were a norm, music could not grow and evolve in new directions but would always be circling around that norm — like an animal in captivity chained to a post. Music is free and limitless — it is forever expanding in new directions. Each one of us feels music differently because of that sacred thing inside us — our individuality. Music will never stop evolving, but century after century will become richer in variety, richer in life experience, in unending difference of feeling. If we compare the opinions of a thousand persons from different countries all over the world, we will find immense variations of opinion as to what is good or bad music. They will sometimes contradict each other completely, with scarcely any two people feeling and thinking exactly alike.[11]

---

[10] Reprinted by permission from *Understanding Your Child* by James L. Hymes, Jr. Copyright, 1952, by Prentice-Hall, Inc., p. 45.

[11] Leopold Stokowski, *Music for All of Us* (New York: Simon and Schuster, 1943), pp. 41-42.

Intelligent and good-natured tolerance on the part of a teacher who has a healthy respect for the opinions of his pupils will do much to ease the tension in a classroom where pupils are actively resisting listening experiences. Such tolerance must be active enough to feature an attitude wherein the teacher is willing to say to his pupils, "Very well, then; you don't like my suggestions about listening to music, so let's compromise. I'll listen to your ideas about the music you want to hear, and more than that, I'll listen to some of it with you. You can tell me what you like about it, and I'll tell you my opinions. Then it's only fair that you should listen to some of the music I like and let me discuss it with you. Let's go fifty-fifty in this situation, and we may find that we like many of the same things about music."

The majority of boys and girls are perfectly willing to co-operate with such an attitude. Their spirit of fair play tells them it's an intelligent approach to solving an unhappy situation.

Last but not least, a teacher who is enthusiatic about the music he presents is likely to find his enthusiasm contagious — if it is sincere. This, combined with a thorough knowledge of the music, is the teacher's best safeguard against failure.

HOUSING AND CARING FOR THE RECORD LIBRARY

The record library should be housed in a central place where all teachers will have access to it. Records should be kept in albums and stored upright on shelves with separators from 8″ to 12″ apart. Preferably, the storage place should have a fairly even temperature and not be subject to extremes of heat and cold, because this causes warping. The best method of keeping track of your record library is a card-index system, whereby each record or album is entered when purchased. Persons borrowing records should sign them in and out; as with books, borrowers may have the best of intentions but prove to be negligent in returning property. Nothing is more frustrating than to look for a record, valuable for illustrative purposes in a situation which has arisen spontaneously in the course of a class, and find it unaccountably missing. Cards bearing the school name and spaces for information relative to composer, title, date of purchase, album number in the library, and other pertinent information can be turned out to your order by any printer. Unbreakable records should be given the widest circulation possible; children should be allowed to take them home overnight if they wish, at the discretion of the teacher. In the case of breakable records, this is a somewhat hazardous procedure, because pupils usually are carrying other school materials with them, and even with the best of intentions, the accident rate is high.

Ideally, a circulating record library should be part of every school, but due to present limited availability of school funds this is impossible in many cases. It is possible to encourage pupils to come in at noon or after school to hear records of their choice; however, because this cannot be a wholly unsupervised activity, it is limited by the extent of the teacher's availability.

Fortunately, school record libraries will, in the future, contain an increased number of long-playing records. These may be used by pupils with less expectation of damage. Teachers should plan to discuss with their classes the care of records in order to encourage intelligent handling.

Records should be marked with album letter and number, or in some similar way. This can be done somewhere on the record label by using white ink and spreading shellac over it.

BUYING A PHONOGRAPH: MONEY FOR RECORDS

Today it is imperative to buy a phonograph which has a three-speed turntable. If the music is to be heard at its best, the reproducer must have high fidelity. Money invested in a good machine is never wasted, while it is almost certain that a cheap machine will not reproduce satisfactory music; many a child has received a false impression of the sound of recorded music because a school skimped on the quality of its phonographs.

Often, community organizations will think it worthwhile to contribute money toward the purchase of phonographs for school use. Parent-teacher organizations and local music clubs seem to feel that contributing sums for the purchase of records and reproducing equipment is a worthy cause; in some cases, these organizations, or others, will contribute a yearly sum in order to assist the school in building a record library.

ABOUT THE BIBLIOGRAPHY

At the end of this chapter are lists of compositions which appeal to the listening interests of many junior-high-school boys and girls for reasons discussed previously. To some readers these lists may appear rather heavy on the side of program music. Many teachers have observed that this age group seems to find a more immediate appeal in music which "tells a story" than in absolute or pure music. Despite the fact that there are those who believe that the latter music speaks directly to boys and girls without the necessity for "approaches" and that it should be stressed in their music classes, judging from the comments of classroom teachers, this is not always true.

Although it is dangerous to generalize in the case of the varied group that makes up public school music classes, it seems likely that the typical restlessness, divided interests, and widely divergent attitudes pupils bring with them into the junior-high-school grades make it more sensible to build upon the type of music they tend to like than to combat aggressive attitudes with the "forced-feeding" of music which is beyond the listening maturity of the majority.

The lists may be particularly helpful to inexperienced teachers wishing to build up a library of records for use in the junior-high-school grades. No list would fit every situation, and in view of the philosophy already expressed (to the effect that lists of materials, as well as methods, should be agreed upon by all who are part of the situation), we ask that the reader consider these lists as "suggested" materials and choose from them with his own pupils in mind and always with the objective of expanding the musical horizons of boys and girls in the direction of the best in music experiences.

A SPECIAL NOTE

Life is often a compromise between the practical and the idealistic. The teaching of music in certain situations resolves itself into just that. In brief, this is the reason for the inclusion in this chapter of the list of popular songs adapted from classics and the list of theme music used for certain television and radio programs, the appeal of which verges on the side of "blood and thunder."

However idealistic the teacher may be, however much he knows in the way of what is best to present in musical materials to boys and girls, in certain situations he must come to grips with bare facts. He may be limited by the musical background of his students, by his own background, by his materials, by unfavorable attitudes toward the music he himself loves. Somewhere, somehow, he must reach his pupils, must speak their language so that he will be accepted by them. The music he himself considers most beautiful sometimes falls upon deaf ears. "It says nothing to us," the pupils may tell him.

If it is true that we must proceed from the known to the unknown, from the familiar to the unfamiliar, then the teacher is justified in using the two listings mentioned above as a *starting point*. If he is a good teacher, his pupils will not remain at that point, else it becomes a *"starving point"* instead.

It is little use for the classroom teacher in the junior high school, faced day-in and day-out by boys and girls who believe they know what they want and like, to tell them that they really do not know what they want, that they really do not like the music they seek out when on their own. They are looking for acceptance, not rejection.

Teachers facing down-to-earth problems are asking for down-to-earth solutions. If we must at times climb to the glory of the best in music by way of the shaky stairs of "adapted" popular songs and compositions made familiar by the use of their themes on mystery programs, at least let us try to make our precarious way to the top rather than rejecting the climb altogether.

If only the best in music were heard over the air, if the music of great composers, unadulterated, were plugged as assiduously as is dance music and hill-billy music, music classes would be paradise for their teachers. But so long as many of our pupils come to us without a background of consistent exposure to the music we wish them to like, music classes must be, in certain situations, a compromise between our tastes and theirs. Lincoln's remark to the effect that God must have loved the common people, since he made so many of them, has a meaning for us. Many a beginning music teacher, with the dew still upon a conviction formed in his methods classes that he must never lower his musical standards, creates a gap between his pupils and himself which cuts off understanding and open-mindedness. Snobbery has no place in music; certainly not on the part of a teacher, who is supposed to be a mature adult. We must go halfway to meet our pupils; we must look into their backyards and visit with them there before we can expect them to come into our better-landscaped gardens.

To state it differently, we must not ask the child to remove his shoes and wipe all the dust off his feet before he enters the concert hall of good music. On the contrary, we must let him come in, dusty feet and all, and sit down with the rest of us, making him feel that his likes in music are not to be rejected and parked outside the hall. Then perhaps, in time he will settle down comfortably and say in his own language, "This is for me!"

The two lists we suggest using as approaches for some classes where children maintain they do not like "long-hair" music may be akin to dusty shoes, but if the children who come to us are wearing them, let's not demand that they remove those shoes too suddenly. For if we do, we may not be able to fit them with a comfortable pair for a while . . . perhaps too long a while.

SUMMARY

The listening experience succeeds to the extent that it produces a favorable reaction in the pupil, and one which he is mature enough to relate with other areas of his every-day life. The true measure of what a child obtains from a listening experience is difficult to obtain, and may not be apparent for many months, even years. If, in listening to music over a period of time the child has experiences which are significant to him, he may eventually develop a degree of independence through which his evolving sense of musical values will mature, bringing him closer and closer to what is finest in music. If a teacher somehow could be miraculously projected twenty years into the future and watch today's pupils attending concerts, listening to radio programs, and purchasing phonographs and records, he would be able to tell at once how well he had succeeded in helping them to identify themselves with great music — the child's cultural heritage.

What each child will gain from his listening experience depends upon his level of intellectual and social maturity, his interests, and his musical capacity and background. Some children may be able to reach the music with no introduction or approach preliminary to the hearing itself, while others may need a carefully considered approach to the music. The musically experienced child will be interested in a more detailed analysis of the music materials with which the composer works to create his effects and will notice such items as the use of themes, dynamics, tempi, form, style, and instruments. The inexperienced child may gain only a musical impression which he lacks the background to clarify. But the approach of the teacher must be so varied and imaginative that it will reach from the total life of the child to the minor segment of life which is the presentation of a musical composition.

The selection of materials also poses the problem of combining interests with the selection of a well-balanced musical diet rich in the essentials which will build the desired foundation for intelligent and discriminating listening.

Also important is the correlation of musical materials with the school life of the child. The listening experience is not essentially and solely a skill-building experience in intent or purpose for the majority of children. It should have a definite relationship with other subjects and other school activities. Growing as it does from the lives of men and their environment, there is something in music for every child — it is related to all experience and knowledge. English and Social Studies are especially adaptable to correlation with both singing and listening material. *The Ride of the Valkyries*, already cited, as a part of Wagner's *Ring* has definite associations with World History as taught in the seventh or eighth grades of many schools. Other legends and folk tales find their counterpart in the music of many composers. Actual historical figures, too, are cited in music, as in Copland's *A Lincoln Portrait*. Only the familiarity of the teacher with available materials, and the school's ability to furnish these materials, will limit the amount of such correlation in the music class. In assisting the child to fit music into the pattern of his life, the teacher is the motivating agent, selecting music which may reach into and then beyond his immediate interests, and presenting it at an appropriate time in a favorable setting. To do this it is obvious that the teacher must know the child and his interests.

The initial problem, that of arousing interest, is a definite test of the skill of the teacher. A further test is his ability to recognize *all* individuals in the class and include them somehow in his unified approach to the music at hand, and at the same time to keep the situation free enough so that each member of the class may react naturally. Growth and maturity proceed at the child's own pace; the child who reacts outwardly only in order to be with the group has not progressed but has adopted an artificial manifestation in order to conform.

The main emphasis in the listening experience always should be on the music itself. Whenever the approach becomes so involved or so detailed that it assumes more importance than the music, the situation is out of balance, and the purpose of the music teacher is defeated. As has been noted, music speaks directly and in its own language to many children. Whenever music can be presented with little or no introduction, preliminaries are not necessary. If it is true, however, that interest aids the learning process, the teacher is justified in proceeding from what is known in the child's life to what is unknown.

Since children are different as individuals, so classes differ. This means that the listening materials chosen for each class (even different sections of the same grade) may vary to a considerable extent, that the same materials may not be used in different classes with the expectation of success even though they have proved successful with one class, and that each class presents a different problem for the teacher's choice of materials. A careful analysis of the class on the basis of these considerations gives the teacher an indication of procedures and materials likely to be successful and meaningful. While we have suggested certain basic listening materials in Chapter 3, we have also indicated that *much* additional material is to be chosen on the basis of class need.

In conclusion, each teacher must remember that his own limits of musical understanding in turn set limits for that of his pupils. It becomes part of each teacher's responsibility to expand his musical knowledge in many directions, so that more and more he will be able to reach the musical interests of his pupils. It also becomes his responsibility to be well read and cognizant of world affairs, if these are to be part of a live classroom. We do not want our schoolrooms to have walls of one-way glass so that those outside can see in, but those inside cannot see out. Boys and girls live not only in school, but outside of school. In music, as in other subject areas, we must bring the two lives together.

A SUGGESTED LISTENING EXPERIENCE PLAN

Here is an illustration of a plan for a listening experience in an eighth-grade music class. This might take one whole period, or part of several. It would probably affect the song repertoire of the class. It is the type of plan which is intended to lead into other areas and to show pupils the background of the music and the material of the composer.

It is not suggested that this plan be used in its entirety or exactly as it appears. It is a plan to be adapted according to materials and time available to the teacher.

A Musical Experience Based Upon the Use of a Recording of
La Cathédrale Engloutie (The Engulfed Cathedral)
from Preludes, Book 1, Claude Debussy

OBJECTIVES
General
To increase the child's enjoyment of music by helping him understand a composition new to his listening experience.
Specific
1. Listening to a new piece of music.
2. Hearing the style of an impressionist.
3. Comparing the musical treatment of a legend and a descriptive treatment of the sea with that of other composers.
4. Exploring the idiom of the impressionistic composers.
5. Analyzing the legend or story upon which the music is based for a sociological meaning.
6. Comparing an orchestration with an original composition.

MATERIALS NEEDED: (as many as are available):
1. The records of *La Cathédral Engloutie* — one orchestral, one piano.
2. A map of France large enough to be seen by all.
3. Several prints of paintings of the sea, plus one or two other pictures.
4. Picture of a cathedral.
5. Additional records (one or all of these, as time permits):
   Four Sea Interludes (Britten)
   Fingal's Cave Overture (Mendelssohn)
   "The Sea and Sinbad's Vessel" — *Scheherazade* (Rimsky-Korsakov)
   Overture to *The Flying Dutchman* (Wagner)
6. Copy of the piano music.
7. Record of Gregorian chant.

REFERENCE MATERIAL:
Book of Bells (Satis N. Coleman)
A Listener's Anthology of Music (Lillian Baldwin)

Prints of the paintings are displayed where the entire class may see them. These *may* be used as a visual focal point, or as a reference during the period of listening to the record. Or, as the record is played through for the first time, you may ask the children to imagine a picture which the composer might have been thinking of or suggesting in his music. Suggest that something is taking place in the music, then ask the class to unleash their imaginations to find out what it is. (Be prepared to receive with due respect any interpretations of the music which come forth!)

After the record has been played, the class, stimulated by leading questions if necessary, will give its views on what the composer was expressing in the music. These views may be brought forth in single words such as adjectives, or in phrases, sentences or paragraphs — all delivered orally. Guided by the teacher's remarks and questions, pupils may attempt to choose the picture which most nearly reflects the mood of the music. When it is brought out that the music has something to do with the sea, and that the mood is mysterious and eerie, the teacher may either tell the class the story associated with the composition or he may proceed to develop the story by questions or suggestions from members of the class. The map is used to point up the fact that the scene is the coast. The origin of the story may have been in legend or superstition. Legends and superstitions are often found among fishing folk, whose long association with the sea has made them experienced with its power to wreak disaster and with which disaster they sometimes associate the supernatural. Fishermen are noted for their "tall tales," and seamen are still reporting rumors of gigantic sea serpents. Ancient charts of the sea sometimes bore drawings of sea monsters.

A discussion of the origin of certain common superstitions as an outgrowth of this musical experience may be a valuable one. This leads directly to the use of the Satis Coleman *Book of Bells* in connection with the tolling of the cathedral bells. Cathedrals and their construction were and are long-term projects; in the Middle Ages a man might devote his entire life to the business of working on one cathedral. In such a situation legends and superstitions often arose. In connection with the bells themselves, Coleman tells a number of stories illustrating the legends and superstitions which grew around their use. To further expand this, it may be pointed out that in the period during which the legend may have originated, the printing press had not been invented, education was for the few not for the many, and among ignorant folk superstition was widely spread. Legends, passed along by word of mouth, may arise easily and grow rapidly.

The foregoing discussion may be used in part or in whole, depending upon the time allotment and the interest of the class. Technical analysis of the music also depends upon the musical level of the class. Certainly such items as the following should be brought out:

1. The basic philosophy of the Impressionist painters and composers. (Compare music of Debussy with that of composers representing other periods.)
2. A discussion of the style of Debussy, emphasizing characteristic features of his music.
3. A comparison of the piano record with the orchestral record. Ask what instruments might be suited to the music of Debussy. Note the use of reed instruments to secure color.
4. Comparing the orchestral version of *La Cathédrale Engloutie* with another orchestral portrait of the sea.

A program for *La Cathédrale Engloutie*, by Huntington Watts, is as follows:

The most mystic of the Preludes, this favorite work makes audible and all but visual the essence of the old Brêton legend that Lalo adapted and expanded for operatic purposes in his *Le Roi d'Ys*. On occasion — so the tale runs — when the sea is transparent in the clear light of morning, out of the waves rises the cathedral of Ys, its bells tolling, its priests intoning; slowly it will return again to the depths where its enchanted sleep will be resumed. The melodic content is Gregorian; the harmony recollective of the medieval *organum*. The effect is, in fact, orchestral. There are three principal musical ideas: one suggestive of plain chant and the organ, as if played by phantom fingers; another representative of the quiet sea; the third like the slow swelling of the waves. A bell-like figure and a ponderous pedal point are heard at the climax. As the cathedral recedes beneath rocking waves, there is an echo of the plain chant, and the conclusion is like the opening, but with seconds added to the harmonies. The moving blocks of hollow chords that Debussy employed to express sombre mystery are utilized to suggest the sunken bells. In its chord successions, the composition represents what was — at that time — a new concept of dissonance: a conception in which dissonance was to be regarded as an end in itself, and not a mere episode on the road to a redemptive consonance.[12]

---

[12] Reprinted by permission. These notes are included in the following record album: Debussy, Preludes, Book I, Walter Gieseking, Piano; Columbia Masterworks Set M-352, Columbia Records, Inc., New York. Although the notes describing this are included here, a recording of *La Cathédrale Engloutie* is not in this album, but may be added: Col. 17077D.

SUGGESTED ACTIVITIES AS AN OUTGROWTH:

1. Reading concerning myth, superstition, legend.
2. Drawings and paintings of the Engulfed Cathedral made by the class.
3. Listening to other compositions by Impressionists.
4. Listening to other music descriptive of the sea.
5. Studying the great cathedrals of the Middle Ages through reading and pictures.

LIST OF MATERIALS

A LIST OF COMPOSITIONS FOR JUNIOR-HIGH-SCHOOL MUSIC LISTENING

Jazz Legato	Anderson
Jazz Staccato	
Fiddle Faddle	
Variations on a Theme by Tchaikovsky	Arensky
Christ Lag in Todesbanden	Bach
Toccata and Fugue in D minor	
Overture to *Egmont*	Beethoven
Rondo a Capriccio in G major	
Symphony No. 3 in E flat (*Eroica*)	
Carmen (excerpts)	Bizet
Airborne Symphony	Blitzstein
Academic Festival Overture	Brahms
Variations on a Theme by Haydn	
Pavane "El Greco"	Braine
Habanera "Lazy Cigarette"	
Young Person's Guide to the Orchestra	Britten
"Four Sea Interludes" — *Peter Grimes*	
Variations on "Pop Goes the Weasel"	Calliet
España (Rhapsody)	Chabrier
Polonaise in A flat major	Chopin
London Suite	Coates
Lincoln Portrait	Copland
Suite for Strings	Corelli
Clair de Lune	Debussy
La Cathédrale Engloutie	
La Mer	
"Ritual Fire Dance" — *El Armor Brujo*	de Falla
"Dance of the Automatons" — *Coppélia* Ballet	Delibes
Brigg Fair: An English Rhapsody	Delius
"Juba Dance" — *In the Bottoms*	Dett
Gossips	Dubensky
Sorcerer's Apprentice	Dukas

Symphony No. 5 in E minor (*New World*)	Dvořák
Music of Stephen Foster (Kostalanetz)	Foster
Songs of Stephen Foster (Nelson Eddy, baritone)	
Donkey Serenade (James Melton, tenor)	Friml
Porgy and Bess Highlights	Gershwin
Rhapsody in Blue	
Pinafore	Gilbert & Sullivan
Funeral March of a Marionette	Gounod
"March of Allegiance" — *Sigurd Jorsalfar*	Grieg
Pleasure Dome of Kubla Khan	Griffes
White Peacock	
Grand Canyon Suite	Grofé
Mississippi Suite	
Turkey in the Straw	Guion
Triumphal Entrance of the Boyards	Halvorsen
Messiah	Handel
Royal Fireworks Music	
Water Music	
Musical Clocks	Haydn
Toy Symphony	
The Planets	Holst
Caucasian Mountain Sketches	Ippolitov-Ivanov
The Music Box	Liadov
Les Préludes	Liszt
Suite No. 2 (*Indian*)	MacDowell
Shadrack (Nelson Eddy, baritone)	MacGimsey
Legend of the Arkansas Traveller	McDonald
Symphony No. 1 (*Sante Fé Trail*)	
A Midsummer Night's Dream (Incidental Music)	Mendelssohn
Fingal's Cave (or *Hebrides*) *Overture*	
A Night on Bald Mountain	Moussorgsky
Boris Godounoff Excerpts (Symphonic Synthesis)	
Pictures at an Exhibition	
Overture to *The Magic Flute*	Mozart
Symphony No. 41 in C major (*Jupiter*)	
The Green-Eyed Dragon (Robert Merrill, baritone)	Newman, Charles
Overture to *The Merry Wives of Windsor*	Nicolai
Moto Perpetuo	Novácek
	(Arr. Stokowski)
Dancing Doll (Lily Pons, soprano)	Poldini
Love for Three Oranges (Excerpts)	Prokofiev
Peter and the Wolf	
Bolero	Ravel
Virgin's Slumber Song (Blanche Thebom, mezzo-soprano)	Reger
Pines of Rome	Respighi

Scheherazade	Rimsky-Korsakov
Lonesome Train	Robinson
Carnival of the Animals	Saint-Saëns
Danse Macabre	
Symphony No. 8 in B minor *(Unfinished)*	Schubert
Fantasiestücke	Schumann
"Polka and Russian Dance" — *Golden Age* Ballet	Shostakovich
Finlandia	Sibelius
"War Dance of the Cheyennes" — *Suite Primeval*	Skilton
Overture to *The Bartered Bride*	Smetana
Moldau	
Irish Washerwoman	Sowerby
Don Quixote	Strauss
Suite from *Der Rosenkavelier*	
Till Eulenspiegel's Merry Pranks	
Circus Polka	Stravinsky
The Firebird (L'Oiseau de Feu)	
Fireworks (Feu d'Artifice)	
The Rite of Spring (Le Sacre du Printemps)	
Through the Looking Glass	Taylor
Marche Slave	Tchaikovsky
Nutcracker Suite	
1812 Overture	
Sleeping Beauty Ballet	
Aïda (excerpts)	Verdi
Overture to *Der Freischütz*	von Weber
"Ho-Jo-To-Ho" — *Die Walküre* (Kirsten Flagstad, soprano)	Wagner
Overture to *The Flying Dutchman*	
Schwanda the Bagpiper (Polka and Fugue)	Weinberger

History

2000 Years of Music (Sachs)
Columbia History of Music (Scholes)

Christmas Music

Carols by the Bach Choir	Jacques (conductor)
Ceremony of Carols	(Britten) Robert Shaw Chorale
Christmas Carols	Royal Choral Society; Sargent (conductor)
Christmas Carols	Robert Mitchell Boys' Choir
Christmas Eve Suite	(Rimsky-Korsakov) Orch. Radio Berlin
Christmas Hymns and Carols — Vols. I and II	Robert Shaw Chorale
Messiah	(Handel) Huddersfield Choral Society

Choral Music (see also Christmas Music)

Choral Caravan	de Paur Infantry Chorus
Ein' Feste Burg	Schola Cantorum
Festival of Choral Music (Selections)	Peter Wilhousky (conductor)
Hymns of All Churches	Hymns of All Churches Choir
Jewish Holidays in Song	Soloists, Choir, and Organ
Spirituals and Work Songs	de Paur Infantry Chorus
Yale Glee Club (Selections)	Marshall Bartholomew (conductor)

Additional Suggestions

Six Dances (Columbia)
Dances, Folk and Square (RCA Victor and Others)
Instruments of the Orchestra (Columbia, Decca, Victor)
Marches: *Sousa-Goldman Marches* (Columbia)
            America's Favorite Marches (Victor)
      (It is suggested that the record library also include representative music from musical shows and motion pictures, as well as selections from so-called "popular" music.)

ART SONGS FOR LISTENING IN THE JUNIOR HIGH SCHOOL

An die Nachtigall (To the Nightingale)	Brahms
Feldeinsamkeit (Alone in the Fields)	
Die Mainacht (May Night)	
Mein Mädel hat ein Rosenmund (My Sweetheart has a Rosy Mouth)	
Der Schmied (The Blacksmith)	
Sonntag (Sunday)	
Vergebliches Ständchen (The Unsuccessful Serenade)	
Mandoline	Debussy
L'Invitation au Voyage (Invitation to Voyage)	Duparc
In the Boat	Grieg
Der Floh (The Flea)	Moussorgsky
"Die Post" ("The Postman") — *Die Winterreise*	Schubert
"Frühlingstraum" ("Dream of Spring") — *Die Winterreise*	
"Der Leiermann" ("The Organgrinder") — *Die Winterreise*	
"Die Wetterfahne" ("The Weathervane") — *Die Winterreise*	
Der Erlkönig (The Erl King)	
Die Forelle (The Trout)	
Heidenröslein (Hedge Rose)	
Litanei (Litany)	

Meeres Stille (Ocean Calm)
An die Musik (To Music)
"Das Wandern" ("Wandering") — Die Schöne
   Müllerin
"Wohin?" ("Whither?") — Die Schöne Müllerin
Mondnacht (Moonlit Night)   Schumann
Der Nussbaum (The Nut Tree)
Waldesgespräch (Woodland Conversation)
Morgen (Tomorrow)   Strauss
Auf ein altes Bild (On Gaizing at an Old Painting)   Wolf
Der Gärtner (The Gardener)
Gesang Weyla's (Weyla's Song of the Island)
Schlafendes Jesukind (Sleeping Jesus Child)
Der Tambour (The Drummer Boy)
Mausfallen-Sprüchlein (The Mouse-Trap)

SUGGESTED MUSICAL MATERIALS GROUPED AROUND TOPICS OF INTEREST

Note: The purpose of this listing of materials is to cite subjects of interest in the everyday lives of boys and girls and to note listening materials associated with them. It is not suggested that all of the listening material noted in any one group be used at any one time; on the contrary, some of it should be used sparingly, such as the material under "Mystery," and so forth. Indiscriminate use easily could be as bad an influence as are movies, comics, television, and radio at times. But since children in the majority appear to be interested in these matters, their use in a matter-of-fact way and their exposition as a part of the surrounding world, presented in a manner which is not overstimulating, may operate to take away some of the importance from the area. In presenting such materials, however, the teacher should always bear in mind the extreme sensitivity of many children and use materials accordingly.

    The use of beautiful music as a part of the child's everyday life is one of the aims of music education. For example, on the Friday before a hike, why not use the Schubert Das Wandern? When the circus comes to town, play the Rimsky-Korsakov Dance of the Clowns. The spirit of mischief and fun shines brightly in Till Eulenspiegel's Merry Pranks. The use of musical material in such a way bridges the gap, where it exists, between the child and the music of the great composers.

    Of course, it is assumed that the teacher, in using such program music, will not neglect the richness of absolute music. Neither are the groupings suggested here supposed to contain all the material available in any particular center of interest. It is hoped the teacher will add other material as it is suggested, or as she locates it in her teaching.

    Some of the compositions listed here may not be available in recorded form at present, but it is hoped that recording companies will issue them in the near future.

	Composer or Performer
I. The Music of Our Country	
American Legends	American Ballad Singers
A Tree on the Plains	Bacon
The Airborne Symphony	Blitzstein
Variations on "Pop Goes the Weasel"	Calliet
Appalachian Suite	Copland
Lincoln Portrait	
Tales of Our Countryside	Cowell
American Songs	Different composers (sung by Helen Traubel)
Symphony No. 5 in E minor (New World)	Dvořák
Porgy and Bess	Gershwin
Frontier Town	Gillis
This Is Our America	
Cowboy Rhapsody	Gould
Grand Canyon Suite	Grofé
Mississippi Suite	
Folk Songs (historical songs and ballads)	Ives (folksinger)
Housatonic at Stockbridge	Ives, Charles
Mark Twain	Kern
I Hear America Singing	Kleinsinger
Suite No. 2 (Indian)	MacDowell
Grandma Moses Suite	Martin-Wilder
Arkansas Traveller	McDonald
Symphony No. 1 (Santa Fé Trail)	
Lonesome Train	Robinson
Oklahoma!	Rodgers-Hammerstein
American Festival Overture	Schuman
Sing of America	Scott (folksinger)
Ozark Set	Siegmeister
Two Indian Dances	Skilton
The Plow That Broke the Plains	Thomson
II. Humorous Characters in Music; Humorous Music	
"Fury Over a Lost Penny" (Rondo a Capriccio in G major)	Beethoven
Adventures in a Perambulator	Carpenter

"*Golliwog's Cake Walk*" (*Children's Corner* Suite)	Debussy
"Dance of the Automatons" — *Coppélia* Ballet	Delibes
Gossips	Dubensky
Funeral March of a Marionette	Gounod
"Intermezzo"; "Entrance of the Emperor and His Court" — *Háry János* Suite	Kodály
Fugato on a Well-Known Theme	McBride
Midsummer Night's Dream	Mendelssohn
"Ballet of the Unhatched Chicks" — *Pictures at an Exhibition*	Moussorgsky
Song of the Flea (sung in English by Lawrence Tibbett)	
Overture to *The Magic Flute*	Mozart
Green-Eyed Dragon	Newman
The Merry Wives of Windsor	Nicolai
"Musetta's Waltz" — *La Bohême* (Act II)	Puccini
"Dance of the Tumblers" — *The Snow Maiden*	Rimsky-Korsakov
Carnival of the Animals	Saint-Saëns
"Dance of the Comedians" — *The Bartered Bride*	Smetana
Till Eulenspiegel's Merry Pranks	Strauss
Schwanda the Bagpiper	Weinberger

III. Heroes Who Fought the Good Fight

Overture to *Coriolanus*	Beethoven
Overture to *Egmont*	
Leonore Overture No. 3	
Lincoln Portrait	Copland
Lonesome Train	Robinson
Two Grenadiers	Schumann
Lohengrin	Wagner
Parsifal	
Rienzi	
Siegfried	

IV. Strong Men and Adventurers in Music

Rákóczy March	Berlioz
Triumphal Entrance of the Boyards	Halvorsen
Scheherazade	Rimsky-Korsakov
Overture to *William Tell*	Rossini

The Spinning Wheel of Omphale	Saint-Saëns
"Bacchanale" — *Samson and Delilah*	
Don Quixote	Strauss
"Siegfried Cleaves the Anvil" — *Siegfried*	Wagner
"Siegfried's Rhine Journey" — *Götterdäm-merung*	

V. Mystery, the Supernatural, Violence, Sudden Death

Carmen	Bizet
The Engulfed Cathedral (Preludes — Book I)	Debussy
Sorcerer's Apprentice	Dukas
Dance of Terror	de Falla
Ritual Fire Dance	
Hansel and Gretel	Humperdinck
Mephisto Waltz	Liszt
Totendanz	
Witches' Dance	MacDowell
A Night on Bald Mountain	Moussorgsky
Khovantchina (Prelude; Entr'acte)	
Tosca	Puccini
Danse Macabre	Saint-Saëns
Der Erlkönig	Schubert
Overture to *Manfred*	Schumann
The Firebird Suite	Stravinsky
Overture to *Der Freischütz*	von Weber
Das Rheingold	Wagner
Parsifal	
Belshazzar's Feast	Walton

VI. What Is Death?

Christ Lag in Todesbanden	Bach
Symphony No. 3 (*Funeral March*)	Beethoven
Marche Funébre	Berlioz
Auf dem Kirchhofe	Brahms
Der Tod das is die Kühle Nacht	
Requiem	
The Trumpeter	Dix
"Death of Ase" — *Peer Gynt* Suite No. 1	Grieg
Ein Schwan	
There Is No Death	O'Hara
Isle of the Dead	Rachmaninoff

Pavane	Ravel
Litanei	Schubert
Swan of Tuonela	Sibelius
Valse Triste	

VII. Festivals; the Circus Comes to Town; Parades;
   Fairs

Fête-Dieu à Seville	Albéniz
Dance of the Bear	Bartók
Skyscrapers	Carpenter
Children's Corner Suite	Debussy
Fêtes (Nocturnes)	
Queen of Sheba Cortège	Gounod
"Mardi Gras" — *Mississippi* Suite	Grofé
"Procession of the Sardar" — *Caucasian*	Ippolitov-Ivanov
Mountain Sketches	
The Fair at Sorochinsk (Prelude)	Moussorgsky
Incredible Flutist	Piston
"Dance of the Tumblers" — *The Snow*	Rimsky-Korsakov
Maiden	
"Festival at Bagdad" — *Scheherazade*	
Circus Polka	Stravinsky
La Procesión del Rocio	Turina

VIII. The Nature of the World Around Us
   A. Water

Mediterranean	Bax
Song of the Bayou	Bloom
"Four Sea Interludes" — *Peter Grimes*	Britten
Reflets Dans L'eau (*Images* — Set I)	Debussy
La Mer	
Sea Pictures	Elgar
Mississippi Suite	Grofé
Water Music	Handel
The Planets	Holst
Sea Pieces	MacDowell
Calm Sea and Prosperous Voyage	Mendelssohn
Fingal's Cave Overture	
Fountains of Rome	Respighi
"The Sea and Sinbad's Vessel" —	Rimsky-Korsakov
Scheherazade	
Meeres Stille	Schubert

The Moldau	Smetana
Blue Danube	Strauss
Swan Lake	Tchaikovsky
Das Rheingold	Wagner

B. Woods, Fields, Meadows, Sky, Plains

Symphony No. 6 in F (*Pastoral*)	Beethoven
In the Steppes of Central Asia	Borodin
Feldeinsamkeit	Brahms
"Clair de Lune" — *Suite Bergamasque*	Debussy
Nuages (Nocturnes)	
By a Lonely Forest Pathway	Griffes
Pines of Rome	Respighi
"Hymn to the Sun" — *Golden Cockerel*	Rimsky-Korsakov
Overture to *A May Night*	
Mondnacht (*Moonlight*)	Schumann
From Bohemia's Meadows and Forests	Smetana
Tales from the Vienna Woods	Strauss
Plow That Broke the Plains	Thomson
"Siegfried's Rhine Journey" — *Götter-*	Wagner
dämmerung	

C. Caves and Canyons

"In the Hall of the Mountain King" —	Grieg
Peer Gynt Suite No. 1	
The Pleasure Dome of Kubla Khan	Griffes
Grand Canyon Suite	Grofé
Fingal's Cave Overture	Mendelssohn

D. Storms

Symphony No. 6 in F (*Pastoral*)	Beethoven
"Cloudburst" — *Grand Canyon* Suite	Grofé
"Storm Music" — *Ivan the Terrible*	Rimsky-Korsakov
Overture to *William Tell*	Rossini
Overture to *Der Freischütz*	von Weber
Overture to *The Flying Dutchman*	Wagner
Die Walküre (Prelude)	

IX. Legends and Myths in Music

Till Eulenspiegel's Merry Pranks	Strauss
"Entrance of the Gods into Valhalla" — *Das*	Wagner
Rheingold	
Overture to *The Flying Dutchman*	

X.   Important Personages
     Caliph of Bagdad   Boïeldieu
     Pomp and Circumstance   Elgar
     Queen of Sheba Cortège   Gounod
     Pleasure Dome of Kubla Khan   Griffes
     "Grand March" — *Aïda*   Verdi

XI. Make-Believe in Music
     Cinderella Suite   Coates
     Children's Corner Suite   Debussy
     Funeral March of a Marionette   Gounod
     March of the Toys   Herbert
     Music Box   Liadov
     March of the Lead Soldiers   Pierné
     Peter and the Wolf   Prokofiev
     Mother Goose Suite   Ravel
     Toy Trumpet   Scott
     Through the Looking Glass   Taylor
     Nutcracker Suite   Tchaikovsky
     Sleeping Beauty Ballet

XII. Industry; Labor
     Skyscrapers   Carpenter
     Pacific 231   Honegger
     Dance of the Workers   McDonald
     Steel Foundry   Mossolov

XIII. Fireworks in Music
     Feux d'Artifice (Preludes — Book II)   Debussy
     Fireworks Music   Handel
     Fireworks   Stravinsky

XIV. Animals in Music (Insect, Bird, Beast,
        Fowl, Fish)
     Adventures in a Perambulator (Dogs)   Carpenter
     Poisson d'Or (*Images* — Set II)   Debussy
     Butterfly   Grieg
     White Peacock   Griffes
     Little White Donkey   Ibert

Coq d'Or	Rimsky-Korsakov
Flight of the Bumblebee	
Carnival of the Animals	Saint-Saëns
Cat's Fugue	Scarlatti
Swan Lake	Tchaikovsky
Light Cavalry Overture	von Suppé
"Immolation Scene" — *Götterdämmerung*	Wagner
"Ride of the Valkyries" — *Die Walküre*	

XV. Religion in Music (see also Christmas Music)

Jesu, Joy of Man's Desiring	Bach
Prelude on *Eine Feste Burg*	Bach-Stokowski
Kol Nidrei (Hebrew)	Peerce (tenor)
Great Sacred Choruses (Selected)	Robert Shaw Chorale
Jewish Holidays in Song	Free Synagogue Choir
Ave Maria	Schubert

XVI. Interesting Scenes and Selections from Operas

Card Scene — *Carmen*	Bizet
"Bell Song" — *Lakmé*	Delibes
"Soldiers' Chorus" — *Faust*	Gounod
"O Isis und Osiris" — *The Magic Flute* (Use the overture as a background for the entire story.)	Mozart
"*Che Gelida Manina*" ("Your Tiny Hand Is Frozen") — *La Bohême*	Puccini
"*Largo al Factotum*" — *Barber of Seville*	Rossini
"Dawn"; "Siegfried's Rhine Journey"; "Siegfried's Funeral Music" — *Götterdämmerung*	Wagner
"Bridal Chorus" — *Lohengrin*	
Cudgeling Scene (available in complete opera recording) — *Die Meistersinger* (Others: "Dance of the Apprentices"; "Cobbling Song"; "Prize Song")	
"Good Friday Spell" — *Parsifal*	
Nibelheim Scene; "Entrance of the Gods into Valhalla" — *Das Rheingold*	
"*Schmiede, mein Hammer*"; "Forest Murmurs" — *Siegfried*	

XVII. Popular Songs Adapted from Other Sources[13]

There's No Tomorrow	*O Sole Mio*	Capua
Till the End of Time	Polonaise in A flat, Op. 53, No. 6	Chopin
No Other Love	Etude in E, Op. 10, No. 3	
My Reverie	*Reverie*	Debussy
Strange Music	*Wedding Day at Troldhaugen*	Grieg
Anniversary Song	*Waves of the Danube*	Ivanovici
The Breeze and I	*Andalucia*	Lecuona
At the Crossroads	*Malaguena*	
Moonlight and Roses	*Andantino*	Lemare
You're Breaking My Heart	*Mattinata*	Leoncavallo
Full Moon and Empty Arms	Piano Concerto No. 2 in C minor	Rachmaninoff
The Lamp Is Low	*Pavane*	Ravel
If You Are But a Dream	Op. 44, No. 1 (*Romance*)	Rubinstein
When I Write My Song	"My Heart At Thy Sweet Voice" — *Samson and Delilah*	Saint-Saëns
Save Me a Dream	Symphony No. 5, second movement	Tchaikovsky
Moon Love	Symphony No. 5, second movement	
Story of a Starry Night	Symphony No. 6, first movement	
Tonight We Love	Piano Concerto No. 1 in B flat minor	
Isle of May	Quartet No. 1 in D, Op. 11	
Our Love	Overture to *Romeo and Juliet*	

XVIII. Some Radio and Television Program Theme Music from Well-Known Compositions

Composition	*Program*
"On the Trail" — *Grand Canyon* Suite (Grofé)	Philip Morris Shows

---

[13] This list was compiled by Dr. Hummel Fishburn, the Pennsylvania State College.

Liebestraum (Liszt)	Dr. Paul
Au Matin (Godard)	Pepper Young's Family
Sixth Symphony (*Andante*) (Tchaikovsky)	Road of Life
Flight of the Bumblebee (Rimsky-Korsakov)	Green Hornet
Donna Diana Overture (Reznicek)	Challenge of the Yukon
Semper Fidelis (Sousa)	Mutual Newsreel
Valse Triste (Sibelius)	I Love a Mystery
March — *Love for Three Oranges* (Prokofiev)	F.B.I. in Peace and War
Ein Heldenleben (R. Strauss)	Big Story
I Will Bring You Music, based on Second Piano Concerto (Rachmaninoff)	Ford Festival
"Cattle Song" — *Plow that Broke the Plains* (Thomson)	Gabby Hayes
"Dance of the Comedians" — *The Bartered Bride* (Smetana)	Star Time
Opening theme, based on Second Hungarian Rhapsody (Liszt)	Texaco Star Theater
Symphony No. 9, fourth movement (Shostakovich)	Treasury Men in Action
Serenade (Toselli)	The Goldbergs
Artist's Life (J. Strauss)	You Are An Artist (John Gnagy)
Toccata and Fugue in D minor (Bach)	Nature of Things (Dr. Roy Marshall)
The Flying Dutchman (Wagner)	Captain Video

BOOKS FOR BOYS AND GIRLS (MUSIC; MUSICIAN;)

Arnold	*Finlandia*	Holt
Bakeless	*Story-Lives of American Composers*	Lippincott
	Story-Lives of Great Composers	
Bauer	*Twentieth Century Music*	Putnam
Bauer and Peyser	*How Music Grew*	
	Music Through the Ages	
Benét	*Enchanting Jenny Lind*	Dodd

Berry	*One-String Fiddle* (recording available)	Winston
Burch	*Modern Composers for Boys and Girls*	Dodd
	Richard Wagner: Who Followed a Star	Holt
Burton	*The Blue Book of Tin Pan Alley*	Century House
Cooke	*The Firebird*	Winston
	The Nutcracker of Nuremberg	
Cunningham	*Paul Lawrence Dunbar*	Dodd
Deucher	*Young Brahms*	Dutton
Ewen	*American Composers Today*	Wilson
	Book of Modern Composers	Knopf
	Haydn	Holt
	Living Musicians	Wilson
	Men of Popular Music	Prentice-Hall, Inc.
	Story of George Gershwin	Holt
	Story of Irving Berlin	
	Story of Arturo Toscanini	
	Tales from the Vienna Woods	
Goss	*Beethoven: Master Musician*	
	Deep-Flowing Brook	
	Unfinished Symphony	
Goss and Schauffler	*Brahms: the Master*	
Gronowicz	*Chopin*	Nelson
	Paderewski, Pianist and Patriot	
	Sergei Rachmaninoff	Dutton
	Tschaikowsky	Nelson
Lawrence	*The Rheingold*	Silver Burdett
	Siegfried (Also other opera stories)	
Lewiton	*John Philip Sousa, the March King*	Didier
Lingg	*Mozart: Genius of Harmony*	Holt
Lochner	*Fritz Kreisler*	Macmillan
Purdy	*Antonin Dvořák: Composer from Bohemia*	Julian Messner
	Gilbert and Sullivan: Masters of Mirth and Melody	
	He Heard America Sing	
	Song of the North	
	Stormy Victory	
	Victor Herbert	

Spaeth	*Dedication*	Holt
	Opportunities in Music	Grosset
Stoddard	*From These Comes Music*	Crowell
Tinyanova	*Stradivari: the Violin Maker*	Knopf
Trapp	*The Story of the Trapp Family Singers*	Lippincott
Vehanen	*Marian Anderson: A Portrait*	Whittlesey
Wheeler	*Ludwig Beethoven and the Chiming Tower Bells*	Dutton
	Frederic Chopin; Early Years	
	Frederic Chopin; Later Years	
	Paganini: Master of Strings	
	Robert Schumann	
Wheeler and Deucher	*Joseph Haydn: the Merry Little Peasant*	
	Curtain Calls for Wolfgang Mozart	
	Mozart the Wonder Boy	
	Franz Schubert	

SOURCE BOOKS FOR THE TEACHER

Bagar & Biancolli	*The Concert Companion*	McGraw-Hill
Baldwin	*Adventures in Orchestral Music* (out of print)	Gilman
	A Listener's Anthology of Music	Silver Burdett
Barlow & Morgenstern	*A Dictionary of Musical Themes*	Crown
	A Dictionary of Vocal Themes	
Biancolli and Bagar	*The Victor Book of the Opera*	Simon & Schuster
Burrows & Redmond	*Symphony Themes*	
Dike	*Stories from the Great Metropolitan Operas*	Random House, Inc.
Ewen	*Music for the Millions*	Arco
Gilman	*Orchestral Music*	Oxford
Hallstrom	*Relax and Listen*	Rinehart & Company, Inc.
Hartshorn and Leavitt	*The Pilot*	Ginn
	The Mentor	
Kinscella	*Music and Romance*	RCA Victor Co., Inc.

Krehbiel	*A Book of Operas*	Macmillan
Lawrence	*The Victor Book of Ballets*	Simon & Schuster
Leonard	*The Stream of Music*	Doubleday
McKinney & Anderson	*Discovering Music*	American Book
Murphy	*Form in Music for the Listener*	RCA Victor Co., Inc.
Newman	*Stories of the Great Operas*	Garden City Publishing Co., Inc.
O'Connell	*The Victor Book of Overtures, Tone Poems, and Other Orchestral Works*	Simon & Schuster
Sachs	*The History of Musical Instruments*	Norton
Schwartz	*The Story of Musical Instruments*	Garden City Publishing Co., Inc.
Stringham	*Listening to Music Creatively*	Prentice-Hall, Inc.
Welch	*The Appreciation of Music*	Harper and Brothers

LISTINGS OF RECORDS AND SOURCES OF INFORMATION ABOUT OBTAINING RECORDS

RCA Victor, Columbia, and Decca catalogs.

Catalogs of other record companies available at record shops.

Long Playing Record Catalog (cumulative: issued monthly by W. Schwann; available at record shops).

Barbour and Freeman, *The Children's Record Book* (Oliver Durrell, Inc.).

Eisenberg and Krasno, *A Guide to Children's Records* (Crown).

Freeman, *Annotated List of Phonograph Records* (Children's Reading Service, 106 Beekman St., New York 38, New York).

Hall, *The Record Book* (Oliver Durrell, Inc.).

Kolodin, *The New Guide to Recorded Music* (Doubleday).

Lumpkin, *Folksongs on Records* (Folksongs on Records, publisher, Boulder, Colorado).

SOURCES OF PRINTS OF PAINTINGS AND PHOTOGRAPHS OF ARTISTS FOR USE AS VISUAL AIDS[14]

RCA Victor, Educational Division, Camden, New Jersey (colored photographs of artists; photographs of orchestral instruments — charts).

Artex Prints, Westport, Connecticut (inexpensive prints of great paintings).

---

14 Note: These are not free materials.

Metropolitan Museum of Art; National Distributor: Book-of-the-Month Club, 345 Hudson St., New York 14, New York (miniature prints of great paintings).

Museum of Modern Art (color reproductions of paintings).

MAGAZINES AND OTHER PUBLICATIONS

Film Music Notes; (official publication of the National Film Music Council, 31 Union Square W., New York 3, New York) (source of information about musical scores of motion pictures).

Opera News (Metropolitan Opera Guild, 654 Madison Ave., New York 21, New York).

Musical America (113 West 57 St., New York 19, New York) (information about current musical affairs and present-day musicians and composers; annual special issue, included with subscription, valuable for summary of musical activities, and also for interesting photographs of many musicians, useful for mounting on colored drawing paper for visual aids in the classroom).

Keyboard Jr. (1346 Chapel St., New Haven 11, Connecticut); also available from *Keyboard Jr.*, at same address:

Television Bulletin
Record Reviews
Film Music

BOOKS FOR USE IN CLASSROOM STUDY OF MUSICAL COMPOSITIONS

Music To Remember	Baldwin	Silver Burdett Co.
Pupils' books for *The*		
Pilot and *The Mentor:*	Hartshorn and Leavitt	Ginn

Prelude
Progress
At Home and Abroad
New Horizons

REPRINTS OF MAGAZINE ARTICLES

"Musical Recordings for World History"   William G. Tyrrell
"Musical Recordings for American History:
I. From Colonization Through the Civil War."
"Musical Recordings for American History:
II. Since the Civil War"

These articles are excellent for correlation of the above topics with music. There are three articles, reprinted from *Social Education*. They may be obtained from: Merrill F. Hartshorn, Executive Secretary of the National Council for Social Studies, 1201 Sixteenth St. N.W., Washington 6, D. C.

7. Pupil Evaluation

THE DILEMMA OF MARKING

School marks (numerical or symbolic letter marks) are the most common way of evaluating the pupil's progress. Yet almost no one is happy about them. A few students who receive high marks may experience a momentary "lift," if they have worked hard and feel the mark is a fair one. Those who receive high marks and know they have been obtained without much work, and even in some cases, unfairly, may develop a feeling of contempt for both the subject and the teacher involved. Parents, teachers, and pupils worry about marks. Yet the custom of dispensing them continues. What is wrong with it? In a brief analysis, here are some of the outstanding faults of marks:

1. Marking requires that a teacher be judge, jury, and executioner. Since maladjusted pupils often look upon the teacher as a jailor of sorts, this completes the teacher's concentration of power in the minds of such pupils, who may eventually adopt a fatalistic attitude and "sit out" the educational process.

2. Marking presents a paradox. Discerning educators realize that each time the teacher marks a boy or girl, he is really passing judgment on his own teaching.

3. If we believe that we teach children according to their individual abilities and needs, we cannot believe that it is possible to stamp them, like apples or oranges, with a grade label — *No. 1*, or lump them together as *windfalls*.

4. A mark is a fixed quantity in the form of an abstract symbol assigned to a boy or girl at a given point. This in itself tends to place him in a category: The whole procedure negates the

growth process, which does not stop at any fixed point but is continuous development.

5. Too often the mark is like a ball passed from the teacher over the head of the pupil to the parent. If the parent does not like the mark, he is likely to become defensive, then aggressive in the way of challenging the teacher's ability. Whereupon the *teacher* may become defensive! All this *mêlée*, in the supposed name of the pupil, usually finds him lost in the shuffle.

6. Instead of regarding the mark as an interpretation of progress achieved in the *direction* of a goal or goals, both pupil and parent are likely to regard the mark itself as a goal. This

may be a direct cause of tension, worry, and cheating in examinations. When marks are used as a club over the heads of pupils, the situation becomes even worse.

7. Marks do not reveal the causes of success or failure (which they may indicate) and thus are not constructively diagnostic. Too often they are used by teachers and interpreted by parents as an end in themselves rather than as a means to an end, which is, of course, furthering the development of the child. For example, a child with all *A*'s on his report card may be working below, and a child with all *C*'s above, the respective abilities of each.

8. Teachers' marks are often unreliable.

These general weaknesses of school marks are bad enough, but the situation becomes even more complicated when we try to mark a pupil's progress in such an area as musical development. Here we have a field in which the over-all goal is, for the vast majority, appreciation. Yet appreciation is almost immeasurable. Intensely personal and subjective in nature, tangible evidence of real growth in appreciation is difficult to pinpoint; we catch fleeting glimpses of it in our pupils from day to day, but it never marches before our eyes as might a parade of solved problems in arithmetic. Even in working with the most inept of instrumental students we cannot say there is no development of appreciation.

WHY MARKS ARE USED

1. Marks are powerful stimuli. Pupils who react favorably to high marks through them sometimes gain in self-esteem and group prestige. Failing marks may stimulate a pupil to do better, but the chronic "failure" is more often stimulated only to a point of giving up.

2. Marks are supposedly easy to understand, since both parents and pupils have a traditional idea of their meaning. Even the youngest pupils soon obtain some concept of mark values because of teacher and parent attitude toward them. And though educators realize that both letter and numerical

marks may not only represent inaccurate judgment but are interpreted in varying ways, parents often prefer them because a more wordy written report is less specific.

3. In schools where pupils are promoted grade by grade, the traditional practice of marking by letters or numbers is the easiest system to handle in terms of both teacher-time consumed and administrative bookkeeping. But whether a pupil's welfare is more important than the time element is really the issue here.

4. It has been argued that since life itself is competitive, pupils must learn to meet competition in performance on the part of their fellow pupils. It has been argued, too, that boys and girls must prepare to meet fixed standards of performance in certain areas of adult life. However, since music educators are coming to realize that by far the largest per cent of the school population will not earn its livelihood through music and that the nature of the junior-high-school music curriculum is largely exploratory, such arguments can hold little value for the conscientious teacher.

WHAT TO DO ABOUT MARKING

Evaluation, in all its phases, should serve the purpose of furnishing a live as possible picture of pupil progress to pupil, parent, and teacher. As well as placing a value upon past performance, it should point the way for future development. No report or evaluation should be arbitrarily pessimistic about the progress of a child unless it suggests ways in which the child may improve his progress. To give failing marks to a child and nothing else, hoping this will result in future improved performance, is like saying, "If I hit him hard enough he'll go down and never get up again." The effect of such marks on children has been that many of them *have* been hit hard enough to go down and never get up again, academically, unless some adult extended a helping hand. Learning is chiefly the impact of live mind upon live mind; if this were not true, we could confine pupils with books and successfully dispense with teachers. Too many teachers overlook this basic fact and assume that in giving the pupil a mark their responsibility is discharged. Any adult mind should be able to find some way to reach the mind of a child and open up avenues of growth; for teachers, this is their reason for being. But a mark in itself may be high or low without this vital process having taken place.

In junior high schools where marks are used, in order to mark effectively, a teacher must orient his thinking in terms of two points:

1. He must mark in keeping with his own educational philosophy. Most teachers either (*a*) mark in relation to a fixed theoretical absolute (100 per cent representing perfection) or (*b*) mark in relation to ability and effort put forth.[1]

It seems more practical to mark in terms of the latter, where music is concerned, because of obvious variables beyond the control of teacher and pupil. Most pupils, we have said, will become consumers of music. But most low marks are based upon pupil performance. By this we mean that a pupil who does not sing well, read music well, recognize the instruments of the orchestra by sound and sight, and so on, is likely to be penalized in the teacher's marking. Yet the reason for his failure to do well may lie in his musical limitations as determined by his native capacity. Or, the boy whose voice is changing may easily slide from an *A* where singing ability is being marked to a *C*, through no fault of his own. Furthermore, to mark a pupil who has an impoverished musical background on the same basis as a pupil who has had many musical advantages is manifestly unfair.

2. He must mark in terms of the objectives of the class he is teaching. If, for example, a teacher's objectives are those which appear in Chapter 3, he may mark on musical participation and give credit for such a simple activity as playing a rhythmic

---

[1] Sometimes a teacher is prevented from marking according to the way he believes best because the school has adopted another system. In such cases, the prevailing practice must be followed. However, each teacher may express himself, and it is possible that the thinking of even one teacher may lead to a revision of marking in a school or school system.

accompaniment on a drum. We have said that one of our objectives is musical enjoyment, and if a child has enjoyed playing the drum accompaniment, whether it has been poorly done or with a high degree of skill, he must receive recognition for this in his mark.

With these points in mind, a teacher will assign to each pupil a mark which reflects the *whole* child as he reacts in the classroom, rather than try to isolate his musical performance and give it a mark.

Music teachers frequently ask other music teachers, "Do you ever 'flunk' a child in music?" The answer most often given by the majority is, "No — if the child has put forth a reasonable amount of effort." Inexperienced teachers may have doubts about passing pupils who are amiable enough in the classroom but show little evidence of actual musical learning. Perhaps one guide for such teachers will be the interest displayed by the child in classroom activities — for the reason that musical awakening in the case of children with an impoverished background or a definitely negative attitude toward music may be long delayed. To fail a child before he has had an opportunity to find himself musically is certainly displaying a fatalistic attitude which has little place in today's philosophy of music education. The majority of music educators to whom the authors have spoken apparently would prefer to err on the side of leniency in assigning marks than to produce an attitude of dislike for music in those children who have displayed reasonable effort in the classroom without producing good musical performance. Children grow by succeeding a little at a time and by recognition of each success whether in terms of praise, marks, or other criteria.

CLASSROOM TESTING

Marks cannot be given without some form of objective evidence, usually tests, notebooks, or other material, indicating concretely what has been accomplished in music class. Unfortunately, much of this material may represent an impressive amount of factual information about music without any musical experience having taken place. Some tests of music achievement may be passed with high marks by pupils who have heard very little music and sung very few songs. In making up classroom tests, one fundamental principle is generally accepted by thinking music educators: *Every question should evolve from a musical experience of the pupils.* Boys and girls do not learn for the purpose of passing tests; through using materials they learn how music may function to make a richer life. We want the pupil to learn that Helen Traubel is a great dramatic soprano, for example, by hearing her sing — not by memorizing this information. We want him to learn that the clarinet is a transposing instrument by bringing it into the classroom and showing what happens when the clarinet plays a song written for voice and piano. We want him to know that the clarinet makes music which sounds a certain way and that it is useful in bands and orchestras besides as a solo instrument. He will remember these things and look for them in his musical life outside of school not by memorizing the spelling of the word and looking at a picture of the instrument, but by exploration in the classroom. Again, we are talking essentially of the difference between verbalism and functional learning. The child should be tested upon the latter for what objective evidence we can obtain of his musical growth.

PUPIL PROGRESS REPORT FORMS

Progress reports on pupils exist in endless variety. They have a common purpose, which is to inform the parent and child of the child's achievement and behavior in the school situation. Some reports include only numerical or letter marks on the various subjects studied by the child. Some rank each child according to his standing in each subject; some note the number of students receiving a particular mark. Some schools send home detailed letters describing the child in his school situation, a procedure which is valuable and revealing since it causes the teacher to think of each child as an individual in many different aspects of his personality, but which, because of the large amount of time it consumes, is impractical in all but small classes. In spite of this, the individual letter which considers many aspects of the child's development both socially and in relation to subject matter has a personal approach which appeals to some parents.

Whatever form the progress report takes it should have one objective; to help both parent and child understand what the child is doing in school and how well he is succeeding. In the belief that traditional report forms succeed in transmitting too small a part of the picture, schools have been experimenting for some time with a "job and behavior analysis" type of report. This lists in some detail the social traits displayed by the pupil and various aspects of the subject matter he is studying. A report of this nature might take the following form:

PROGRESS REPORT — MUSIC [2]

GENERAL MUSIC CLASS

Code: S (Satisfactory) U (Unsatisfactory)[3]
I. Classroom Attitude and Response
   A. Interest in music activities   _____
   B. Attention to classroom work   _____
   C. Co-operativeness and effort   _____
   D. Care of materials   _____

II. Participation
   A. Individual classroom activity   _____
   B. Participation in group activity   _____
   C. Extra activities (follow-up and extension of classroom activities on own initiative)   _____

III. Achievement
   A. Listening Experiences   _____
   B. Use of singing voice   _____

---

[2] The authors assume that schools using such a report as this will re-word each item in terms of school and class objectives as well as prevailing philosophy. Such report forms should not be standardized.

[3] The particular code (including the number of symbols used) should be developed by the individual school concerned.

Progress Report — Music *(continued)*:
    C. Music reading   _____
    D. Musical interpretation   _____
    E. Rhythmic activities   _____
    F. Application of musical knowledge to outside
        activities (radio, television, concerts)   _____

INSTRUMENTAL MUSIC (Group or Individual Instruction)
    I. Tone Quality   _____
   II. Music Reading   _____
  III. Performing Ability; Enjoyment of Instrument   _____
  IV. Group Co-operation   _____
   V. Care of Instrument   _____
        Explanatory Comments:

It should be observed that a report on both general music class and instrumental activities is provided in this form. Some schools prefer to furnish separate reports. However, combining the two areas on one form tends to bring about closer co-operation in cases where the pupil is taught by different instrumental and general music teachers. Remarks about participation in other music groups may be written in as comments.

The reason for using two symbols instead of three or more ("Excellent," "Satisfactory," "Unsatisfactory") appears to be that the more symbols used, the closer the approximation is to the *A, B, C* system. Individual comment will take care of superior performance or other marked deviation.

Pupils must understand the significance of such symbols as *S* and *U*. This should be explained in terms as specific as possible; otherwise the report loses its diagnostic and motivating value. (Just what each symbol means should be decided by the entire faculty of a school and included in the progress report. It also should be discussed in each class.)

The report illustrated could be abbreviated by combining two or more of its items under each heading. Brevity certainly is a desirable feature of progress reports. The danger is that the broader the item in scope, the less likely it is to be understood by pupil and parent.

Certainly there is no point in telling ourselves that by using "Unsatisfactory," "Satisfactory," and similar terms we are escaping a marking system. We can say that it may be a move in the right direction — that use of the progress report form directs the teacher's attention toward consideration of many aspects of the pupil's personal and social, as well as academic, growth. Also, in accepting general symbols as a rating device instead of number or letter categories, we may be admitting that no one can total the sum of a child's classroom behavior like a list of groceries at the checker's counter — something which should have been admitted long ago. These symbols give the teacher more room; he is not forced to squeeze the child into so small a niche. It seems sensible to suppose that the child will be more comfortable with increased space, too!

On every report of this type there should be a place for teacher comment. Such comment should clarify the marking of items in which the pupil is doing unsatisfactory work or not working up to capacity. In attempting to convey the message to the parent, the teacher should answer two questions:
1. Why is the child's work unsatisfactory?
2. What can he do to improve it?

Where this cannot be accomplished on the report form, the parent should be invited to visit the teacher for a conference.

It has been said that both parents and pupils should understand the report form. One way to help children with this problem is to hand out mimeographed copies of the report form, explain each item, and ask the pupil to rate himself on it. (The majority of pupils take this procedure seriously; they often rate themselves lower than would the teacher.)

This prepares the child for the report which reaches his parents and helps him discuss it intelligently with them. Other ways in which parents can be educated to understand the newer type report forms are through explanatory letters, home-room parents' meetings, and Parent-Teacher Association meetings; some schools have sent pupils to explain the new progress reports to service clubs, church groups, and other community organizations. Other schools prefer to do the same thing with teachers as representatives.

If, in addition to this type of report form, a parent wants a letter or percentage equivalent describing his child's work in the class, or his rank in the class, the teacher should give him such an equivalent. Some schools feel it is necessary to translate such general designations as E, S, and U into numerical equivalents for permanent school records.

We feel that in report forms, as in other areas of school life, weaknesses of pupils have too often been stressed without recognizing strengths. Yet, through recognition of these strengths, boys and girls gain confidence and go on to remedy their weaknesses. On every report the teacher should recognize the pupil's good points. No businessman would think of totaling only his liabilities and ignoring his assets, yet many a child dreads the day reports go home because teachers are sometimes so concerned about their pupil's shortcomings that they see little else. In other words, the progress report should report *progress*.

TESTS OF NATIVE MUSICAL CAPACITY

Carl Seashore[4] distinguishes between ability and capacity as follows: "The term 'capacity' has reference to the inborn or native power; the term 'ability' is used to designate acquired skill in the use of a capacity." However, the two terms are often used interchangeably.

Seashore[5] clearly states that musical talent exists very unequally in individuals. He also states that the musical mind is a normal mind. In testing the musical capacity of any individual, then, we are looking particularly at one aspect of the total personality. Theoretically, we are securing as a test result a measure of "pure" native capacity, although it seems possible that by the junior-high-school age tests of musical capacity will be affected in some part by the musical experiences of each

---

[4] From *The Psychology of Musical Talent* by Carl E. Seashore, copyright, 1919, by permission of the publishers, Silver Burdett Company, New York, pp. 14-15.

[5] *Ibid.*, p. 6.

individual and by the ability developed through these experiences.

Tests of musical capacity (also called talent or aptitude tests)
attempt to measure certain basic components which determine
the total index of an individual's innate musicality. The Seashore Measures of Musical Talent,[6] for example, test pitch,
loudness, time, timbre, rhythm, and tonal memory. The
Kwalwasser-Dykema Music Tests,[7] also designed to measure
native musical capacity, test tonal memory, quality discrimination, intensity discrimination, tonal movement, time discrimination, rhythm discrimination, pitch discrimination, melodic taste, pitch imagery, and rhythm imagery.

The purposes of testing for native musical capacity in the
junior high school may be listed as follows:

1. To predict what may reasonably be expected of each
child in the way of musical accomplishment.

2. To determine areas of potential strength in order to provide for each child musical activities in which he may engage
with satisfaction. For example, a child may rank low in pitch
discrimination but fairly high in rhythm discrimination. The
wise teacher will try to provide rhythmic activities from which
such a child will derive enjoyment. At the same time, he will
not forget that the child will receive pleasure from the stimulus
of pitch in relation to his capacity. No child is incapable of
such response unless he is totally deaf.

3. To identify the musically gifted. We list this separately,
although it is implied in the preceding point, because here the
teacher has a great responsibility. Some boys and girls who
have had little musical opportunity may have latent aptitude
which, when discovered, may be developed. The implication
is obvious when we realize that the school is the only agency
which can reach all children in an attempt at such identification.

4. To check scores obtained on aptitude tests given in the
upper elementary grades. It seems possible that junior-high-

---

6 Information on various tests cited is given at end of chapter.

7 *Ibid.*

school pupils may be better able to co-operate with test directions.

5. To aid in vocational guidance, which usually begins in the junior high school. Pupils considering a career in music may be more intelligently guided when an evaluation of their musical aptitude is available. Guidance in the choice of senior-high-school courses may be expedited through use of test scores. However, no test of musical aptitude yet devised is significant to such an extent that a score may be considered final predictive evidence of future success or failure in the pupil's school music experiences.

6. To assist teachers who consider effort in assigning marks, some indication of the musical capacity of the pupil aids in determining the relationship between achievement and effort.

7. To guide the interested pupil in the selection of an instrument.

A test of musical aptitude, administered to all pupils in the seventh grade, may be recorded on the pupil's cumulative record. It should be emphasized here that while this is one factor influencing his musical development, low scores should not be considered a deterrent where the teacher's efforts to make music a vital part of the child's life are concerned. The simplest way to look at this business of musical aptitude is that we all react to music differently because of our native capacity. The important thing is that unless a definite physical handicap exists, we all have the power to *react*. This should be enough to stimulate the efforts of each teacher. Music is no longer considered hallowed ground where only the talented few may walk — it belongs to the masses and to every child who enters the public schools. *No test score can alter this fact.*

TESTS OF MUSICAL ACHIEVEMENT

Standardized tests of musical achievement attempt to measure the amount of knowledge and skill pupils have developed in music. These are intended for use by teachers interested in learning how their pupils compare on a large scale with others of the same status. Since it has been stated in preceding chapters that different music classes may have quite different objectives and musical activities, the least important of which may be at times the acquisition of technical skill and information, it cannot be recommended here that such tests be used in every situation. However, they may serve to call to the attention of teacher and pupil areas of musical information which are generally considered to be useful. If through the administration of such a test a teacher finds, for instance, that a class is deficient in musical terminology, we cannot advocate that he thereupon gear his teaching to the understanding of this alone. He may feel, however, upon examination of his teaching materials and methods, that he has either neglected developing an understanding of such information or has taught it ineffectively. Whereupon he may devise methods of improving his teaching. But it must still be done in the same basic manner: Understanding of technical information should develop from musical experience. No test, standardized or otherwise, should determine what is to be taught in the classroom.

In addition to tests of aptitude and achievement, attempts have been made to measure music appreciation. However, it cannot be said that the teacher may hope to learn much of his pupils' indices of appreciation through the use of formal tests of music appreciation. Here and in the matter of measuring attitudes toward music, two highly important areas, he must rely largely upon his own individual knowledge and observation of the pupil.

Generally speaking, the teacher should be extremely careful not to overemphasize the importance of test results. Except diagnostically (and then only rarely), we do not favor disclosing to junior-high-school pupils scores on tests of musical aptitude, because those who rank low may feel, "What's the use? I don't have it, so it's useless to try." Such an attitude may effectively cut off the ability of the child to express himself through music. Self-expression, a goal of music educators, does not necessarily demand a high degree of musical talent. In fact, after years of teaching and observing junior-high-school pupils, the writer can say that it is often the pupil with only average talent who realizes more musical satisfaction and enjoyment than might be expected from his musical activities. This is frequently true with pupils displaying no outstanding aptitude in any area. When such boys and girls succeed in identifying themselves with a musical activity, the success carries great weight in their adjustment problems. In the case of a pupil who is clearly not making good use of his aptitude, however, it may be wise to tell him that he is capable both of better work and experiencing more musical satisfaction than is evident.

Music teachers sometimes state that those pupils who do superior work in music also do superior work in other subject areas. It is possible that in some cases intelligent pupils with only average or even below-average musical aptitude work so efficiently with what aptitude they possess that they progress at a faster rate than do more musical pupils who are less intelligent. Work habits, motivation, and inner drive also affect individual musical achievement.

Insufficient research exists concerning the gifted (I.Q. above 130) pupil with a high degree of musical talent. Even though teachers may expect to find few such pupils in a lifetime, they can perform an invaluable service by identifying these individuals. These are the potentially creative members of the human species in terms of great contributions to the field of music; they may be the openers of new frontiers. Every effort should be expended to identify and educate them with whatever resources are at the command of both school and community.

USING A CUMULATIVE MUSIC RECORD FORM

Musical growth is a continuous process and one which should not proceed in a series of starts and stops. It is advisable to provide some form of cumulative record which will cover the student's musical activities and reactions during the junior-high-school period. A form such as the one illustrated here may be adopted by the school, and if information is recorded each semester, or at least at the beginning and end of the school year, teachers may find it both revealing and interesting. For example, a teacher perplexed by a ninth-grade boy who refuses to participate in singing activities may examine his record for his seventh- and eighth-grade teachers' comments. Perhaps his attitude is one of long standing, which has had to be solved anew by each teacher. Perhaps it is a new attitude, arising from his uncertainty over the use of his changing voice. In either case the record, if it has been conscientiously kept, will furnish some leads. A new teacher may find such records invaluable in that they supply a background of information on pupils, which otherwise would be forthcoming only after several weeks of classes. They also furnish a long-term record which is useful in evaluating musical progress at the end of the junior-high-school period.

Such a record may be drawn up in the form of a single card for each year of the junior high school (illustrated); in this case the card of the preceding year should be attached to the current card. The comparatively small size of this card makes it convenient for filing. For schools which prefer to keep the entire junior-high-school record on one card, a record card approximately 9″ x 12″ may be drawn up for the entire junior-high-school period, with spaces for evaluating or commenting on all pertinent items.

Devices and techniques discussed in Chapters 2 and 3 should be considered as resources in evaluating pupil progress; the pupil-inventory, as it appears each year, may reflect changing attitudes and, indirectly, growth. Class self-evaluation may furnish similar information. Even the process of reviewing objectives may be revealing in terms of individual reaction. The pupil interview often furnishes substantial indication of growth in musical taste and appreciation. Conferences with private music teachers are often valuable sources of information. All in all, no opportunity to obtain formal or informal pupil reaction should be overlooked.

CUMULATIVE INDIVIDUAL MUSIC RECORD

Musical Aptitude Test——————— I.Q.——— School Year———
Name——————————— Age—— Grade—— Home Room———
    (Last)   (First)
Previous Musical Experience (Lessons) ———————— ——————
                                    (Instrument)   (Years)
Musical Organizations (School and Others)————————————
Private Lessons This Year————— Teacher ————————
School Instruction ——————— Instrument ———————
Singing Ability ————————————————————————
Reading Ability ——————————— Listening Attitude ————
Special Likes and Dislikes ————————————————————
Significant Personal Behavior Traits ————————————————
Estimate of Musical Ability ————————————————————
Progress During Year: Instrumental ————————————————
                       Vocal ————————————————————
Recommendations ——————————————————————————
(Use reverse side for additional comments)

SUMMARY

School marks present definite problems in any field, but particularly in music, where the goal is appreciation. Traditional marks are still used in many schools; the junior high school is caught between a broadening philosophy of marking in the elementary school and a rather conservative philosophy in the senior high school. The type of mark used should be determined by the philosophy of the school, which in turn should be developed with the best interests of the pupil in mind.

All marks should serve a diagnostic purpose, and should be regarded not as a final judgment but as a basis for future progress. Too much emphasis must not be placed upon the acquisition of factual information and skills in music; attitudes, interest, and effort must be considered if we are really meeting the life-like goal of consumer (as well as performer) education.

Classroom testing should be based upon the actual musical experiences provided for all children in the classroom. Every classroom test should provide an area of questioning which the less advanced pupil will answer successfully, but at the same time, the more advanced pupils should find in the test some questions which will challenge them to use their musical experience and ability.

Progress reports, which attempt to give the parent a whole picture of his child's progress in school, appear to be more functional than traditional report cards. Both child and parent should be given every opportunity to understand the significance of such progress reports, both in terms of items and marking code. A definite effort must be made to bring about general acceptance of the new type of progress reports.

Tests of musical capacity are useful in estimating what may be expected of a child in musical achievement and in guiding him vocationally. Such tests should not be regarded as furnishing conclusive evidence and should never lead a teacher to place any child in the "hopeless" category.

Standardized tests of musical achievement have a limited value because too often they are chiefly concerned with measuring factual information rather than musical experiences, and because musical opportunities vary in different schools.

A cumulative record of the junior-high-school pupil's musical experiences is a valuable source of information and guidance for the music teacher.

The whole process of pupil evaluation should be regarded as a functional tool contributing to the musical growth of the child. Where it acts as a deterrent factor in his progress, it is not only misconceived but misused.

BIBLIOGRAPHY OF TEST MATERIALS

Tests of musical talent

Drake Test of Musical Talent, A Musical Memory Test (Public School Publishing Co., Bloomington, Illinois)

Kwalwasser-Dykema Music Tests (Carl Fischer, Inc., New York City)

Seashore Measures of Musical Talent (The Psychological Corporation, New York City)

Streep Test of Musicality, E. Thayer Gaston (Streep Music Co., Inc., Kansas City, Missouri)

Musical Aptitude Test, Harvey S. Whistler and Louis P. Thorpe (California Test Bureau, Los Angeles, California)

Tests of musical achievement

Beach Music Test (Bureau of Educational Measurements, Kansas State Teachers College, Emporia, Kansas)

Diagnostic Tests of Achievement in Music, M. L. Kotick and T. L. Torgerson (California Test Bureau, Los Angeles, California)

Gildersleeve Music Achievement Test (Bureau of Publications, Columbia University, New York City)

Hutchinson Music Test (Public School Publishing Co., Bloomington, Illinois) (Out of print)

Knuth Achievement Tests in Music, Grades VII-XII (Educational Test Bureau, Educational Publishers, Inc., Philadelphia, Pennsylvania)

Kwalwasser-Ruch Test of Musical Accomplishment, Grades IV-XII (State University of Iowa, Bureau of Educational Research and Service, Iowa City, Iowa)

Providence Inventory Test in Music, Richard D. Allen, Walter H. Butterfield, and Marguerite Tully (World Book Co., Yonkers-on-Hudson, New York)

8. The Junior-High-School Instrumental Program

The organization of the junior high school, with its emphasis on exploratory courses, gave instrumental music a great impetus. With the rapid growth of the junior-high-school movement, pupils were encouraged to participate in all kinds of instrumental classes and organizations which were changed from extracurricular status to become a part of the class schedule. Some of the modern junior-high-school organizations are superior to similar high-school organizations of a previous decade.

Pupils enter into the instrumental program with amazing enthusiasm and need very little motivation for participation. The instrumental program, which contributes to the realization of the following objectives, has a distinct contribution to make. The list is quoted in its entirety since it seems to be fairly representative of the purposes of instrumental music throughout the country.

1. To provide *every interested* pupil an opportunity to explore the field of instrumental music.

2. To provide an outlet for the gregarious instinct.

3. To teach good citizenship through emphasis on teamwork.

4. To provide a desirable leisure-time activity.

5. To develop mental health through pleasurable and satisfying experiences.

6. To encourage good health habits through emphasis on posture and breathing.

7. To perform good music artistically, consistent with the ability of the group.

8. To encourage further study of an instrument stressing the need for technique as a means of attaining better appreciation of music.[1]

RECRUITMENT, SELECTION, AND GUIDANCE
OF PUPILS

Instrumental teachers have been so eager to develop well-balanced organizations in the high school that they have not only used the junior high school as a recruiting ground but also have imitated high-school groups in drilling intricate marching routines. In so doing, they have lost sight of one of the most important objectives of instrumental music education, namely, as previously stated, to provide every interested pupil with an opportunity to play the instrument he prefers. Because of the lack of instruments, many pupils have been denied the right to play; because of these economic reasons, many pupils who need pleasurable and satisfying experiences conducive to good mental health and desirable leisure-time activities for favorable sociological reasons are not able to play. This is where music education has failed.

"Music for every child, and every child for music" has been the slogan of the Music Educators National Conference for many years, but we have not made instruments available for all interested pupils; we have failed to keep our pledge. Music teachers often face the realistic problem of raising funds for

[1] Edith M. Keller, *Ohio High School Standards*. (Columbus, Ohio: State of Ohio Department of Education, 1946), pp. 39, 44.

the purchase of instruments. Here are helpful suggestions for accomplishing this:

1. Enlist the aid of your PTA in the buying of instruments.
2. Organize a Band Mothers Club.
3. Interest civic minded clubs in the project.
4. Present your needs to service clubs.
5. Include the purchase of instruments in the annual budget.
6. Have paper drives.
7. Give concerts and ask for free-will offerings.

Recruitment of pupils is most important in schools which are organizing an instrumental program and in schools suffering a low ebb in enrollment. In such cases, the instrumental teacher must be a "Pied Piper," seizing every opportunity to interest pupils in playing an instrument. The recruiting program succeeds best when it is understood and supported by the school principal. First of all, be sure to gain his willingness to support your program. Enlist the aid of the vocal teacher and make it clear that the vocal and instrumental classes can thrive in the same school if both teachers co-operate and never exploit the pupils. Give demonstrations of instrumental music in the general music classes and in the assembly. Sound films shown in assembly are most effective; one example is entitled "The First Chair." It may be obtained free of charge for use from C. G. Conn Ltd., Elkhart, Indiana. It describes the manufacturing and the sound of wind instruments. Survey the entire school body by using questionnaires which will give you needed information. Often pupils who play, or are interested, are not enrolled in the music classes because of poor articulation between the elementary school and the junior high school.

A clinic for exploring instruments, conducted in the spring as an introduction to summer beginner's classes, or in the fall to begin the year's instrumental program, would give the pupil and the teacher definite ideas whether or not music is a worthwhile experience for him. During this clinic, pupils may become interested in a more unusual instrument and through this experience make a much wiser choice. Parents are reluctant to invest money in buying instruments until they know that it is a real desire and not a whim that prompts the pupil to participate.

Favorable attitudes toward music are one of the basic prerequisites for admission to instrumental study. Pupils who sincerely desire to play may go farther with music, and will certainly derive more pleasure from it than those who may be able to pass the required tests well, and have more talent, but have little interest in learning to play. In addition, dependability, industry, and co-operation are some of the most valuable qualities in learning to play an instrument. Some teachers include in their basis of selection reasonable intelligence, mechanistic ability, and evidenced interest in vocal music. The latter criterion is not always reliable, since some pupils prefer playing to singing.

Although certain physical characteristics are desirable as a basis of selection, the following experiences seem to refute the reliability of such criteria. Teachers have found that spastic and polio victims, who did not have the physical characteristics deemed essential, were aided in overcoming their physical handicaps by the study of an instrument. When permitted to play and march with the band, their determination to participate caused them to develop a self-satisfying skill in performance believed unattainable. One university student played his trumpet out of the corner of his mouth. In spite of a seemingly impossible embouchure, he proved himself to be one of the university's finest performers. The will to play, based on strong motivating factors, is of as equal importance as physical characteristics.

Tests are sometimes used by teachers to determine the selection of the players and may be used both as prognostic and diagnostic evidence of musical ability. Among the tests used by many teachers are (see also bibliography in Chapter 7): (1) Pan American Music Aptitude Test (Pan American Band Instrument Co., Elkhart, Indiana); (2) Gretsch-Tilson Musical Aptitude Test (Fred Gretsch Manufacturing Co., 60 Broadway, Brooklyn 11, New York); and (3) Gaston-Test of Musicality

(Streep Music Co., 913 Grand Avenue, Kansas City 6, Missouri).

The guidance program must be concerned with discovering and advising talented pupils and with placing them in classes suitable to their achievement levels. It should attempt to help a pupil plan his course in keeping with his needs, interests, and abilities, since pupils who fail in playing one type of instrument have a good chance of succeeding with some other kind. The teacher must guide pupils in the purchase of a good instrument best suited to them and advise them how to avoid charlatan dealers and inferior instruments. The teacher must be sure he is right before he advises a parent to purchase an instrument, because repercussions coming from dissatisfied pupils and parents are disheartening and detrimental to the program. In no instance should a teacher become so unprofessional as to sell instruments and supplies.

Often it is difficult to interest pupils in such instruments as the baritone, the bass, the French horn, and the oboe, if they are unknown in the school and the community. They should be purchased by the school and played in the assembly and the general music class to motivate their use. Some pupils will be willing to transfer to playing these more unusual instruments when they realize how important they are to the success of their organizations and how little opportunity they may have with an instrument that overbalances the melody in number. Trumpet players, by way of example, learn to play the baritone and the bass readily.

When instruments owned by the school are loaned to pupils, they and their parents should sign an agreement to keep the instrument in good repair. Blanks furnished by the school should give definite information concerning the instrument and the cost of rental, if there is a fee. They should be recorded in every detail and kept on file. Teachers who desire information concerning these forms, will find specimen blanks in *High School Music*.[2]

---

2 Peter W. Dykema and Karl W. Gehrkens, *High School Music* (Boston: C. C. Birchard and Co., 1941), pp. 518-520.

CLASS LESSONS

Class lessons have been accepted by most instrumental teachers as an efficient means for teaching beginners how to play. Some pupils cannot afford individual lessons, and they are much too expensive to be furnished by the school. They lack the social values of class lessons, which also stimulate wholesome competition.

Some teachers who put techniques first, claim that class lessons permit bad habits to be formed easily and that good and poor players are put in the same class. To remedy this situation, another class may be organized to accommodate slower learners. The experienced pupil is often a lead player and should be encouraged to study with a private teacher, since he is able to do more solo work and thus can make more progress with individual lessons. But, while studying with a private teacher, he should continue to play in the school groups because he needs ensemble experience.

Two classes a week are recommended if class periods are forty-five minutes in length. If the class periods are only thirty minutes long, three classes a week are necessary to promote more rapid growth.

The homogeneous class is one in which like instruments are taught. Due to technical problems, string classes should be smaller. Often, common problems face the pupils, and learning them together saves time for the teacher. There is no doubt that the homogeneous class, which can be approached as an ensemble, is comparatively easy for the beginning teacher to manage.

The heterogeneous class is one in which unlike instruments are taught. A mixture of strings may be taught as a heterogeneous group. Teachers can teach a group numbering as many as thirty. The mortality rate in this type of group often is higher with less experienced pupils because there are many instruments played and there are fewer players on each instrument. This group may not only become an ensemble, but it may also easily develop into a second band or orchestra. Because of the variety of instruments it is much easier to schedule than the homogeneous group, but at the same time it is more difficult to teach since it easily becomes a problem to keep all pupils busy. It is claimed that progress is slower than in the homogeneous class and that technique is on a lower level. But regardless, the heterogeneous class is sometimes preferred because pupils may learn something about instruments other than their own.

It must be up to the individual administrator, supervisor, and teacher to decide which type of class suits the school better. It can be seen that either type of class has its advantages and disadvantages.

Summer classes

In many places, instrumental music has been accepted by the entire community to such an extent that the instrumental music program continues throughout the year and teachers work for eleven months. During the vacation months organizations and class lessons are organized or continued. In some communities this is an excellent plan because pupils are freer to practice and can more easily attend rehearsals. Pupils often join with adults to form a community organization which, giving periodic concerts, easily wins the financial support of the local businessmen and the community.

Teaching the class lesson

Although instrumental music education is started in the upper grades of some elementary schools, there are a considerable number of pupils in the junior high schools who have not had the opportunity to learn to play. It seems that it is easier to obtain school-owned instruments for use in the junior high than in the elementary school, and they are made available to more pupils. The influence of the high-school band is felt, and administrators desire for their schools the support and good will of the community which a thriving band engenders. Thus, we find classes organized to teach all kinds of instruments. Many are taught with the main objective of how to teach pupils as quickly as possible to play an instrument needed most in the band. Thus, little thought has been given to the problems of learning, and educational principles accepted in other areas of learning have not been utilized in teaching instrumental performance.

Visitation to instrumental classes and an examination of some methods reveal that some teachers use a *mechanistic* approach, which is based on an atomistic psychology. The books used are based on a logical procedure which organizes the structural elements of music in a step-wise manner. One can recognize these "method books" easily by the usual topical sequences such as how to hold the instruments, the names of the staff and the clef sign, and the playing of whole, half, dotted half, quarter and eighth notes in various meters. All this, in addition to written exercises involving these so-called fundamentals, is drilled and memorized by the pupil before he plays a familiar tune or makes what he knows is music.

This kind of teaching is an inheritance from the former old conservatory type of teaching once prevalent in America, and is still used by many sincere teachers. The following experience illustrates how futile isolated drill may be when learning to play an instrument. A teacher was attempting, with little success, to teach a trumpet and clarinet group to play in tune the tones G, A, B, G, which were written on the board. One pupil remarked that the tones weren't hard to play because they were the beginning of *Are You Sleeping?* The teacher caught on, and finding that everyone knew the tune, asked the class to sing it. The next time they played it he was amazed because every pupil was able to play it in tune; their ears told them how it should sound. This rather vividly points out that musical experience should precede attempts to play symbols, if one wishes a musical rather than a mechanical result.

Another illustration of the mechanistic type of procedure may show the reader how overemphasis on isolated notes loses musical meaning. A high-school band teacher was teaching a group of clarinet pupils how to play the French folk song, *At Pierrot's Door.* The song had been taught by note and the playing followed the teacher's mechanical 1, 2, 3, 4. The result was a series of disconnected tones all with equal accent and with no dynamic effects. The writer asked the pupils if they knew the song. Receiving a negative reply, he told them the story of the night wanderer who begged for shelter within Pierrot's door. After hearing the song sung they sang it with two "strides" to the measure and with a quiet tone like the "moon's pale shimmer." When they compared the singing with the playing, they said they liked better the way they sang it. Then they tried to play it in the manner in which they had sung it. The results were so much more meaningful that even the principal, along with the supervisor, sensed the improved qualities of the playing. The most disappointing outcome was that the teacher never sensed the musical differences, while the pupils, the principal, and the supervisor realized that note-playing is unsatisfying to both the player and the listener.

Visits to other classrooms reveal that instrumental music is taught with a very different emphasis, based on a psychology in direct opposition to the mechanistic approach. These teachers believe that music is a language art, and is learned best by using principles of linguistic learning. A visit to a primary-school or to a high-school foreign language class shows that teachers start beginners with conversation in the language the pupils are to learn. They are not concerned with the "A, B, C's" or the syntax of sentences at first; rather they "just talk" about familiar objects and experiences. Since musical meanings and values are vital to musical expressiveness, emphasis is placed on these factors during the first experiences with playing.

Symbolism is used, drilled, and learned as the experience develops. Real music, such as folk songs, hymns, and other easy familiar music, is used at once with no lengthy preliminary discussions on notation or on how to hold the instruments. They sing, and they play. All valuable skills and knowledge are taught through the attempts to play real music. Music is fun! The whole song is attempted first, thus using an organismic approach. There is no logical sequence of techniques or knowledge in this type of teaching, since skills and factual knowledge, which are most important, emerge through rote and imitative learning. This type of teaching is called *developmental, functional, or direct method*.

This approach uses three types of learning: manipulative, repetitive, and linguistic. By manipulative we mean how to hold and finger the instrument. These skills can be developed as one learns to play music (not exercises), but should not be taught as preparation for playing. Repetitive learning, of course, refers to drill — doing the thing until it becomes automatic. The melodies played are musical rather than mechanical, and the message of the music is always in the foreground. The drill involved is used to make the music more beautiful. It should not be divorced from the musical setting. This means that teachers should forego the overused "warming up" drills with beginners, since psychologists tell us there is little transfer of training from drilled factual knowledge and skills taught in isolation to new, related, musical experiences. When one learns to play a melody through imitation or by rote, having first heard the tune sung or played, one is using linguistic learning. This learning emphasizes the expression of feeling whether it is in learning a language, how to sing, or how to play.

One young instrumental teacher found it difficult to motivate his pupils to practice the usual exercises found in the "method" book, and in spite of promises of rich musical rewards which come from daily practice, they came to class reluctantly with none to their credit. They continued to lack interest, and some became behavior problems within the group.

The teacher decided to use copies of a song collection from which the class selected several easy, familiar songs they thought they would enjoy playing, since they had learned them in the general music classes. The teacher guided them in their choice by suggesting which ones might be too difficult at this time. Several songs were selected, and all agreed to try to have them learned by the next lesson. When the class met again the

teacher was the most surprised of all those present. Not only were most of the group able to play their chosen songs, but they were willing to work together "to make it sound good." The problems of classroom control were gradually eliminated, and there was little need of urging them to practice from then on. Some pupils wanted to play a harmonic part, and this became a powerful motivating force in these class lessons. Music became enjoyable rather than drudgery for both pupils and teacher.

These illustrations serve to show how much better we learn when we make and play authentic music and learn the symbolism of music experientially. One pupil remarked to his teacher after the class had a lesson devoted to formal drill on notation: "When do we start some music?" The wisdom of our pupils often causes us to evaluate what we are doing and, from the results derived, decide whether to use a linguistic (song or rote) approach or a mechanical (note) method.

Suggested lesson plan

Before the lesson is started it is helpful to have the class librarians number every fifth measure so the pupils can find the rehearsal places more easily. This also saves considerable time.

The following plan is offered as suggestive, but in no case should it be followed slavishly:

1. Using a tuning bar or piano for B flat for band or A for orchestra, pupils should tune their instruments while the teacher checks when necessary. A short period of time may be devoted to "warm-up," when it is deemed necessary.

2. The familiar composition to be used should be played through in its entirety.

3. Errors in rhythms, tone, pitch, dynamics, and phrasing should be corrected through drill. Exercises may be necessary to correct these errors.

4. Introduce a new composition. Give the background of the music and the composer, and if possible, play a recording of

the number, calling attention to unusual and characteristic rhythms.

5. Have the group play through the entire composition and then drill on it as suggested in step 3.

6. Close the lesson with some familiar composition popular with the class. Often this may be material sung in the general music class.

Materials, equipment, and teaching aids

The instrumental field, abounding with books which use mechanistic methods, is woefully lacking in the rote or ear approach. Teachers of instrumental music are urged to use familiar tunes in their beginning classes. As soon as the pupils are able to play to some degree, the teacher should aid the pupils in playing very simple accompaniments to the songs that are being learned in the general music classes. This motivates the singers as well as the players. Often these accompaniments are based on tonal and rhythmic figures taken from the song.

When the players are experienced enough, they can be taught to play the simple parts written for instruments in several of the junior-high-school vocal texts. The instrumental teacher should teach these accompaniments in the instrumental classes and use them with the vocal groups in their general music classes. This stimulates all the participants, and will aid in breaking down those barriers existing between vocal and instrumental activities in some junior high schools.

When pupils play well, they should be used in the general music class as part of the listening program. They can illustrate the tone quality of various instruments as they play some composition which is worth knowing and enjoying. Every effort should be made to use instrumental music by correlating it with all school and music activities. It should not be relegated to band and orchestral performances or serve for the glorification of the director. It should function for everyone in the school and the community.

Teachers are urged to make their selections of music and

music books after having examined the material carefully to determine whether or not it uses the procedures which they approve, whether or not the music is genuine or "manufactured" (exercises set with words to teach certain technical problems), and whether or not it serves better the homgeneous or heterogeneous type of class organization. Usually one may secure examination copies from the publishers, or they may be ordered from large music houses which handle publications of various publishers. *The Business Hand Book of Music Education,* published by the Music Educators National Conference, lists these various firms.

One of the problems teachers face is how to obtain a good tone from beginning players. One reason pupils play with such poor tone production is that they have had little opportunity to hear good tone. There are some excellent recordings to use as models of good music, nice tone, and fine performance to motivate and set a standard for students. Ruban, Inc. has just such recordings available, played by a university band. Boosey and Hawkes also has some recordings of its publications to aid in teaching.

A representative list of material follows, for which a key to the publishers will be given at the close of this chapter.

MATERIALS AVAILABLE FOR
INSTRUMENTAL CLASSES (HETEROGENEOUS OR HOMOGENEOUS)

ALL STRINGS OR VIOLIN

Beginning Strings (Het-Ho) — Whistler-Nord	CF[3]
Bow and Strings (Ho), Vols. I & II — Hermann	BEL
Easy Steps to the Orchestra (Het-Ho), Vols. I & II — Kiefer and Taylor	MIL
Gamble Class Method for Strings (Het-Ho) — Fischel-Bennett	GHM
Instrumental Horizons (Het) — Herfurth	SB
Modern Orchestra Training Series (Het-Ho) — Church-Dykema	CCB
String Class Method, Book I (Het-Ho) — Isaac	COLE
Songs for Strings (Ho) — Dalley	NAK
Spotlight on Strings (Ho) — Mignin	WIL
Strings from the Start (Het-Ho) — Jones-Dasch-Krone	CF
Tune a Day (Ho) — Herfurth	BM

---

[3] For an explanation of these code letters see pages 298-299.

WOODWINDS, BRASS AND PERCUSSION

Bennett Band Books (Het-Ho) — Bennett	FILL
Easy Steps to the Band (Het-Ho) — Taylor	MIL
First Steps in Band Playing (Het) — Whistler-Hummel	RU
Modern Band Training Series (Het-Ho) — Church-Dykema	CCB
Our First Band Folio (Het) — Cheyette	RU
Rubank Elementary Band Course (Het-Ho) — Van Deusen, *et al*	RU

The instrumental music room and its equipment

Since instrumental music is one of the newer subjects in the junior high schools, many schools have no rooms or equipment adequate for rehearsals or teaching. Teachers have had to teach in the boiler rooms and have had to rehearse on the stage with all kinds of gymnasium classes on the opposite side. In spite of these handicaps, instrumental teachers have taught and developed organizations, many of which play good music with a great deal of musicianship.

A good teaching room is an inspiration to pupils and teachers. The room should be located where it will cause the least possible disturbance to other classes. It is most difficult to schedule classes if the room must serve both vocal and instrumental classes, and a problem arises if all the materials and equipment for music education must be stored in one room. In any room, adequate storage shelves, stalls, cupboards and acoustical treatment should be provided for instruments and music. If there is a desire on the part of the school administration to build or remodel a music room, it would be expedient to secure a bulletin called *Music Rooms and Equipment*.[4] Very few architects know what is needed in instrumental rooms, so it is advantageous to seek expert information.

Straight, short back folding chairs are serviceable, especially when the chairs must be moved occasionally. Music stands, fingering charts, piano, phonograph, elevated risers and recording equipment are necessary. Blackboards, pictures of noted conductors, players, and composers, a tuning bar (A for

---

[4] *Music Rooms and Equipment* (Chicago: Music Educators National Conference, 1949).

orchestra, B flat for band), records, a podium, and a larger stand with a shelf for the teacher are essential to a good instrumental program.

THE ORCHESTRA

With bands becoming closely allied with athletics plus winning public approval with their fine appearances, they have easily surpassed orchestras in size and number, although orchestras were started earlier in American schools. Another reason why we now find orchestras outnumbered is that pupils can learn to play brass, reed, and percussion instruments more quickly than strings. Often, instrumental teachers are unprepared to teach strings, and, as a result, no string instruction is offered except that given by private teachers. Thus, we see why orchestras are in a dilemma and are a real problem to all who are concerned with instrumental music education in the junior high school.

To have a junior-high-school orchestra requires a good string program in the elementary schools and good articulation between the two schools. It has been done, but it is difficult to have an orchestra in the junior high school and depend entirely on the strings taught at this level. In order to make string classes available to elementary-school pupils some junior-high-school teachers spend part of their time teaching in the lower grades. This is one way to meet this problem, if instrumental teachers cannot be secured for the elementary school.

In their eagerness to have orchestras, teachers too often put their pupils in organizations before they are ready. Students with but one semester's experience in strings or many other instruments are not sure enough tonally or rhythmically to play the "umpahs" or after beats of the second parts. What is more discouraging to the pupil than to try to play the second violin part when he is not ready to play it? He is never given a melody to play, and soon loses interest. It is distressing to the teacher, and often the whole affair ends in a fiasco. A much longer class experience might have saved the pupil for music, if the teacher had not been too eager to have another member in the orchestra or band.

Due to the earnest efforts of administrators, supervisors, and teachers, orchestras seem to be increasing in number in some schools. These people realize that the orchestra can contribute much to developing a genuine interest, both as a performer and as a listener, in orchestral music in school or later in adulthood. The power of the orchestra to afford desirable social experiences for adolescents and its ability to integrate the school and community are realized by those concerned with the school's curriculum. Also, orchestral music should be a part of the all-school program and should be integrated with the general music classes. In this way it becomes a potent motivating factor for both the orchestra and the general music classes.

Seating plans

Teachers should not adhere to a rigid balance of instruments for a junior-high-school orchestra. It would be disastrous for a pupil to work hard to learn an instrument and find to his dismay that the teacher, having filled the quota of instruments on each part, will not take him into the organization. In other words, since music should exist solely for the pupil's benefit, take everyone who is prepared to play and secure the best balance possible by playing an overbalanced part lightly. One group may play certain sections, and the other group may play other sections during public performance.

It should be remembered that no one seating plan will function for every orchestra. However, by way of suggestion, here are two plans to use as guides.

Selecting materials

When the teacher faces the problem of selecting materials, there are numerous things which must be kept in mind in order that the music may be educational and functional. In the first place, remember that no list of recommended materials will fit every junior high school, not even all of the junior high schools in a school system. Teachers and supervisors should remember this above all and not try to have uniformity between varying schools.

1. Select only music which has clearly printed notation. This is doubly important with beginning players.

THE SMALL ORCHESTRA

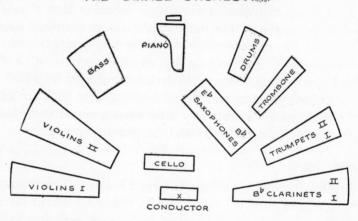

THE LARGER ORCHESTRA

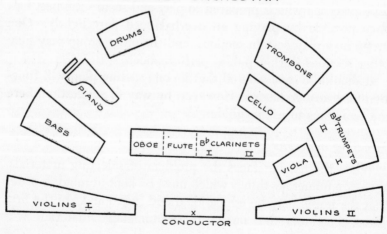

2. Know the ability of your group before selecting the music. Music which is juvenile is unsatisfactory to the group, while extremely difficult music is just as discouraging to young players. It should be challenging but not disheartening.

3. Music for violins should be limited for the most part to the use of the first position, unless there is a rest in the music during which time the position change can be made.

4. Sharp keys should be used more than flat keys, since the violins use more open strings in sharps. Some collections of music limit the number of sharps to three or four.

5. The meters used should be simple ones, such as $\frac{2}{4}$, $\frac{3}{4}$, $\frac{4}{4}$, and $\frac{6}{8}$. Avoid compound meters and also meters of 5 and 7.

6. The rhythmic patterns should not be more difficult than those used in the general music vocal classes, which means using generally familiar patterns.

7. Avoid music that features the weakest sections of your group.

8. The ranges used in the music should not be extreme, that is, neither too high nor too low. The following ranges are recommended by Stephen M. Clarke [5] for inexperienced players:

9. Select a variety of types of music because adolescents, having so many interests, soon tire of one type.

10. Select music that is suitable for the occasion. Music for Armistice Day is quite inappropriate for a pep rally. A wide variety of music is necessary to meet these school and community uses.

---

[5] Stephen M. Clarke, *Some Principles and Suggestions for the Teacher of Instrumental Music in the Junior High School* (Unpublished Master's Thesis, Columbus, Ohio: Ohio State University, 1951), pp. 59-60.

11. Reserve a limited place for novelty and popular tunes.

12. Since pupils' tastes are influenced by those of their parents, who will be the major part of any audience, consider the taste of the community.

13. Select some real music, that which has stood the test of time and is our musical heritage. This is in bold contrast with the cheap manufactured music which, written to develop a skill, has nothing to say. Pupils have a right to play and enjoy the easy classics, pure folk tunes, and celebrated marches which are available for young orchestras.

14. Beware of music written "in the style" of great composers, but do use compositions of the masters simplified to the playing ability of amateurs. However, in order to make the music sound modern, the original tonal and rhythmic characteristics should not be added to, nor lost, in the simplification.

15. The inner parts should be interesting, not a monotonous repetition. An occasional melody or counter melody is most important to young players.

Sources for obtaining material lists

There are many sources for obtaining lists of materials suitable for orchestra and bands. Many commendable new materials are made available by publishers who employ trained personnel to send materials for examination when requested by teachers. Addresses of publishers are included at the close of this chapter. Some other sources are as follows:

1. Music Educators National Conference (64 E. Jackson Blvd., Chicago 4, Illinois)

   This organization publishes the *Music Educators Journal* in which lists of new music are evaluated. Also available for $1.50 are the Selective Lists of Music published by the National School Band, Orchestra and Vocal Associations.

2. Educational Music Bureau (30 E. Adams St., Chicago 3, Illinois)

   Available is the *Educational Music Bureau Guide*, which lists music materials of all publishers.

3. *Educational Music Magazine* (30 E. Adams St., Chicago 3, Illinois)

   This magazine lists new, evaluated materials.

4. *The Instrumentalist* (Glen Ellyn, Illinois)

   Write for mimeographed and bound lists of materials available for subscribers to the magazine.

5. *The School Musician* (28 E. Jackson Blvd., Chicago 4, Illinois)

   Reviews and evaluations of new materials are published in this magazine.

6. The State Department of Education (Columbus, Ohio)

   A Supplementary List of Materials for Junior and Senior High Schools, representing the reliable selection of many supervisors and teachers, is available on request.

The following short list is given to show how varied the materials should be. They represent many forms and such styles as the march, the overture, the suite, the dance, the light opera, and the operetta.

ORCHESTRA LITERATURE

Bach	Chorale-Fugue, *All Glory Be to God on High*	CF [6]
Balfe	*Bohemian Girl*	SF
Bizet	Selections from *Carmen*	SF
Cadman	*Festival March in C*	OD
De Lamater	*Golden Rule Overture*	Ru
Gershwin	*The Man I Love*	Har
Gould	*Indian Nocturne*	CF
Grieg	*Triumphal March*	SF
Handel	Handel Suite	GS
	"Largo" — *Xerxes*	OD
Humperdinck-		
Isaac	"Prayer" — *Hansel and Gretel*	CF
Ketelby	*Bells Across the Meadows*	BHB
Lambert	*When Johnny Comes Marching Home*	CF
Romberg	*Stouthearted Men*	Har
Schubert	*Moment Musical*	OD
Yon-Baron	*Gesu Bambino*	JF

THE BAND

Bands have a distinct place in junior high schools. Their association with athletics, their contribution to all-school activities

---

[6] For an explanation of these code letters see pages 298-299.

such as drives and patriotic assemblies, their participation in community parades for bond drives, Memorial Day Services, festivals, and fairs has given them the support of both young and old in the community. Hearts beat fast with pride and joy when parents see their children, clothed in colorful uniforms, march by in step to the rhythmical and tuneful music they are playing. Band Mothers Clubs and Band Parents Associations sponsor the financing of bands, even to the purchasing of uniforms, equipment, instruments and music.

Bands are here to stay; the present problem is how to improve them. Too often, bands play only marches, all of which are played with the same tempo, tone quality, and dynamics which are as loud as possible. Too many band directors use their bands only for marching, paying little attention to the concert possibilities of their organizations. Marching bands easily can become concert bands as well, if directors desire to make the change.

Pupils often are put into band organizations before they are really prepared to play. Many directors of bands in larger junior high schools organize second bands, which serve as a feeder for the first. It is in this organization that they develop skills necessary in playing in a good musical organization. Many elementary schools have class lessons in instruments which motivate the pupils to work hard in order to belong to the bands. In this way, a better articulation is made between class lessons and the band in the junior high school and between the junior high school and the elementary school. There is very little other motivation necessary to stimulate the pupils to join a successful organization.

Problems concerning recruitment, selectivity, equipment, teaching aids, lesson planning, and selection of music have been discussed previously under class lessons and the orchestra. For further information consult Van Bodengraven, *Organizing a School Band* (Iron-Snell Printing Company). Since it seems to be easier to teach wind instruments than strings, bands often make a better showing in a shorter time. Whether the band or the orchestra should be organized first is a debatable question which can only be decided by the school administration and the music director in terms of community and school conditions.

Seating plans

Again it is advised that the seating of the organization be made in terms of the number of players, the instruments represented, and the kind of rehearsal room used. Teachers are urged to experiment with the seating of the players in relation to the music played and the balance gained. One cannot say exactly how many reed players are required to balance the brass section, since from an educational standpoint one should use all the players who are prepared to play. Serving the pupils is more important than balancing an organization. Some semblance of balance may be obtained by having the brasses play with a lighter tone. You might like to try these plans as a point of departure.

Marching bands

The marching band is a most important activity in the music education program, and has been so popular with music directors, parents, and administrative officials that it has dominated the entire music program in many schools. The smartly uniformed band with its drum majors, majorettes, and twirlers thrill any audience. But, unfortunately, it sometimes competes with the antics of a circus band. On the other hand, junior-high bands, aping high-school and college marching techniques, have developed such finesse that often the emphasis is put on the marching and maneuvering to the neglect of the music. Furthermore, some junior-high groups try to play music suitable for senior high school. This is unfair to the pupils. The variation in size of the pupils and their poor co-ordination make precise drilling difficult. It is true that a limited amount of

THE SMALL BAND

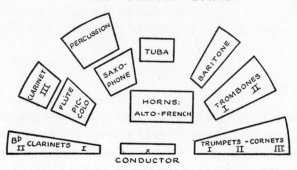

THE LARGER BAND

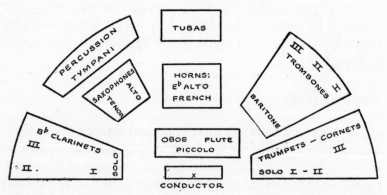

pageantry is good for early adolescents, but when a program is devoted largely to marching maneuvers and drill to the neglect of playing good music well, it is certainly a questionable procedure.

The sources on page 289 are among the many good ones from which teachers may find help in learning how to teach the fundamental movements necessary for marching and how to make formations that function according to the numbers available.

Church and Dykema	*Modern Band Training Series — Manual*	CCB[7]
Dvořák	*Band on Parade*	CF
Norman	*Instrumental Music in Public Schools*	TP
Prescott and Chidester	*Getting Better Results from School Bands*	CF
Righter	*Gridiron Pageantry*	CF
Righter	*Success in Teaching School Orchestras and Bands*	PAS
School Music Competition	*Festivals Manual*	MENC
Schilling	*New Formations for Marching Band — The Instrumentalist*, Glen Ellyn, Illinois	
Smith and Capel	*Marching Maneuver Series*, Vol. 2	GHM

Selecting materials

The same care should be exercised when selecting band materials as that suggested under selection of orchestral materials on pages 282-284. The ranges suitable for winds were included in the discussion of wind instruments in the orchestra, and should be considered when a composition is selected. Sources for obtaining band lists are the same as those suggested for the orchestra. A wide variety of music, including songs, overtures, operetta selections, dances, chorales, and marches, should be used.

The materials chosen should be useful in many of the school's activities. A program given by the band and the school vocal groups, with opportunities for the entire student body to sing, is a thrilling project. Pupils enjoy singing with band accompaniment; assembly programs devoted entirely or partly to singing with band accompaniment is an experience pupils never forget. Try it! Vocal and instrumental teachers should do everything possible to unite these two areas in school with community activities.

BAND LITERATURE

SONG BOOKS WITH INSTRUMENTAL ACCOMPANIMENTS

American Collection	Ru[7]
Americana Holiday Collection	Ru
Golden Book of Songs	HMc
One Hundred Songs to Remember	NAK

[7] See pages 298-299 for explanation of code letters.

COMPOSITIONS

Bach–Holmes	*Two Chorales*	Ru [8]
Bennett	*Cole Porter Selections*	Har
Buchtel	*Americana*	NAK
Danks–Yoder	*Silver Theads Among the Gold*	Ru
De Lamater	*Country Gardens*	Ru
Franck	*Panis Angelicus*	CF
Gluck–De Lamater	*Dance of the Happy Spirits*	Ru
Gould–Yoder	*Pavanne*	Mil
Gounod–De Lamater	*Soldier's March*	Ru
Grundman	*Two Moods*	BH
Herfurth	*Whistle While You Work*	GHM
Klein	*The Booster*	Fill
Leoni	*Overture Orientale*	Bel
Long	*Stephen Foster Rhapsody*	Ru
Pierné	*March of the Little Lead Soldiers*	BH
Roberts	*Pomp and Chivalry* (March Processional)	CF
Sibelius–De Lamater	*Finlandia*	Ru
Sullivan	*The Lost Chord*	CF
Sullivan–Yoder	*H.M.S. Pinafore*	Ru
Waldteufel–Morton	*Skater's Waltz*	Asch
Williams	*Folk Song Suite*	BH
Yoder	*Grieg Melodies*	Bel
	Mozart Melodies	Bel
	Southern Cross Overture	Bel
	Thirty-Five Famous Chorales	NAK

All-city bands and orchestras

Numerous cities offer added opportunities to talented pupils by organizing all-city instrumental and vocal groups. These groups meet on Saturday mornings in some central location, and are conducted by the school music teachers and the supervisor. The bands and orchestras play some of the very finest music and afford experiences which their own schools cannot offer.

These all-city organizations have a great influence on the musical taste and standards of performance of the community, and their appearance at the most worthy community affairs attests to the high regard in which they are held. Rochester, New York, has been a pioneer in this movement which has

---

[8] See pages 298-299 for explanation of code letters.

spread to many other cities. The same idea underlies the district orchestral festivals, which are held in some of the districts of the Ohio Music Education Association, for example. The enthusiasm for fine music is carried back to many schools, and is proving to be one of the strong factors in renewing interest in orchestral music.

Rehearsal suggestions

Some music teachers will have only bands, and may not refer to the materials concerning orchestras. Thus, it seems wise to repeat the rehearsal suggestions, to some extent, along with those which pertain only to the band.

All rehearsal should be planned carefully if pupil growth is expected. The routine should be varied to meet the project at hand. Lack of planning results in disorder and poor work.

All needed materials should be ready for use; racks, chairs, and music should be in place. Pupils should have the responsibility of preparing for the rehearsal and for storing the materials, in case the room is shared with classes other than instrumental music. To have the organization of the materials work smoothly, the teacher must plan and then teach the pupils to execute it. Often a list of the music which is to be rehearsed is posted so that librarians and the entire group know what music will be needed.

Unnecessary noise, horn tooting, and disorder should not be tolerated. Neither is silence wholesome. One very successful junior-high-school teacher has an understanding with his groups that they may talk quietly until he is ready to rehearse. When he steps upon the podium that is an automatic sign for all conversation to cease. When he steps down during a rehearsal the group may take a "breather" and converse quietly. He permits no unseemly behavior, and all pupils work well for and with him. Young teachers should heed these suggestions, because lack of control soon becomes license.

Begin promptly and tune carefully. There is no one way to tune. Often section leaders give the pitch from a tuning bar

(B flat for band and A for orchestra). The teacher may check the pitch in sections, checking with individuals only when necessary. Encourage string players to tune their own instruments. If this is taught in the beginning class, many pupils will be able to do their own tuning. This period of tuning should be done as quickly as possible to avoid delays which can destroy a rehearsal.

The first number should be one that is well known and a favorite, and, if possible, something such as a chorale, which is fine for securing sonority. Occasionally, it may be a number requested by the pupils, but in any event it should be one that will win the co-operation and attention of all the players. Play through the entire composition. Comments on the playing, or retrials of places where improvement is desired, are in order. Have no lulls and work rapidly. Before leaving the number, play it through in as finished a manner as possible.

It is wise to follow the first number with a new number. It should be presented so as to arouse the interest of the players. No discussion of technical aspects of the music will do this. Something about the composer, the type of music it is, or better still, a recording of the composition played in a superior manner will do much to arouse interest in the music. Try it through in its entirety, noting carefully what is done well and what corrections need to be made in tone, pitch, phrasing, rhythm, and dynamics. Use scales, chords, and intervals if they are functional in the drill process, which should be both short and quick on the most glaring errors. Drill may be done in sections, and then the sections may be put back into the complete registration. Leave the composition before the players are weary of it, yet still have acquired a feeling of accomplishment and success with it.

Closing the rehearsal with a partially learned but much liked composition leaves the players in a good frame of mind. If they leave humming the melodies they have learned, it is a fairly good indication that the rehearsal has been successful.

To vary the routine, do something different in the next rehearsal. By way of suggestion you might record a performance of a number and then play it back so the pupils may evaluate it before the next rehearsal. Vary the music enough to hold interest and repeat it enough to ensure musical growth.

ENSEMBLES

Ensembles are another means for meeting individual differences in pupils. The great differences in musical ability, with gifted pupils being held back by many inferior players, are often the cause of the lack of interest in the larger groups. Ensembles function in adult life and provide a carry-over from the school into the community. Through ensembles, music education supplies wholesome recreation and develops a taste for good music in both the performer and the listener.

Ensembles, taught by the teacher, may be scheduled as a class. In some schools, pupils rehearse under the supervision of the teacher, but are lead by a pupil. It is excellent for ensembles to meet at the homes of pupils, playing the music selected by both the players and the teacher. It should be remembered that chamber music is house music and is heard best when performed within the confines of a small room such as a home affords. Ensembles are excellent groups for performance before small clubs and can appear where large groups are impractical.

The kinds of ensembles which can be organized are dependent on the number of good players available. The following groups are used, and have literature for them: flute trios, clarinet trios, clarinet quartets, trumpet trios, three trumpets and piano, brass quartets, saxophone quartets, trombone quartets, and string groups.

Sources for obtaining lists of materials suitable for ensembles are identical with those listed for the orchestra on page 285. In every case, the materials may be somewhat more difficult than those played in the band or the orchestra yet not as difficult as that played by the more experienced high-school groups.

EQUIPMENT AND STORAGE

The storage and care of instruments, music, equipment, and uniforms is of great importance to the success and efficiency of the instrumental program. The cheapest instruments are an unwise investment, because pupils learn poor tone quality during their first playing. It is likewise unprofitable to purchase the finest instruments for beginners and in so doing limit the number which may be bought. Medium priced instruments function very well for beginners.

When instruments are purchased, there must be adequate storage place for them. Filing space must also be provided for music, books, and records. Also, there must be lockers for uniforms. Teachers should make every effort to organize the storage of all equipment and materials in such a way that pupils may assist in their care. Junior-high-school pupils take responsibility seriously and are able, with good leadership, to preserve and make available for efficient use every bit of material necessary for success. The instrumental teacher needs to be a good organizer and, above all, an excellent housekeeper.

Two good sources concerning equipment and storage are recommended. Chapter XXIX of Dykema and Gehrkens, *High School Music*, and The Music Educators National Conference Bulletin, *Music Rooms and Equipment* (also mentioned on page 279), are valuable.

SCHEDULING AND ACCREDITING

In many schools, music is an integral part of the curriculum and has its rightful place in the schedule. Its status is determined by the attitude of the school administration and the value placed upon music by the pupils, the staff, and the community. In other schools, music is considered extracurricular, much to the disadvantage of everyone interested in music. In that case, rehearsals are held before and after school, and having to compete with athletics and work, music becomes the loser.

When a music activity is first introduced, it may have to begin outside the schedule, but should not remain so. An understanding administrator will be sympathetic to requests by pupils, parents, and the teacher to include the activity in the schedule.

The six-period day presents difficulties in making music available to all students who wish to elect it. However, some teachers claim it can be and is being done in schools in which there are duplicate academic classes. Those schools which have supervised study may alternate the study periods so that they come the last half of one period and the first part of the following period. This makes time for music and other arts. It also solves the problem in schools that have hour periods.

Elective classes which rotate, or are offered during alternate years, may be scheduled opposite music with no harm to either subject. It should not be expected that an entire school should be idle just to accommodate the music class.

Those schools which employ so-called traveling or circuit teachers often rotate the periods to avoid the continual absence of pupils from other classes. For example, the violin class might meet at 9 on Monday and at 9:40 on Wednesday. Teachers of other subjects are far more co-operative when this rotary plan is used.

The entire problem is solved when schedule makers place music in the program first and organize other classes in order to permit pupils to elect music. The lack of co-operation in building such a schedule is one of the most frustrating and discouraging problems in music education. It is hoped school administrators will do everything in their power to make music available for every pupil.

Most music classes and organizations in the junior high school are credited on the laboratory basis. That means that all music courses which meet daily for one year and do not require outside preparation receive one-half credit. When classes meet only two periods a week, one-fourth credit is given. In many small schools, classes meet only once a week, which, poor as it is, is better than none. In this case a pupil may elect another music class and be eligible for one-fourth credit toward graduation from high school. It seems to be a usual practice to give grades in music the same as they are given in other subjects.

Some schools prefer the point system because of the inequality of giving one-fourth credit for two classes a week. In this system, each of the sixteen units toward graduation is valued at twenty points; sixteen units would be the equivalent of 120 points. With no outside preparation a unit is valued at ten points. In other words, each class period counts two points. Under this system two music periods a week are worth four points; as previously stated, the total required for graduation would be 120 points.

Many schools accredit work done in music outside the school. This varies in many states, for although it is not a new idea, it is not generally practiced. To make this problem work successfully, school music and private teachers must work together within the frame work of the state organization to which they belong. The teacher who is interested in providing credit for work done outside of the school is advised to read the recommendations made in the *Ohio High School Standards*.[9]

THE INSTRUMENTAL TEACHER

After reading this chapter on instrumental music, the young teacher may feel inadequate to the responsibilities which he must assume in carrying out the music program suggested. No beginning teacher is able to carry on all the activities required in a well-balanced curriculum, but with determination to grow in the ability to teach, he can develop skills in teaching and performance which will make him more efficient and eminently successful.

In personality qualifications, the instrumental teacher must have a liking for, and an understanding of, youth. He must know how to establish leadership with his pupils and how to win and retain the respect of the school administrators, co-

---

[9] Edith M. Keller, *Ohio High School Standards* (Columbus, Ohio: State Department of Education, 1946), pp. 97-98.

workers, parents, and the community. He must believe that what music does for the pupil is more important than what the pupil does for music.

In addition, a teacher needs a good background in general education to understand the learning processes and all the personality factors affecting it. Although essential, good musicianship is not enough, for besides knowing what is good music, one must be able to impart its spirit if one may truly be called a teacher.

One need not be an expert performer on all the instruments one teaches. It is generally believed that one should be a good performer on one instrument and a generalist on many. This belief is based on the idea that if a teacher is a good musician, has had excellent training on one, and limited training on many, he will have enough skill and knowledge to assure his success with beginners.

He will need to be a good organizer and have enough business acumen to buy equipment and materials wisely. After these have been purchased, he must be able to keep them in good working condition and available for use under any circumstances. Being able to carry on this program successfully is one of the most rewarding compensations any teacher may expect. What other field offers so much to so many?

SUMMARY

In general, we find that the objectives of the junior-high-school instrumental program are established to provide an exploratory experience for all interested pupils, in addition to providing avocational, and to a limited degree, vocational training to talented students. Recruitment, selection, and guidance of pupils are the first considerations in beginning the instrumental program. Sometimes enlistment of financial aid from community and parent organizations is necessary. These pursuits require much thought and attention, and should be governed by the actual needs, interests, and abilities of the junior-high instrumentalist.

The class instrumental lesson as well as large and small ensembles, obviously, are organized and taught with modern psychological principles in mind. Here again a wise junior-high-school philosophy is mandatory.

Materials and equipment demand much attention if the program is to succeed. Materials, whether of the beginning class or of an advanced ensemble, should take into consideration the sociophysiological maturation of the students as well as their technical proficiency. It behooves the instrumental teacher to procure equipment and maintain physical facilities in good order.

Scheduling of instrumental music classes is one of the major problems of many junior high schools. Often the program is begun on an after school or Saturday morning basis and later is included in the regular curriculum. Most schools solve this problem as it seems feasible within their program.

No successful junior-high-school instrumental program is possible without a good instrumental teacher who has the junior-high-school viewpoint. Musicianship and a good teaching personality comprise the basic components of this individual.

DIRECTORY OF MUSIC PUBLISHERS

Asch	E. A. Ascher, 1155 Broadway, New York
Bar	C. L. Barnhouse Co., High Ave. and L Street, Oskaloosa, Iowa
Bel	Belwin, Inc., 250 Maple Ave., Rockville Center, Long Island, New York
BH	Boosey & Hawkes, Inc., P.O. Box 418, Lynbrook, Long Island, New York
BM	Boston Music Co., 116 Boylston St., Boston
BO	Bourne, Inc., Music Pub., 799 Seventh Ave., New York
BMI	Broadcast Music, Inc., 580 Fifth Ave., New York
CCB	C. C. Birchard & Co., 285 Columbus Ave., Boston
CF	Carl Fischer, Inc., 62 Cooper Square, New York
EV	Elkan-Vogel Co., Inc., 1716 Sansom St., Philadelphia
Fill	Fillmore Music House, 528 Elm St., Cincinnati
Fs	H. T. Fitzsimmons Co., 615 N. LaSalle St., Chicago
GHM	Gamble Hinged Music Co., 218 S. Wabash Ave., Chicago
GS	G. Schirmer, Inc., 3 E. 43 St., New York
HMc	Hall & McCreary Co., 434 S. Wabash Ave., Chicago

Har	Harms, Inc., RCA Bldg., Rockefeller Center, New York
JF	J. Fischer & Bros., 119 W. 40 St., New York
Lud	Ludwig Music Pub. Co., 323 Frankfort Ave., N.W., Cleveland
Mil	Mills Music, Inc., 1619 Broadway, New York
NAK	Neil A. Kjos Music Co., 223 W. Lake St., Chicago
OD	Oliver Ditson, c/o Theodore Presser Co., Bryn Mawr, Penna.
PAS	Paul Schmidt Music Co., 88 S. 10 St., Minneapolis
Pro	Pro Art Publications, 143 W. Broadway, New York
RAH	Raymond A. Hoffman Co., 118 West Ohio St., Chicago
Rem	Remick Music Corp., RCA Bldg., Rockefeller Center, New York
Ric	G. Ricordi & Co., Inc., 1270 Sixth Ave., New York
Ru	Rubank, Inc., 5544 W. Armstrong Ave., Chicago
SB	Silver Burdett Co., 45 E. 17 St., New York
SF	Sam Fox Publishing Co., 1250 Sixth Ave., New York
TP	Theodore Presser, Bryn Mawr, Pennsylvania
Vic	Victor Publishing Co., 1322 Congress St., Chicago
Wil	Willis Music Co., 124 E. Fourth St., Cincinnati, Ohio
Wit	M. Witmark & Sons, 54 W. Randolph St., Chicago

9. Teaching Aids

Since Music Education is concerned with developing appreciation, understanding, knowledge, and skills of performance in pupils, it can be said that any device used by teachers to promote these learnings may be called a teaching aid. Teachers have used various aids for a long time, but their effectiveness was realized after World War II. Education has been influenced greatly by the success with which they were utilized in training the armed forces. In Chapters 3 and 6 references were made to various teaching aids which are necessary for carrying out a well-balanced music program; in this chapter these aids will be discussed in detail.

Although many music teachers have used maps, pictures, slides, demonstrations, concerts, and various performances to vitalize and enrich their teaching, they have not always taken advantage of the many excellent teaching aids available in the community because they do not know what resources are at their disposal. One community has a violin factory, but the music teachers do not use it in vocal or instrumental studies. To see how violins are made, hear how they sound, know what the famous old violins are called, see where they were made, or to realize in what ways the modern violin differs from the old ones would make a deep impression on adolescents. Also, such a trip might serve as a starting point for a fine unit on instruments. In another community there is a museum containing an unusually fine collection of Indian instruments and other Indian relics, but few music teachers use the museum as a teaching aid.

Local newspapers often print articles on music concerning local concerts, radio, and television programs devoted to music and musical happenings. These are excellent aids, possibly forming the basis of curricular studies and discussions.

The magazine *Keyboard Jr.*, published in New Haven, Connecticut, is devoted to interesting musical subjects which please junior-high-school pupils. Some teachers use this magazine in their classes. As a result, many pupils look and listen to the Firestone television and radio programs, which are discussed in this magazine.

There are many fine illustrative pictures which may be found in numerous magazines, such as *Life, Holiday,* and *The National Geographic.* These pictures can be mounted on manila or colored cardboard and filed for use in the study of the music of various nations and cultures. The pictures can be used in their exact size or reflected by a projector, and become a valuable teaching aid. Teachers need to be on the lookout constantly for illustrative materials in newspapers and magazines. A complete set of twenty charts of instruments are made available by the RCA division of Radio Corporation of America (Camden, New Jersey). Miniature replicas of these charts, which pupils enjoy using in note books, may be secured from J. W. Pepper and Son (Philadelphia).

A music room, appropriately located and adequately equipped, is one of the most important teaching aids to the success of a music program.[1]

Within the music room, no piece of equipment is more important than the piano around which may be centered various teaching aids. Proper attention should be given to the selection,

---

[1] See *Music Rooms and Equipment.* Music Educators National Conference, 64 E. Jackson Blvd., Chicago 4, Illinois.

care, and use of the piano. Too often, pianos are left untuned throughout a whole year, and then it is difficult to use them with either vocal or instrumental groups. They should be maintained at American Standard Pitch, which is A-440, by several tunings each year. A grand piano is preferable because of its quality of tone and the unobstructed view it affords the teacher. If the piano is mounted on a frame equipped with rubber casters, it can be moved easily so that it may be used in the many locations required by various groups. Large upright pianos may be used, but they are not entirely satisfactory. However, there are several kinds of small upright ones built for classroom use, which are satisfactory in pitch and tone.

SELECTION OF TEACHING AIDS

Teachers should choose aids most carefully. First, be sure that the materials are functional in your teaching situation. An aid that is good for one school is not necessarily equally effective in another. There is such a continual development of materials that they are soon outmoded. Whenever possible, try out the aids in your classroom or see them demonstrated, so that you are sure of their excellence. Too often, administrators claim that a music teacher selects materials which the next teacher feels are inadequate. To determine what materials are best, get some expert advice from a reputable teaching aids laboratory where experiments are conducted. Many cities, colleges, and universities maintain these experimental centers and are willing to advise teachers.

There is such a variety of excellent sources and kinds of aids available that few people can know all of them. *Preparation and Use of Audio-Visual Aids,* by Haas and Packer, Prentice-Hall, Inc. (New York), is most helpful in selecting such equipment. *Building an Audio-Visual Program,* by Schreiber and Calvert, Science Research Associates (Chicago), offers good suggestions for organizing a teaching aids program.

Seldom are music teachers required to select projectors or motion picture machines, since they serve the school at large, but there are some aids, which, functioning especially for music education, must be selected by the music teacher. Music teachers should co-operate in every way in promoting the development of a visual-aids program. They can work on the audio-visual committee, and they can contribute financially by giving a special concert or by participating in an all-school drive for funds.

AUDIO-VISUAL AIDS

It is necessary that we understand what is meant by the term audio-visual aids. In every case they are aids for instruction. By an *audio* aid we mean that the material used is heard but is not seen. The radio is an example of this type of aid. A *visual* aid, which is seen and not heard, is exemplified by the film strip. An *audio-visual* aid can be both seen and heard; television is an excellent illustration of this type. Some universities and public schools used such aids before World War II, so the idea is not new. But music education, like all areas of education, has been influenced by the success the armed forces has had with them. There seems to be little opposition to their use, but educators are still in a quandary in regard to their selection and purchase. Since they are being improved constantly, directors and teachers need to know the most improved models available. Due to the fact that all of them have been adopted so recently, techniques for their use are still in the experimental stage.

Audio-visual materials should always be considered only as a means to the ends desired. They can never take the place of an enthusiastic, efficient music teacher, nor should they become the curriculum. They are only tools in every sense of the word, tools to make learning more meaningful. They contribute to learning but are not a substitution for it. They are powerful in motivating a class to learn, and with their use, learning is achieved more rapidly, more effectively, and with more facility.

A film showing unfamiliar instruments brings these instruments into reality and removes vocabulary barriers set up when teachers use the same names. Music education contains many words that are foreign to pupils, and the use of them by teachers often blocks the learning of some children. (Percy Grainger avoids this by using many English words in his compositions to convey dynamic meanings, instead of the typical Italian words which have little significance for pupils.)

For those pupils who live in remote communities and do not have an opportunity to see and hear orchestras, choral groups, folk dancing, artist concerts, or ballets, audio-visual aids bring these musical experiences into reality. No vivid verbal expression given by the teacher can create such a lasting impression as the one possible through the use of these aids. Television has proved this fact. Whether or not we approve, all these mechanical devices are having a powerful educative influence on adolescents inside and outside the classroom.

Suggestions for the selection and use
of audio-visual aids

There is a "happy medium" which should be observed in regard to the number of aids used. The policy of "all or none" should be avoided. Never should their overuse be permitted to become a fad or a frill. There is a rightful place for these aids, and teachers need to be sensitive to their place in education.

Be sure to *preview* all materials, unless you have seen and heard them previously. The catalogues may have what seems to be a fine description of them, but they may be entirely unsuitable for your use when you see or hear them. When pupils feel that their time is wasted, it is better never to have used the material.

In choosing an audio-visual aid the age of the class must be kept in mind. Nothing is more insulting to a junior-high-school class than to have juvenile materials presented to them. There may be a temptation to use well-liked materials which are too mature for the class; this, too, is disliked by adolescents. Know your class!

The teacher should plan for the use of the materials some time ahead of their actual presentation. Many films are rented, and unless they are available when they are needed, their effectiveness is lost. Often there is a waiting list for popular educational films in state loan, or rental film libraries or depositories, and as a result, they are slow in delivery. Holding the films is too expensive. In a city system, teachers in other areas may want a music film for their classes at the same time a music teacher wishes to use it. Book the materials early with the teacher who is in charge of audio-visual aids in your school.

In some schools, all classes are taken to a special room where the materials are presented. If the music room has the necessary equipment available, plan for the operation of the machine. If you are required to operate it, be sure you know how to do so before presenting the material to your classes. Have everything well-organized so that there is no confusion. If you have student operators, as many schools do have, check with them to be sure all is in readiness. Good planning is a necessity for the success of the program. Check the ventilation carefully, being sure the room has plenty of fresh air and a temperature not in excess of seventy degrees. Too often, pupils are crowded into too small a space with a torrid temperature. This is detrimental to learning.

Audio-visual aids should be used, only if they contribute to the unit which the class is studying. When teaching aids are presented as isolated and unrelated experiences, they have little educational value. It is the teacher's job to tie class work and the aids together in order to enhance their unitary power and avoid isolation. Remember that they should not be selected for their recreational experiences but for their educational values. However, the two ideas are not incompatable, because educational materials can be pleasurable as well as educational in character. In fact, educational aids should have emotional appeal, since we learn "all over" — through the emotions as well as through the senses. Knowledge gained through audio-visual aids is experiential as opposed to *memoriter learning*, which is plain drudgery for some pupils.

These aids are particularly useful in presenting a new unit, in stimulating interest, and in presenting new ideas available in books and recordings. Often, they are used effectively in the culmination of a unit. They can put the study into true-life situations. Stephen Foster lives again when a sound film about him is used; a film strip causes the "ballets" of the mountain folk to have more meaning, deepens appreciations, and widens human relationships. All these suggestions should be kept in mind when audio-visual aids are used.

Presenting audio-visual aids

Because of a lack of preparation and differences in background, the same teaching aids may evoke very different responses from two sections of a grade. Thus, to be really effective, teaching aids need the help of the teacher, who should develop a pupil readiness before the material is presented. Be sure your class knows what they are to see and hear, and you should explain how it relates to their unit of study. Suggest what things they should look and listen for and create within the group a desire to see and hear the film. Emotional and aesthetic qualities as well as factual knowledge should be emphasized. Set the stage and then let the material have full sway. It seems unwise to interrupt any sound material, no matter how eager you are to have your class notice something that is characteristic. Run the film through without a break. Re-run it if pupils are enthusiastic and if you wish something to be noticed particularly.

After the material has been shown, *follow-up activities* should be encouraged. Request the pupils to give their impressions to the class; these pupil responses can well become the basis of class discussions. Teachers should stimulate and enter into these discussions, always remembering that pupil evaluations are most important in music education. Sometimes you may wish to give a written test on the things heard and seen, but do not forget that if this procedure is used continuously interest will be killed.

FILMS

Films are used in many areas in junior high schools, but music teachers who have had skill in performance as their chief objective have been slow to realize their worth in the classroom. Now that more good films are available, teachers are urged to consider them for use in the general music classes, for the development of good choral groups, as a means for recruitment for instrumental classes, and for class teaching of instruments.

There are a few films which will always be effective and can well become a part of the permanent film library. The cost of films makes it necessary for teachers to purchase only those which will be useful in many ways. For example, Instruments of the Orchestra — *Variations and Fugue,* by Benjamin Britten (BIS), can be used to meet the uses indicated in the preceding paragraph and for this reason is worthy of being purchased.

Many schools will prefer to rent films rather than to purchase them. Other films, the permanency of which is doubtful, should be rented. Some state departments of education and universities loan films to schools, charging only for their transportation. Check these suggested sources to supplement your audio-visual aids department.

Sometimes, teachers are located in communities which are partly isolated and cannot get in touch easily with the new films as they appear on the market. For these teachers, the following reliable sources, which list and evaluate films and often include teaching suggestions that are invaluable, are given:

1. *Educational Film Guide* (H. W. Wilson Co., 950 University Ave., New York, New York). Films for rent or sale.
2. *Evaluation of Sound Films for Music Education* (University of Nebraska, Lincoln, Nebraska).
3. *Film Music Notes* (31 Union Square West, New York, New York). There are articles on films, special bulletins, and teaching aids in the magazine.
4. *How to Use Films in Music Education* (Music Educators National Conference, 45 E. Jackson Blvd., Chicago, Illinois). Included is information on what is available, the cost, and the use of films.
5. *Music Educators Journal* (This publication is obtained from the source mentioned in 4 above.) The magazine contains articles on recommended music films. The "Audio-Visual Forum" is a regular feature in the journal.

At the end of this chapter a suggested list of films used successfully in schools will be found. A directory of sources of films is included.

Film strips

Film strips, also called strip films or slide films, have been in use in some areas for over thirty years, but they have not been used as much in music education as have some other teaching aids. Industry and the defense and war training programs have used them to advantage. They are stationary pictures on a continuous film and, as such, have some advantage over films or motion pictures because the individual frames can be moved forward or backward as desired and held for any length of time. This allows for discussion by the teacher and the class at the time of showing. The pictures are arranged in sequence with captions between the pictures. The number of pictures on a film varies from twenty-five to one hundred, depending on the number of captions or descriptions used. The single frame strip is popular, since the film runs through the projector vertically. The double frame strip runs through horizontally because the tape and the bottom of the pictures are towards the film's edges.

This visual aid is especially good for teaching some phases of instrumental music, such as good sitting position, how to hold the instrument, the proper embouchure, and how to finger the instrument. Nine 35-mm. film strips with a Teaching Guide, produced by the Bureau of Audio-Visual Instruction, Pan American Band Instruments (Elkhart, Indiana), are available for teaching instruments. Color film strips called *Rhythm Magic* and *The Musical Forest* may be purchased from Young America Films, Inc. (18 E. 41st St., New York 17, New York). These sets contain three film strips. The Bureau of Audio-Visual Instruction of the University of Nebraska (Lincoln, Nebraska), has prepared two excellent 35-mm. film strips called *Trumpet and Cornet, Part I* and *The Violin, Part I*. Teaching guides and the film strips can be secured for a nominal fee.

Sound film strip, sometimes called sound slide film, is like the film strip, but it has sound produced simultaneously with the film by a phonograph record or transcription. They are synchronized with the pictures, with a faint bell sound to tell the operator to show the next picture. Sometimes the captions or explanations are omitted on the films and put on the record. If it is desired, the film may be used without the sound. This type of film is more effective for music education, since the sound of the music makes the picture doubly educational. There are several manufacturers who furnish new sound slide film projectors which automatically advance the film to the next picture. Your local dealer will be happy to give you the necessary information. The Los Angeles city schools produced and used a sound film called *Instruments of the Orchestra* with success; there is a distinct need for more such sound slide films. In case you wish to make your own film strip or sound slide film, you will find excellent advice in Chapter Two of *Preparation and Use of Audio-Visual Aids,* by Haas and Parker, previously referred to in this chapter.

THE OPAQUE PROJECTOR

Pictures, which have a great place in educating the American public today, are used to advantage in many classrooms to bring ideas into reality. Music Education is concerned with many cultures, places, and nationalities about which verbal ideas expressed by the teacher are not enough to stimulate interest and develop appreciations. Pictures used as illustrations have something to offer educationally when circulated through a class, but their effectiveness is heightened immeasurably if they are projected on a screen for the purpose of class discussion. Too, their enlargement increases their value by making details discernable.

The opaque projector makes this possible, and, since it offers unlimited use to most departments because of the free materials which it can project, it should be one of the first aids to be purchased by any school. However, the combination slide and opaque projector is more useful because the teacher or operator may insert a small picture up to 6 × 6 inches and get a very good enlargement. The names of some manufacturers of this device are as follows:

1. The American Optical Co., Buffalo, New York
2. Bausch and Lomb Optical Co., Rochester, New York
3. Charles Beseler Co., 243 E. 23rd St., New York, New York (This company has an opaque projector, "Vu-Lyte," which can accommodate pictures 8½" x 11½" — a decided advantage.)

*Using the opaque projector
with pictures and slides*

Check the size of the slides or pictures that are to be shown to be sure that they fit the platon. To avoid confusion, always arrange the materials in the order of showing. Place the screen and projector so that there is a straight line between them. The projector needs to be placed high enough so that the picture will extend above the heads of the viewers. A well-darkened room is more satisfactory; the lighter the room the brighter the lamp must be. Always check every bit of equipment before the class period to ensure a satisfactory learning situation.

Teachers should use judgment in selecting pictures, the sources of which were discussed earlier in this chapter. Some pictures should be mounted and filed to insure their preservation. A description of the picture and a suggested use for it should be placed on the back. In this way, the material is always available when it is most effective.

Song slides

Song slides projected on a screen have been used for years, by music teachers, to make assembly singing more vital and efficient in organization. The use of slides eliminates the need for song sheets and music books and helps solve the problem of making the words of the songs available to all.

To make the "sing" successful arrange the slides in the order which will arouse interest, lend variety to the program, and gain the co-operation of the entire student body. Check every piece of equipment, the projector, screen, and the lighting. Failure of the equipment to operate in a crucial place may kill all desire for singing, and the joy of group singing can be permanently destroyed. Good ventilation is essential if the co-operation of pupils is expected; a room temperature above seventy degrees is not conducive to vigorous participation in singing. If you have a pupil trained to operate the projector, which may be one of a number of good types, go over the entire program with him before it is presented to the student body.

Song slides $3\frac{1}{4}'' \times 4''$ may be secured from Sims Visual Aids Co. (Quincy, Illinois). They have excellent black and white slides of most American community songs written in parts.

The arrangements are standard; so, the accompanist may use accompaniments other than the voice parts after the songs are learned.

Pupils, with the aid of the teacher, can make slides of school and currently popular songs which are not available on slides. The work involved is not difficult, and the materials are very inexpensive. The complete operation takes little time and is excellent training for students. The necessary materials can be purchased from theatrical, stationery, or photographic supply stores. Type the words of the song on cellophane through carbon, or on radiomats. Then place the mats between two pieces of clean glass which will fit the projector and secure in place with binding tape. Ordinary binding tape may be used, but Scotch tape has proved satisfactory. About sixteen inches of tape, for a 3¼" × 4" slide (allowing an inch for security) should be laid flat on a table, adhesive side up. Moisten binding tape a little. Even all the edges of the glass and place in the middle of the tape, starting at one end of the tape. Turn the slides over the tape and press firmly both sides, especially at the folded corners. Permission should be gained from the publishers before attempting to copy the words for slides in order to avoid infringement of copyrights. The melody and words of many folk songs are public domain, and only the arrangements are copyrighted.

RECORDS AND RECORD PLAYERS

Records, which have been used in schools for many years, make an unquestionable contribution to music education. Their use, along with sources for purchasing them, was discussed at length in Chapter 6, to which the reader may turn for reference at this point.

To make recordings acceptable to junior-high-school pupils, an adequate phonograph is needed. Pupils have little respect for the finest record if it is played on a poor machine. The record situation is in such a condition at the present time that it is unwise to purchase any phonograph which does not have 78, 33⅓, and 45 r.p.m. speeds. These machines will play the old records, which many schools still own. If the speaker is adequate, a portable machine is often preferable to the console type. In addition, select a machine which is easy to operate because many pupils serve as operators.

Some phonographs worthy of consideration are:

1. Audio-Master (Audio-Master Corp., 341 Madison Ave., New York, New York)
2. Admiral (New three way radio-phonograph — see your dealer)
3. Califon (Califon Corp., Hollywood, California)
4. Webcor Fonograf (Webster-Chicago, Chicago, Illinois)
5. Newcomb R16 (Newcomb Audio Products Co., 6424 Lexington Ave., Hollywood, California)

RECORDERS

Of all the audio-visual aids, the magnetic recorder is one of the most frequently used devices. It has been used long enough to prove its value, and although it is being improved constantly, it is definitely out of the experimental stage.

Tape recorders seem to be very popular with music teachers. They are preferred because the playback can be done at once after the recording is made. Both instrumental and vocal teachers use tape recordings to perfect operettas, performances, concerts, contests, and festivals. The pupils can hear their errors and are more sensitive and receptive to criticisms.

In addition, for advertising purposes teachers use tape recordings when a program is played over the school's central sound system. Sometimes a piano accompaniment is recorded for a choral number and used later with the choir. Instrumental teachers often record marches and use the tape later, when marching maneuvers are being learned. The use of the machine seems to be limitless.

Recordings are permanent, and will stand hundreds of playings. Too, they may be erased, and a new recording made in one operation. The magnetic tape recorder is so small and light in weight that it can be easily carried from room to room. It is so simple to operate that a teacher can set it in motion and devote his time to the rehearsal, or, a pupil can be trained quickly to run the machine. If the tape tears it can be repaired simply with inexpensive Scotch tape.

Teachers should make a careful examination of all available recording and playback equipment before making their selection. A small list of tape recorders follows:

1. The Bell Tape Recorder (Bell Laboratories, 555 Marion Road, Columbus, Ohio)
2. Ekotape (Webster Electric Co., Racine, Wisconsin)
3. Revere (Revere Camera Co., 320 E. 21 St., Chicago, Illinois)
4. Soundmirror (Brush Development Co., 3405 Perkins Ave., Cleveland, Ohio)
5. Web-Cor (Webster, 5610 W. Bloomingdale Ave., Chicago, Illinois)

THE BULLETIN BOARD

Bulletin boards are most useful to music teachers for exhibiting materials shown in class, thereby making it possible for the pupils to enjoy and study them at their leisure. Fine display materials are: music maps, posters, post cards of places famous in the music world, photographs of musicians, pictures of instruments and musical events, notices of coming performances in the community and on television and radio, and newspaper clippings concerning local and national performances. On the lighter side, some humorous cartoons should be included.

Some classes elect a bulletin board committee, advised by the teacher, to prepare materials which they and the group collect. (Often this is an excellent way to find out what things interest the pupils.) These materials may be used later in making individual and group notebooks, or filed for future use by the teacher. Display items, which should be changed frequently in order to pique "reader interest," should be arranged harmoniously. They can fit into some classification which bears a clever title concerning the center of interest or unit.

There is no average size for a bulletin board that can be

recommended for classroom use. This must be determined by the amount of wall and blackboard space available. The bulletin board can be made in the school shops from soft wood, cork, or Celotex covered with burlap, the small expense being far outweighed by the educational values of this excellent teaching aid. For more detailed information, consult Marjorie East, *Display for Learning*, Dryden Press.

RADIO AND TELEVISION

Radio has a powerful influence on American life and is recognized as a valuable tool in modern education. When we realize that over ninety per cent of America's homes have radios, that most automobiles have them, and that they are used in many industries, we know that it plays an important role in the lives of Americans. The current slogan "Everywhere you go there's radio" is apropos at this time. We should remember, however, that it is not a substitute for the teacher but, rather, a most effective aid when it is put in the hands of a clever teacher. In no case should the radio be turned on and left to charm the listeners. Good radio lessons require pupil preparation before a broadcast and a discussion afterwards. Sometimes tests on the program may be used effectively.

Television has swept the country, linking it from coast to coast. Its advancement has been so rapid that it has surpassed the greatest hopes of its sponsors. The most rampant critic of television is forced to admit that television is here to stay. Many educators are profiting by their experience with radio and are realizing that television should have a distinct and forceful place in education.

In the classroom

Radio programs are available to schools in both urban and rural communities. In spite of many untrained teachers, the isolation of some schools, and the presence of but one music supervisor, music comes to the pupils even by battery-powered radio if electricity is not available.

There are many programs, which are arranged for children, broadcast by colleges and universities. Schools of Wisconsin, Kentucky, Ohio, and Indiana are among those which have conducted these musical programs. Some cities, notably Cleveland, Ohio have operated their own radio stations, and have their own music programs directed to children in various grades in the elementary schools. They have used radio as an excellent supervisory activity and have found it most effective and not too expensive.

There is a dearth of musical programs suitable for junior-high-school classroom use. "The Standard School Broadcasts," sponsored by the Standard Oil Company, are fine programs and are used extensively in some parts of the country. Teaching guides and musical maps are sent free to teachers who request them. Their brochure, *Musical Portraits of Famous Americans*, can be secured by addressing Standard School Broadcasts (225 Bush St., San Francisco, California).

Before they are recommended to pupils, it is wise to secure information about suitable radio programs. If local radio stations do not have the dates and time of the programs, this information accompanied by teacher's manuals and broadcast notes may be obtained by addressing the following:

1. American Broadcasting Co., Radio City, New York
2. Columbia Broadcasting System, 485 Madison Ave., New York
3. Mutual Broadcasting System, 1440 Broadway, New York
4. National Broadcasting Co., Radio City, New York
5. Station WQXR, Times Square, New York

Television has not found its way into classrooms to any great extent. Recently the Federal Communications Commission has earmarked 242 television station assignments for "non-commercial educational purposes." Educators are hopeful that the development of these educational television stations will make worthwhile telecasts available to many schools.

It remains to be seen whether the direct-view models with sixteen to twenty-one-inch screens, or the projection model which throws a picture on a screen, are more practical for classroom use. Much development can be expected in television, and it is possible that color will be generally available later. For the present, there are plenty of black and white direct-view consoles and table models from which to choose to meet the needs of any school. (See also Chapter 10.)

Radio transcriptions

Since many desired radio programs are not available when classes meet, transcriptions, which are merely recordings of radio programs made on discs or tape at the time of the broadcast, can be used later during class time. Often, they are filed, and become a part of a permanent library of recordings. They make the finest music available for classroom use and are inexpensive, since transcriptions may be recorded free of charge if they are not used commercially.

Radio stations which use transcriptions for rebroadcasting make some of them available for school use. A fifteen-minute program can be recorded on a sixteen-inch disc, because most transcriptions are made on a turntable that revolves at 33⅓ revolutions per minute. Like a record, the wanted places on transcriptions can be found easily and replayed for study. Transcriptions can play a most important part in music education by bringing choral and instrumental music of all kinds to the classroom.

Outside the classroom

Most of the programs which seem to be suitable for junior-high pupils are broadcast and televised after school hours. The evening programs of "The Voice of Firestone" are excellent for both adults and young people. Often these programs are discussed in *Keyboard Jr.*, a music magazine published for pupils. Some teachers use this magazine in their classes and prepare their pupils for listening to the programs at home. The Saturday afternoon broadcasts of the Metropolitan Opera, the broadcasts of the Westminster Choir, and the Band of America programs are all excellent for young people. Other programs are available and teachers may secure information concerning them by writing for *Radio in Music Education,* available from The Music Educators National Conference (64 E. Jackson Blvd., Chicago); price, twenty-five cents.

Americans were thrilled when the coaxial cables and relay towers across the country made the signing of the Japanese Peace Treaty in San Francisco visible, by television, to the entire nation. General MacArthur's famous speech before Congress was heard and seen by millions of viewers, and the Senate Crime Investigation Committee's hearings were likewise viewed in millions of American homes.

The "Voice of Firestone" hour is seen on the television screen with the whole program, featuring both the orchestra and chorus with eminent soloists, becoming an educative and thrilling experience. Program notes concerning the Firestone programs are available for the writing by addressing The Firestone Rubber Co. (Akron, Ohio). Some of the programs are arranged especially for pupils and are understood better if the teacher prepares his class before the broadcasts and discusses them afterwards. Another fine program featuring famous singers and players is "Meet the Masters." The effectiveness of opera on television was proved by the première performance of Menotti's *Amahl and the Night Visitors,* given on Christmas Eve, 1951. Until we have learned how to use television in the schools, we can at least stimulate its wise use outside of school by preparing our classes for viewing such worthy performances as these.

Teachers are often amazed when they are told by their pupils what radio and television programs they enjoy. Frequently, pupils are not aware that there are better programs available. A list of good radio and television musical programs, with the hour and station, should be posted on the bulletin board and discussed in class. Making the list would be a good class or committee project. Using class time to discuss interesting programs which pupils have heard and seen is a good way to raise their level of appreciation. Comments by class members are often very effective in suggesting inherent musical values. In these discussions the taste of all individuals should be respected, and, in doing so, pupils can be influenced in their choice of programs. Teachers should use "wise influencing" in teaching this important phase of appreciation.

Some schools are using television to foster better public relations by having school groups appear on local television programs. Music has a very important place in television shows, and the music organizations in the junior high school can be used to familiarize parents with the school's activities.

Universities have pioneered in presenting noncredit courses on television. Now, Western Reserve University, located in Cleveland, Ohio, offers credit for home study by television and is using this medium for teaching courses leading to a degree. One may expect a wider use of television as more programs are directed toward education and as more sections of the country have television stations.

Industry has made use of television in its training programs. Verbal direction becomes reality when the operations to be learned are viewed by the trainees. All kinds of musical performances could be aided by television. Again, it should be borne in mind that this new aid will never take the place of radio, films, tape recordings, records, or a good teacher.

Broadcasting and telecasting[2]

Teachers have only to announce that the pupils may broadcast a musical program and at once interest in the project is kindled. Music needs the social outlet which a radio or television program supplies. The broadcast offers one of the finest opportunities for creative education, and teachers will find that the powerful incentive aroused by a broadcast will stimulate the music education program as few activities will do. Sometimes a program may be given over the school intercom-

---

[2] Despite the eagerness of pupils to participate in broadcasts and telecasts, teachers should be careful not to overrehearse in order to reach artificial standards. For discussion of other problems related to this area, see Chapter 10.

munication system, or it may be used on a regularly scheduled school broadcast over a local radio station. Some school administrators use the radio to develop better public relations, and music is given a place in the program.

A pupil-teacher committee should plan the program carefully, using some theme as a center to interest the audience. If a script is used, pupils must be rehearsed carefully so that the spoken and musical parts of the program are related effectively. In this preparation a tape recording can be of great assistance. The performance before a microphone is different from a stage performance, and there is a technique to broadcasting about which every teacher must be informed. Such matters as arrangements of voices, instruments, and accompanists should be checked carefully with the studio engineer before the broadcast.

Telecasting, partly because of its newness, has a most stimulating effect on any group that is asked to appear before the television cameras. Pupils will rehearse unlimitedly in order to sound and appear well, and no detail of performance is too difficult to perfect when a television program is in preparation.

Such select groups as the school choir may appear en masse, and the entire group will cooperate in every respect because they will be seen and heard by their peers, their parents, and the entire community. Teachers should embrace as many of these opportunities for television appearances as possible, since they motivate the group to do its best work.

When the general music class is asked to present a program, some pupils who do not sing well are often left out of the presentation. For them music becomes a closed book, and their attitude toward music easily becomes negative and sometimes antagonistic. Teachers should find something in which those poor in performance can participate. Exclusion for a few may far outweigh the valuable experience the participants gain.

Every detail in appearance as well as musical effects must be considered. Whenever possible, a trial rehearsal should be held under the expert direction of the telecast staff. From the rapid development of telecasting techniques by broadcasters, music educators may learn how to use television to promote pupil learning in all areas and with varied groups.

FOLK INSTRUMENTS

For too long a time music education has operated on the idea that only art songs, symphonic literature, and symphonic instruments have musical and educational values (excluding other types, such as folk songs and the music of folk instruments). There is no use trying to deny the fact that folk instruments have always had a distinct place in the folk music of all nations. Who can suggest a symphonic substitute for the cowboy's guitar, the Italian's accordion, or Arthur Godfrey's ukulele? Can you imagine a Latin American song without maracas, claves, or drums to heighten its rhythmic effects? Adolescents hear these instruments every where outside the school; so, why not bring some of the simpler ones into the classroom? If we believe that appreciation must grow from the level on which a person lives, surely it is the better part of

wisdom to use these levels as points of departure on the high road of appreciation.

Many junior-high-school pupils play the banjo, guitar, harmonica, and the ukulele. They need only a little urging to bring them to school to play chordal accompaniments for the singing of folk songs or for folk dancing, which will delight everyone, knowing that the school program recognizes their use. One cannot carry a piano about to play accompaniments, but these simple instruments made famous by Andreas Segovia, Arthur Godfrey, and John Sebastian can enliven a school program which otherwise may have little attraction for large numbers of students. Some modern textbooks include chord directions for these instruments. Through their use some teachers win their pupils' love for the famous three B's (Bach, Beethoven, and Brahms). Students hear all types of music on the radio and television and, being accustomed to adjusting to various types of music without a lift of an eyebrow, can adjust as easily in the classroom. Music teachers need to learn that it isn't an "either, or" program that is the winner, but rather a varied program which offers something for everyone.

The Auto-harp is used in many schools for playing simple chordal accompaniments. By way of example, "Red River Valley" is enhanced by such an accompaniment. Some boys who never sing are pleased to learn to play this stringed, zither-like instrument, which plays the I, IV, V, and V$_7$ and some minor chords in several keys when its bars are pressed while being strummed. These bars are constructed to dampen all tones except those in the particular chord they produce. This simple instrument, which provides an excellent way for teaching a feeling for the bass, is inexpensive enough so that several can be afforded. You will want more than one because pupils ask to take them home to practice. This instrument, which may be obtained in a large or small size, may be purchased from the Willis Music Company (Cincinnati, Ohio), or from the manufacturers, Oscar Schmidt, Inc. (89 Ferry St., Jersey City, New Jersey.)

ORGANIZING TEACHING AIDS

The extent to which teaching aids are used in schools varies so much that one will find no uniform pattern to follow. This is a good thing. Every music teacher should be interested in the use of teaching aids and should be willing to co-operate in every way in securing materials and making them available to all members of the teaching staff.

There are schools that have a well-organized teaching aids committee that operates with one teacher acting as the chairman. If you are a new teacher in this type of school, ask the chairman about materials which are available for music education. Express your willingness to co-operate and offer the services of the music department to secure funds for needed equipment and materials. Such willingness to co-operate begets cooperation.

There are many schools in which there is no organization of teaching aids. Each teacher must acquire all the materials necessary for his own use. As a result, teachers do not know what equipment is available other than their own and are unwilling to share what they "own" through length of service for fear they may be in use elsewhere when they desire them. This is a typical situation. To correct such a state, propose the organization of a teaching aids committee when it is advantageous. This committee should be headed by a dynamic and interested elected chairman. Suggest that all school-owned aids be collected and ask your principal for both storage space and a room in which to use these materials. This development may come slowly, since working together for the common good is not a watchword in some schools.

The committee should hear from members of the teaching staff in regard to the purchase of needed equipment and materials. The first purchases should be useful to many areas, and often, simple and less expensive materials should be secured. Your committee must decide whether to purchase an opaque projector, a slide and film strip projector, a recording and play back machine, a phonograph, or a movie projector. Machines are of no value unless there are materials to use with them; so, all purchases must be selected most carefully. How to finance a budget for purchasing these aids will require the co-operation of administrators and teachers.

After the project is well on its way, it must be decided whether one teacher shall operate the machines, or whether pupil operators shall be trained. In one school an administrator returned from taking a summer school course in visual aids and required each teacher to learn how to operate all the machines the school possessed. Needless to say, the teachers disliked the suggestion. There had been no united effort of the staff for discussing the value of the aids, no staff participation in the selection of them, and no in-service training in their use. Since American schools teach democracy, democracy should be lived within the school. There is no better way for teachers to learn democratic living than in organizing teaching aids to foster educational growth in pupils, teachers, supervisors, and administrators.

SUMMARY

A teaching aid is any device used by teachers to promote learning. An audio aid is any material heard but not seen. A visual aid is one which is seen and not heard, while an audio-visual aid can be both seen and heard.

Education has been influenced greatly in the use of these aids by the success with which the armed forces used them during World War II. Many aids are found in the community and are available in newspapers and magazines.

Teachers should be well informed concerning the various types of audio-visual aids and their cost before selection of them is made. Their use and educational value should be understood throughly before they are purchased. These aids can never take the place of a good teacher, but their effectiveness is greatly heightened by class preparation and follow-up activities.

Films are a very valuable aid, and may be rented when their purchase is prohibitive. A list of recommended films and a directory of their sources is included at the close of this chapter. Reliable sources for evaluating new films are listed. The chapter contains comments concerning the meaning of a film strip and its use.

The opaque projector, and its use with pictures and slides, is discussed. Slides may be made by pupils and teachers when copyrights do not prohibit their use.

Records for the listening program are found in Chapter 6; here a list of record players worthy of consideration is included.

Recorders are a most valuable aid in music education, and the various ways in which a music teacher may use them are discussed. Sources for purchasing reliable recorders are listed.

The bulletin board is one of the most effective aids for exhibiting valuable materials. Suggestions for its use and types of materials suitable for display are listed.

Radio and television within and outside the classroom and their great influence on pupils are noted. Teachers are urged to use pupil experience with these two media for curricular studies and for the development of appreciation.

Folk instruments often frowned upon by music teachers have a contribution to make to music education. Their place in the classroom is discussed, and suggestions are made concerning their use.

The chapter concludes with a discussion in regard to the music teacher and the organization of the teaching aids. Teachers may contribute generously to the development of teaching aids and, in turn, promote more effective learning by their use.

SELECTED LIST OF MUSIC FILMS [3]

1. *Andante et Rondo*, Piatigorsky (cellist). (OF, b&w) Plays a von Weber composition.
2. *American Square Dances*, Coronet (10 min., color). Shows typical dance steps, defines terms and calls (do-si-do, grand right and left promenade).

---

[3] Used in five Ohio school systems. See page 328 for explanation of code letters.

3. *Brass Choir,* EBF (11 min., b&w). Howard Barlow, conductor.
4. *Coolidge Quartet* (string ensemble), EPC (1 reel) "Andante" from String Quartet in E Flat Major by Carl Von Dittersdorf; "Fugue" from Beethoven's Quartet in C Major, Opus 59, No. 3.
5. *Cradle Song,* Fouré, HFS (b&w). Vallin, celebrated singer.
6. Mildred Dilling (harpist), EPC (1 reel) Zabel's *The Fountain;* Hasselman's *Fireflies;* Welsh air, *March of the Men of Harlech,* arranged by John Thomas.
7. Emanuel Feuermann (cellist), Lib (1 reel) Dvořák's *Rondo,* Opus 94; Popper's *Spinning Song.*
8. *Finlandia,* ST (1 reel). Sibelius at home, with a musical background of *Finlandia* and the Second Symphony.
9. *Great Waltz* (collaboration with MENC), TFC (2 reels) (b&w). Music of Johann Strauss: *Beautiful Blue Danube, Artist's Life, Die Fledermaus.*
10. Carroll Glenn (violinist), EPC (1 reel) Weiniawski's *Mazurka;* Tchaikovsky's *Canzonetta;* Hobay's *Hi, Katie (Mejre Kati).*
11. Igor Gorin (baritone), OF (1 reel) "Largo Al Factotum" from Rossini's *The Barber of Seville.*
12. *Gypsy Revels,* TFC (1 reel) (11 min., b&w). Songs and dances of czarist Russia.
13. *Hymn of the Nations,* UWF (28 min., b&w). Produced by U.S. Office of War Information. Toscanini conducts NBC Symphony Orchestra, Westminster Choir.
14. José Iturbi, EPC (Part I) (1 reel) Albeniz's *Sevilla;* Chopin's *Fantasie Impromptu.*
    José Iturbi (Part II) (1 reel) Three pieces for harpsichord by Jean Philippe Rameau; on the piano, Liszt's *Eleventh Hungarian Rhapsody.*
15. Instruments of the Orchestra, BIS (2 reels). The London Symphony Orchestra "takes itself apart" to show what makes it tick. Each instrument is played separately by a member of the orchestra. Then all the instruments are blended for an orchestral selection. *Variations and Fugue* by Benjamin Britten; *On a Theme* by Purcell.
16. Michel Piastro and His Orchestra, BIS (1 reel), Reel I: Gounod's *Ballet Music;* Saint-Saëns' *Thy Sweet Voice;* Luigini's "Ballet Egyptian."
    Michel Piastro and His Orchestra (1 reel), Reel II: Lehar's *Gold and Silver Waltz;* Strauss' *Tales from the Vienna Woods;* Tchaikovsky's *Arabian and Russian Ballet.*
17. *Malaguena,* HPS (28 min., b&w). Jacques Thibaud, violinist, plays the composition by Szyamanowski.
18. *Music in America* MOT (17 min.), Educational Forum Series. Folk music, opera, jazz, music in schools.
19. *Musical Instruments of India,* SFC (1 reel). Identifies some of the

most popular instruments of India (whose music dates back to antiquity) and gives brief examples of their melody.

20. *A Night at the Opera* ("Inside Opera") with Grace Moore, TFC (3 reels) (28 min., b&w). Excerpts from *La Traviata, Carmen, Madame Butterfly;* excerpts from *One Night of Love* by MENC.

21. *Percussion Group,* BBF (11 min., b&w). Each instrument is played. Tuning of tympani, snaredrum, tambourine, tom-tom, castanets, gong.

22. *Schumann Story* (3 reels) (30 min., b&w). Excerpted from *Song of Love* by MENC, TFC. Schumann's immortal music and his wife Clara's playing of it.

23. *String Choir* (Symphony Orchestra), MP. Close-up of violin sections, violas, cellos, and basses. Place of strings in orchestra.

24. Symphony Orchestra, Howard Barlow (conductor), EBF (11 min., b&w). Excerpts from *Lohengrin, William Tell,* and *Tannhäuser.*

25. *Symphony of Young America.* Borrow from National Music Camp (Ann Arbor, Michigan). Sound and color of activities of National High School Music Camp at Interlochen, Mich. Rehearsals, concerts, and conductors at work.

26. *Songs of the South.* Borrow from the Atlantic Refining Company.

27. *Songs of the West.* Borrow from the Atlantic Refining Company.

28. *Songs to Remember.* Borrow from the Atlantic Refining Company. Requests to local office.

29. *Second Hungarian Rhapsody,* Liszt (played by Paderewski), OF (3 reels) (each 10 min., b&w). Chopin's *Polonaise* and *Moonlight Sonata.*

30. *This Is Our Earth* (*Lord's Prayer*), UWF (4 min., b&w). Produced for U.S. Dept. of Defense; sung by U.S. Air Force sergeants.

31. *Vronsky & Babin* (duo-pianists), EPC (1 reel), Reel I: Brahm's *Waltz in A Flat;* Rimsky-Korsakov's *Flight of the Bumblebee.*
Vronsky & Babin (duo-pianists) (1 reel), Reel II: Borodin's "Polovitsian Dance" from *Prince Igor.*

32. *Vocal Music,* EBF (1 reel) (60 min.). Reviews structure of vocal instrument and illustrates common faults found in beginning students. Describes basic techniques of singing.

33. *Woodwind Choir 9* (Symphony Orchestra), Howard Barlow (conductor), EBF (11 min., b&w). Excerpts from Brahms and Beethoven.

The following films are worthy of consideration: [4]

1. *Introduction to Jazz,* CUF (12 min., b&w, and color). Produced by Theater Arts, U.C.L.A. Traces the evolution of jazz from African origins through New Orleans period.

---

[4] See page 328 for explanation of code letters.

2. *Magic Fire Spell,* CLU (Color), Werner Jannsen Symphony; *Story of the Metronome,* CLU, Werner Jannsen.
3. *Music Deeply Rooted in American Folk Ways,* EBF. Four films for all levels.
4. *Rehearsal of Telephone Hour,* AT&T (24 min.), free loan. A rehearsal for "Bell Telephone Hour," featuring Pinza, Thebom, and Vorhees with orchestra.
5. *Salzburg Fiesta,* AM-C (12½ min., b&w). Folk songs and dances from Austria.
6. *Science in the Orchestra,* McG-H (three films). The London Orchestra, Muir Mathieson, director.
7. *Story of a Violin,* CAN (21 min., color). A 12-year-old breaks his violin, a skilled violin maker is seen making a new one. Bach's Gavotte in E.
8. *String Choir,* MP. Close-up of violin sections, violas, cellos, and string basses. Place of strings in symphony.
9. *Story of the Writing of "The Star-Spangled Banner,"* TFC (20 min., b&w).
10. *Tanglewood Story,* UWF. Excellent showing of rehearsals at Tanglewood Festival; Koussevitzky, conductor.

DIRECTORY OF SOURCES OF FILMS

AF	A. F. Films, Inc., 1600 Broadway, New York
AM-C	Audio Master Corporation, 341 Madison Ave., New York
AT & T	American Telephone and Telegraph Co., 208 W. Nash St., Chicago; requests to local telephone office
BIS	British Information Service, 30 Rockefeller Plaza, New York
BBF	Brandon Brandon Films, 200 W. 57 St., New York
CAN-FB	National Film Board of Canada, 620 Fifth Ave., New York
Clu	Clune Studios, 5358 Melrose Ave., Hollywood, California
Conn	C. G. Conn Ltd., Elkhart, Indiana
Coronet	Coronet Instructional Films, 65 E. South Water St., Chicago
CUF	University of California, Educational Film Sales, Los Angeles
EPC	Eastin Pictures Co., 707 Putnam Bldg., Davenport, Iowa
EBF	Encyclopaedia Britannica Films, Inc., 1150 Wilmette Ave., Wilmette, Illinois
EFG	Educational Film Guide, H. W. Wilson Co., 950 University Ave., New York
HFS	Hoffberg Productions, Inc., 362 W. 44 St., New York
ICS	Institutional Cinema Service, Inc., 1560 Broadway, New York
Lib	Library Films, Inc., 25 W. 45 St., New York
MOT	March of Time Forum Edition, 369 Lexington Ave., New York
MP	Carl P. Malinke Productions, 215 E. 3 St., Des Moines, Iowa
OF	Official Films Inc., 25 W. 45 St., New York
SFC	Scientific Film Co., 6804 Windsor Ave., Berwyn, Illinois
ST	Sterling Films, Inc., 316 W. 57 St., New York

TFC   Teaching Films Custodians, Inc., 25 W. 43 St., New York
UWF   United World Films, 1445 Park Ave., New York
WEST   Westinghouse Electric Corporation, 306 4 St., Pittsburgh, Pennsylvania
YAF   Young America Films, Inc., 18 E. 41 St., New York

10. Music in the School and Community

MUSIC AND SCHOOL MORALE

Music can do much to bring about good school morale. It is potentially capable of pervading the school atmosphere and, from there, spreading to the community. Basically, the only requirements for such a situation are first, an enthusiastic and diligent teacher or group of teachers and second, essential materials. Even lacking the latter, the authors have known schools where a music teacher or teachers succeeded in raising the level of school morale; it simply took longer to do so.

Reasons for believing the preceding are:

1. Music is fundamentally to be enjoyed. If it is taught with this in mind the burden of academic activities, a heavy one for many children, is lightened each time the child comes to a music class or organization. Such enjoyment does not preclude real work and actual learning on the part of boys and girls, however.

2. Music can be used to broaden the significance of any subject in the curriculum; it may find its way into every classroom. Conversely, other subjects may be used to make the music class

more vital and significant. Today we know that music is not an isolated or "special" subject. It has grown stronger in the curriculum because it is not. The Latin teacher who always borrowed the Christmas carol books for her ninth-grade class and the science teacher who related his unit on sound to musical instruments and the human voice are only two examples of classroom teachers who were aware of music's significance. The music teacher who played the Jerome Kern *Mark Twain* Suite when the class was reading *Huckleberry Finn* obviously had made a point of knowing what was taking place in English classes. These activities are not mentioned primarily as examples of correlation, but rather as indications of ways in which music may bring increased interest and vitality to the life of a school.

3. Music should be regarded as an activity subject, one in which boys and girls may express themselves energetically through singing, playing, rhythmic activities, and group discussion. If any one word could express the key to success with junior-high-school pupils, particularly boys, that word might be *action*. Music has this, plus significant spiritual and social appeal.

4. It is doubtful whether any thinking teachers conduct music organizations without encouraging a real attempt at student government. School systems where senior-high-school organizations function successfully on this basis have learned from experience that the foundation of such government should be laid at least in the junior high school and probably in the earlier grades. Character development, ability to assume responsibility, and understanding of democratic procedures are three outcomes of such student government. Furthermore, music *classes* may learn and practice the rudiments of democratic government. In a school where large numbers of boys and girls are involved in the music program, such experiences should affect school morale.

5. Since music offers a real basis for school-community relationships because of the large numbers of parents and other taxpayers brought to the school through musical programs, boys

and girls may achieve a sense of accomplishment and fulfillment through their musical activities. And in group performances, no one fails . . . when the group succeeds, *all* members of the group succeed, from the strongest to the weakest.

MUSIC AS A UNIFYING SUBJECT

To make music function throughout the music program the music teacher must know what is happening in other departments and in other subject areas. The most direct way to accomplish this is to exchange and discuss course-content outlines with department heads (or subject teachers, where there is no department head). Explain what you would like to do in relating the work of the music class to the work of other classes and ask what music can contribute to the other teacher's classes. Examine text and reference books used in other subjects; make it clear that your library of records and your song textbooks are available for use by fellow teachers. Although it is not always possible or desirable to plan lesson-by-lesson correlation with other subject areas and activities, many courses suggest obvious leads for emphasis in music classes; for example, world history is taught in some schools in the seventh grade, American history in the eighth grade. The co-operation of the school librarian is invaluable in setting up special bookshelves for reference reading combining two or more areas.

The old fear that music will lose its identity in such a program still disturbs some music teachers. However, since it has been established that children's minds are not separated into walled-off compartments labelled music, mathematics, history, and so forth, and that the ability to perceive relationships is both an objective and a basis for learning, such fear is groundless. We do not maintain that a music class cannot be interesting unless it is conducted in this manner: The level of interest in the classroom depends largely upon the teacher. We do maintain that music has a responsibility beyond that of pumping musical skill and information into the child: Its basic responsibility is to contribute to the development of the child, and this can be done best by making the pieces of the puzzle — school and its subject matter — fit together.

It is apparent, too, that once the teacher begins to bring the weight of other subjects to bear upon music, it assumes a new authority. Furthermore, many educators believe that this is the natural way to proceed; music did not develop as an isolated subject in man's history, with human beings working feverishly on music for a few years, then art, science, or literature for a few more. The roots of music lie in the everyday life of mankind, composer, laborer, artist, and scientist. This is the way it should be brought to children.

INTERCLASS ACTIVITIES

Although we have said in preceding chapters that each class, even on the same grade level, may be following different procedures and using different materials, classes should maintain a relationship with each other so that there is an exchange of ideas and experiences. A common way of doing this is to have one class present for another class the culminating activity of a project or unit. The form taken by such an activity will vary; it may be a musical show, panel discussion, quiz show, classroom concert, or similar presentation. Such exchanges are mutually stimulating. For example, at the end of a semester the eighth-grade music sections in one school exchanged programs, with each class presenting a sample of the musical activities of the class during the semester which was ending. This served not only as a review for each class but in cases where the classes had worked with some of the same materials showed different ways of handling them.

Not only may there be an exchange between music classes, but also between various departments. In the case of the science teacher who presented sound, members of the class used their musical instruments to contribute to the subject. Another way in which this might be done would be to have the science class present the physical basis of sound while a music class carried on with its musical aspects. A field trip to examine the workings of a church organ and hear a short recital might bring such a project to an interesting conclusion.

Like most procedures in good teaching, the foregoing requires understanding teachers and careful, thorough planning. It is not a cure-all to be applied in every situation. Teachers must be particularly cautious where classes are grouped homogeneously. Such groupings may make for increased interest at both advanced and retarded levels by removing the pressure of more musically experienced and facile pupils from their slower fellows, and also by removing the drag of the less experienced and/or less talented from the relatively advanced. But an exchange of programs between such classes may be disastrous to the confidence and self-esteem of the slower groups, unless activities are shared which may not only be done with satisfaction, but also received with some degree of enthusiasm and respect. Likewise, it is important that in all presentations of this nature the objectives of the group be clearly explained, both for the sake of the "audience" and as review for the group making the presentation. An evaluation by both groups of how successfully these objectives have been reached is likely to prove a worthwhile procedure.

PERFORMANCE LEVEL IN THE JUNIOR HIGH SCHOOL

Here is a controversial topic which has caused many tears to be shed, not only by exploited pupils, but also by misguided teachers. A performance should be a sharing experience; something we enjoy doing is shared with others for the purpose of mutual enjoyment. A satisfactory resolution of the question swings on two points: standards of the audience, whatever they may be, and attitude of the teacher toward the development of the child or children who are performing.

Particularly where the adult audience is concerned, a large part of the teacher's task involves developing a receptive attitude and establishing the viewpoint that pupil performance should *not* be judged by professional standards. This does not mean talking down the pupil's talent and ability; it does mean making a clear distinction between the professional and the pupil-amateur in terms of audience criticism. In this connection it is readily apparent that radio and television, where each listener and viewer is a self-appointed critic, have influenced attitudes. For instance, on many so-called amateur programs the audience is invited to participate directly in passing judgment. But invited or not, anyone capable of turning on a radio or television set is a critic — he may approve or reject. Such attitudes are likely to carry over unconsciously into the school audience situation. The teacher who is working with a pupil already knows the ability of the pupil, and should know that performance is justified only as a means of growth through self-expression. But the teacher cannot assume that the audience knows this. Whenever a pupil or an organization performs, it is the teacher's responsibility to see that the audience understands the purpose of the performance, not in technical terms, but in general terms of the music program's objectives. Informal introductory talks concerning pupils' musical experiences and goals will do much toward developing both school and community understanding of today's school music philosophy.

With regard to the second point, teachers themselves may be confused at times about pupil performance standards. "Perfectionists" may unintentionally pressure pupils toward goals which are not within their capability. The results of a performance which falls below such artificial standards may be, in their effect upon the pupil, failure and discouragement. The defense of such teachers is that the school music program must maintain and "sell" itself through certain standards of performance.[1]

A growing dissatisfaction with this argument exists, especially on the part of some administrators and music educators who

---

[1] It must be noted that teachers, at times, "inherit" difficult situations of this kind in which they may change the *status quo* only gradually and tactfully.

express the belief that what goes on in the music classroom is as important as what takes place on the concert platform. This is a wholesome viewpoint, since public performance should grow out of regular classroom work and not at the expense of it. The latter has been the case with teachers producing concerts under such pressure that regular classroom work has been almost neglected for weeks.

Teachers sometimes believe that because of public demand for performances at many types of community meetings the work of performing organizations must come first. The answer to this lies in a definite effort to educate the community to the real aims of music education in a philosophy which places the welfare of all the children first and does not primarily set out to develop the highly talented minority into virtuosi. One school solved this problem in part by initiating "open rehearsals" in order to relieve the pressure of a performance load that was too heavy. The only variation from the regular school rehearsal was the inclusion of an explanation made by the director or a student officer regarding the work of the organization, its objectives, and regular activities. The reaction of many parents was that they liked these open rehearsals better than formal performances; they were more lifelike, and parents saw their children in a situation closer to the regular school situation.

Parents, who comprise the majority of school audiences, are on the whole sympathetic and understanding. But even they are likely to judge all pupil performers on the same basis, and one teacher found it advisable to say to audiences something like this:

Tonight we are fortunate enough to have four different accompanists for our junior-high-school choir. Some have studied piano longer than others — some have worked harder than others — no two have had the same teacher. Let's not try to decide which is best. Instead, let's realize that each one is doing a good job of helping the choir and give each credit for playing to the best of his ability. Music is something we enjoy together — we don't have to compete with each other in order to have a part in it.

The guiding principle in deciding what constitutes acceptable performance should be what the child can do with satisfaction at his own level of maturity and ability.

SELECTING AND DEVELOPING GOOD PERFORMING SITUATIONS

The teacher who puts the welfare of children first will choose very carefully the situations in which they perform. The desire to perform publicly appears to be strong in junior-high-school boys and girls. Psychologically we can understand this, since it is a means of gaining public approval and group prestige. Actually, teachers must be on guard to prevent public performances which may result in dissatisfaction on the part of the performers. Boys and girls usually know when they have done an acceptable piece of work. But if public appearance results in tears, cases of jitters, surliness, and other signs of tension, it is obvious that more harm than good is being done. Although a certain amount of tension is inevitable in many children before such appearances, extreme nervousness is certainly unhealthy. More nail-biting, handkerchief-twisting, and knee-trembling have been tolerated by music teachers in the way of performance experience than ever can be justified in the name of child development. When a child can do a thing well and has confidence in his ability to share it with others, he should be encouraged to do so with a sympathetic audience and to evaluate his performance with the teacher, since its chief purpose is that of future growth — not public entertainment. The teacher should always be present, not only for this purpose, but also for moral support.

There are few teachers of even a year's experience who have not had to answer the question, asked by an anxious pupil just before a performance, "Weren't *you* ever afraid?" Once, at a first performance by a boys' quartet the teacher left, just before the boys went on, in order to go to the back of the auditorium and listen. When the quartet appeared, the boys had their arms around each other's shoulders. After they had sung, the teacher

went backstage. "That was a good idea . . . arms around each other's shoulders," he commented. "How did you think of it?" One singer grinned and said, "We had to. My knees were shaking so they had to hold me up!" This was a school assembly at which the boys had been requested to sing, and, fortunately, they were well received. Later the boy told the teacher, "Next time my knees won't shake so much!" And they didn't. But with an unfriendly audience and unsympathetic companions the result might have been a different story. Often boys who shy away from singing individually or in mixed classes will be eager to do so in boys' ensembles. This drive for recognition, as well as the urge to *sing together*, may be used by teachers to help pupils' musical growth.

It is important to remember that, since the urge to perform is so strong, we cannot wait for a performance until a pupil or a group is letter perfect. Much of the music children sing or play should not go through the polishing process; it comes under the heading of increased musical experience. Children learn musically by experiencing a large amount of music; for example, it is commonly said, "The only way to learn to read music is to *read music!*" Finding audiences for pupils who enjoy performing but are not *accomplished* performers is important. The classroom itself is a good place for this — classroom concerts may be organized with members of the class performing, also with members of other classes contributing. Bringing senior-high-school pupils into junior-high-school assemblies and classes is mutually beneficial. Amateur programs are popular with junior-high-school pupils. Inviting parents to visit the classroom or assembly serves two purposes: They constitute a somewhat more important audience, and they become acquainted with classroom or assembly procedures. Every community has situations in which audiences are happy to hear the music of young performers and do not expect perfection; some of these are old people's homes, service clubs, fraternal groups, stores at Christmas (street carolling with instrumental ensembles is also popular at Christmas), and exchange programs with nearby schools.

The type of program which children themselves plan and carry out not only develops group co-operation, but also initiative. Children, who can be thoughtlessly cruel to the less talented members of the group, can also be resourceful and kind when it comes to finding something for all the children in the group to do in a performance. Time and again groups have been observed to assign important parts in a program not to the most talented, but to a child who needs the experience or the "lift" which comes from having the confidence of the group expressed in his ability. Not only will children choose such individuals, but they also will freely aid them in preparing for their parts. This is one of the most valuable phases of a democratically conducted program.

Some schools have successfully planned and presented all-school music festivals each year.[2] The most effective of these are based upon interdepartmental co-operation, with the production growing out of classroom work, and extensive pupil participation in the selection of performers and materials. Such productions vary from minstrel shows and talent or variety shows to operettas and original productions, with script and music written by the pupils. The most difficult feature of such productions is allowing the pupils to really assume a large part of the responsibility instead of tolerating a teacher-dominated situation for the sake of expediency. We cannot possibly unleash the real power of children, whether it be creative, executive, or both, unless we give them opportunity and a reasonable amount of freedom to develop it. *Latent aptitude lies sleeping in every classroom, sacrificed to efficiency and verbalism.* A striking example of this took place in an eighth-grade music class which was discussing *Das Rheingold.* Sitting in the class was a nonparticipant, a boy with little confidence in his singing voice and a general disinterest in listening and rhythmic activities. The discussion veered to the difficulty of staging Wagnerian operas because of the unusual stage effects demanded by the composer, and the teacher discussed with the class several

---

[2] For additional discussion of such projects, see Chapter 4.

situations in which almost impossible effects were required in stage directions. Slowly the boy came to life, and when the teacher asked, concerning a problem of staging, "How do you think this could be done?," he voluntarily arose, went to the blackboard, and by drawings and diagrams explained how *he* would do it. This later led to assignments as stage manager, and throughout his high-school career the boy, through class recognition of his newly discovered interest and ability, associated himself with the staging of plays and musical productions. His interest in music grew, too, because of the teacher's confidence and interest in him. Such is the miracle of discovering the individual which awaits every teacher.

Both operettas and the original school show arouse in pupils and community a high level of interest. Either may be good or poor, musically. Few operettas, however, justify the time and effort expended upon them, and there is comparatively little opportunity for originality and creative effort in most of these productions. A limited number of individuals receive prominent parts, and participants have been known to go through six weeks or more of rehearsals as chorus members without even understanding the plot, their activity being confined to following the chorus leader off and on the stage, singing a few songs over and over, and mechanically performing prescribed dance routines. A large amount of operetta literature plays down to the musical taste of both participants and public, yet the cast is usually so overtrained that the music stays with them for years. Teachers who prefer operettas to other types of school productions should be careful to make sure the music contributes something of lasting value to the education of the participants. This also applies to the libretto.

Many music teachers face the problem of preventing pupil overload of public performance. When a group or organization is successful and popular, it is likely to be swamped with requests for appearances. Again, the pupil is more important than the performance. There must be enough time between performances so that pupils will be able to enjoy learning new music — nothing contributes more rapidly to the downfall of morale than singing or playing the same numbers over and over again. Furthermore, this limits the musical growth of pupils. All requests for performance should be referred to the members of the group; adults sometimes forget that boys and girls have lives of their own and plans which cannot always be changed in order to fulfill performance requests. Then, too, besides music there are other subjects and activities in the school program, the demands of which must be respected. (We strongly recommend that all public performances be cleared with the school administration before scheduling, in order to prevent conflicts with other school activities.) Sometimes it is necessary to say "No — thank you!" Every teacher should be prepared to do so in order to safeguard pupil welfare, even though refusals are not always received with good grace.

It is wise to make known the policy of the school with regard to pupil performances, through the media of newspapers, PTA meetings, and similar channels of public information. Pupil handbooks are commonly used in today's schools; handbooks containing information both for parents and the general public are a good means of bringing about understanding. Information concerning the music program should include the time, length, and number of rehearsals pupils are expected to attend outside school hours, and the hour at which parents may expect children to return home. Long after the rehearsal has been dismissed, many a music teacher has received telephone calls from parents asking where their children are — we must admit that it is natural for the gang to collect at the corner drugstore for a jukebox session after rehearsal. One way to solve this problem is to plan for a few social gatherings after rehearsals and particularly for one following a performance. Most boys and girls will tell you that their enjoyment of a musical organization is social as well as musical; one director schedules a covered-dish supper once a month for the school choir with dancing to records or other entertainment following. These suppers are organized by the students; with a choral group, for example, salads, vegetables, meat, and dessert are furnished by different sections in turn. Any member of the organization may bring along one or more friends. Such suppers provide an excellent opportunity for the teacher to meet pupils outside the rehearsal situation. Parents may be of great assistance in social functions of this kind; their participation should be encouraged.

Special open rehearsals to which parents are invited also help bridge the school-home gap. Many directors mail or send home a copy of out-of-school rehearsal schedules well in advance of the first rehearsal. This not only tells the parent where his child is, but also prevents conflicting plans.

PROGRAM BUILDING ON THE JUNIOR-
HIGH-SCHOOL LEVEL

In addition to types of programs mentioned, school concerts by band, orchestra, chorus, small ensembles, and glee clubs are a prominent part of the music program. Audiences seem more receptive to the concert which includes several such organizations rather than to a program consisting of all band, orchestral, or choral music; better pace and more variety are possible here, provided there are no long pauses for stage changes. To avoid this, small groups may be presented in front of the curtain, or even with a background of larger organizations.

Concerts no longer must be characterized by an atmosphere of formality. In fact, directors who understand that parents are often more nervous than their performing children do everything possible to relieve tension by making the situation informal through verbal explanatory remarks. Such simple procedures as changing the position of a piano or rearranging an organization's seating while the audience looks on, so that all children may be in full view at some time during the concert, do much to make for a friendlier atmosphere.

In the traditional type of program it was common practice to place heavier numbers at the beginning of the program. Unfortunately, this is the time when any organization is under the greatest strain. Unfortunately, too, the heavier or more serious numbers of a concert are not always those which evoke the most enthusiastic applause. Therefore, after putting forth a serious effort which culminated weeks of rehearsal on a number, boys and girls often have been let down by indifferent audience reaction.

Although this traditional type of program arrangement is still used, another arrangement is that which attempts to evoke a sympathetic audience reaction by programming first one or two numbers which will be well received and make for a relaxed audience and performing group, after which heavier musical numbers are performed. Audiences, particularly those composed largely of parents and relatives, need the release from tension which comes from liberal applause following the successful performance of a musical composition. It is after this has occurred that the audience really relaxes in the confident expectation of enjoyment to come. Needless to say, the performers react in much the same way. This does not mean first doing a humorous number or a selection from a musical comedy and following it with, for example, *Jesu, Joy of Man's Desiring*. It means building the program first with the ability and interest of the performing group in mind and, second, with due consideration for the probable response of the audience.

We also believe that boys and girls who have grown into a real appreciation and love for such a number as a Bach chorale should be prepared for the fact that, although it may have far greater musical value than some of the lighter music they perform, audiences are ignited into applause by those compositions which have a more obvious musical appeal. Whereas the performers have had time to grow into an understanding of the serious music, members of the audience have not — they hear it once, and it is gone. Applause is far from being the final criterion of musical worth and performing success: Audiences are influenced in this by such factors as a lively tempo and increased volume at the end of a number, both of which are likely to excite more applause than slower or quieter numbers. In fact, an eminent musicologist, Percy A. Scholes, says:

... it must have been often noticed by every observant concert-goer that the volume of tone in the last quarter-minute of a performance largely governs the volume of applause that follows, a very loud ending usually "bringing the house down" whatever the merits or demerits of the composition or performance as a whole (a high note at the end of a vocal piece sometimes has the same effect).[3]

Pupils should be helped to understand that the value of the music they perform is not altogether determined by the volume of applause which follows.

How long should a junior-high-school program be? Not much longer than an hour and a quarter, and if it must err in any direction, it should be in the direction of brevity. It is far better to have an audience leave wanting more than to have them fidget their way through the final group. Furthermore, many junior-high-school organizations are not select groups; instead they are considered as experience groups in which a sincere desire to participate is a worthy basis for admission if the pupil has anything at all to contribute. Long programs are taxing for such groups, both in terms of preparation and execution.

SCHOOL ASSEMBLIES

Music should be a part of all school assemblies, and a thoughtfully planned part. It should be more than a perfunctory singing of the *Star-Spangled Banner* (which is almost impossible in range for changing voices) and a closing song. Music can make a real contribution to the assembly program through group singing, a legitimate purpose of which is to bring about group solidity and to create a friendly feeling of relaxation and enjoyment. Much depends upon the leader of the singing, and even more upon the accompanist. Part-singing is not necessary for assembly singing, but is desirable because it encourages pupils to use reading skills acquired in the classroom. It should also serve to encourage harmonizing by ear. For part-singing, the

[3] Percy A. Scholes, *The Oxford Companion to Music* (Second American Edition) (New York: Oxford University Press, Copyright 1938 and 1943), p. 40.

assembly should be seated in sections by voice rather than in the traditional grade and homeroom arrangement. Some music educators feel that best results will be secured by seating boys in the front of the auditorium, both because of the discipline factor and because there are usually fewer part-singing tenors (or alto-tenors) and bases. Although the girls' voices are lighter in quality, they carry through better from the rear. Boy sopranos usually prefer to be seated separately from girl sopranos; sometimes they prefer to be called "high tenors."

The group singing situation should be approached by the leader with the attitude of "Singing is fun — let's enjoy it!" A basic song repertoire similar to that suggested in Chapter 3 for all grades will furnish songs everyone knows as "warm-ups"; so-called "ice-breakers" or action songs also do much to get the group with the leader. When song slides are used, it has been noticed that flashing a slide upside-down on the screen immediately draws a chuckle from the group; one director, capitalizing on this, had several colored slides of the cartoon variety, which "accidentally on purpose" appeared on the screen when least expected. This always led to good-natured repartee between the leader and the operator of the slide machine, enjoyed by both participants and assembly.

Music teachers who hope to become good community or group song leaders might well take a cue from the ease and spontaneity which characterize camp singing. Not only is there a feeling that the singing is voluntary and from the heart, but the songs sung are those which are favorites with the campers; that is, the group has a voice in determining the selection of songs. This is a sound approach to use in assembly singing; it can be done by encouraging pupils to talk to the song leader about song selections, or on an organized basis by asking home-room teachers to report the song choices of their pupils. A song suggestion box may be placed in a prominent location to obtain further song suggestions.

For assemblies centered around special topics music teachers should make an effort to find appropriate music. Sports assemblies suggest the use of the school band, with the singing of school songs. The Christmas assembly may well become a traditional program, with choirs and glee clubs appearing in a setting created by the art and shop departments. (In schools where there is a minority sect, any service which has to do with a religious season should recognize this group as well as the majority.)

Music assemblies are often good audience situations for music groups in need of a performance. Here, for example, we can combine the two purposes of performance and education by "taking apart" the band, chorus, or orchestra and explaining what makes up the various instrumental or vocal sections of musical organizations. Some directors like to present previews of annual concerts in the school assembly a short time before the concert; this not only provides publicity, but also gives the performers an opportunity to experience audience reaction.

MUSIC AS PART OF THE SCHOOL
ACTIVITY PROGRAM

School activity programs usually include many clubs; these have a natural appeal for pupils of junior-high-school age. Music clubs of various kinds may be organized, ranging from a German Band Club, Swing Music Club, or Barbershop Quartet to a Madrigal Group or a Classical Music Club. The high degree of interest often generated when adolescents or preadolescents with similar tastes voluntarily come together may spark the entire music program in a school. For instance: A music teacher new in a school found himself confronted with a class in which the boys sang, but with little display of enthusiasm. Part of their attitude seemed to stem from an expressed dislike of the song texts in use ("The music was too dull," they said), and part of it from resentment of the girls in the class, who undoubtedly sang better than the boys. The situation came to a head one day when the regular teacher was absent; the boys refused to sing. This was the best thing for all concerned, because the problem was now out in the open. "Let's have a club," the teacher suggested, after a discussion of the situation when he had returned. "No one *must* belong, but those who really want to sing may join, and the members may chose the songs. We'll have a boys' club and a girls' club; part of each class will be a rehearsal for each. For those who do not wish to join, we will have special activities. Singing is for those who like it, and it must be terrible to have to sing and not enjoy yourself!" Only four or five boys joined the club at first, but in a week or so the club had grown to include about twelve of the boys in the class. By this time the group was largely self-governing. They decided their club was big enough and voted to admit no more. This had the effect of causing more of the boys to demand admission! After lengthy discussion, these boys were included. Both boys' and girls' groups flourished, and in brief, gave the entire music program new vitality. (The same boys, two years later, became the leading spirits in the boys' section of the senior-high-school *A Cappella* Choir.) The year following the club's organization it was sponsored by the activities program and carried on outside music class. Such was the effect of a club which was organized to solve the problem of a group of boys who had said they were not interested in singing!

It has been the experience of the writers that music clubs in the junior high school spring up like mushrooms, even in the least favorable of environments, when the teacher understands the psychology underlying their appeal. Teachers should notice that the factor of size seems to be important for three reasons: First, a club limited to a certain number seems to be exclusive. Each member feels a bit more important; there is something in most human beings which reacts favorably to being one of the chosen! We may object to this, but we may also satisfy the needs of our boys and girls by seeing that there is a club each of them can "make."

The second reason is that these small organizations make for good school-community relationships. They can appear in situations where a large group would be unwieldy.

A third reason is that the teacher learns to know each pupil better in a small group, the importance of which cannot be overemphasized. However, clubs should be large enough either in size or in number of organizations to meet the needs of the pupils.

Junior-high-school music teachers would do well to recognize the value of music clubs and to utilize it in building the music program.

SCHOOL-COMMUNITY RELATIONSHIPS
IN THE MUSIC PROGRAM

Every child who goes home from a music class is a messenger conveying an impression. Indications are that the majority of parents want their children to have music. Therefore we may assume that they want them to like music. (But notice that there appear to be few parents who are interested in having their children recite key-signatures to them or tell them the dates of composers' births!) If parents approach the music program with such a friendly attitude, we must attempt to fulfill their hopes and expectations.

Today's schools are in desperate need of intelligent understanding by the lay public. In the search for newer and better ways of teaching, too often parents have been closed out of the circle. Yet, good schools are now both more functional and more lifelike in their approach to the educational process. Much the same situation exists here as with dissenting teachers; the standard of learning known to parents is the way in which they learned, and once having survived the educational process, they may assume that there is something wrong with other ways. To illustrate from another field, in the thinking of parents it may be a failure of the school if a child does not know the name of the first chief justice of the Supreme Court, but the fact that he knows how to use reference books in order to find such information when he has a functional need for it is either not discovered or seems unimportant. Education based upon a problem-solving approach may not result in an impressive mass of factual information, although today's children are testing as well or better in many cases than did their predecessors of earlier generations. But, we believe that today we are preparing children to face the problems of democratic living more realistically and to solve them with greater wisdom and facility.

Unfortunately, our schools have failed to throw a spotlight on the implementation of the new educational philosophy. For example, in one school a small, extracurricular instrumental ensemble aided by the teacher set up its own rules and regulations. One of the rules provided that if a certain number of absences and tardinesses accumulated without sufficient reason, the offending member would be suspended. Eventually the rule was violated, and, by group action, the offender was suspended. His parent's remark to the teacher was, "I wouldn't object if you had suspended him, but I don't think the members of the group should have had any voice in the matter." The failure here lay in the teacher's neglect of public relationships; the parent did not know how the group was conducted and what educational values beyond musical ones the teacher was working to meet. As long as the lay public is furnishing the children, no new educational philosophy will be established until that same public understands and accepts it.

How can the music program gain a foothold in the understanding of the community? First, by convincing our pupils that they are having a good school experience, since they are the daily messengers. But we cannot stop here; children are likely to take even the best of school life for granted if they have always known it and have no basis for comparison. So we must attempt to bring the parents into contact with the school. This is not as easy as it sounds. Try as we will to have "Parents' Days" in schools, "Back to School Weeks," and so on, these usually result in being artificial showcases. Teachers should try as much as possible to bring the parents into the everyday live classroom situation, with no attempt to make it better than usual. One teacher who asked the members of a class to bring anything from home which had to do with music has never forgotten the little girl who raised her hand and asked, "May I bring my parents?" She then explained that they played piano duets. They came into the class and delighted its members with a few spirited selections. More parents, if encouraged, might take musical instruments from their cases and bring them into the classroom. We also should remember that many parents have record collections, sing in church and community choirs, have traveled in other countries where they have had musical experiences, or attended memorable concerts in our own country — all of which are food for classroom discussion.

Even when there is no musical experience to draw upon, we have a generation of fathers whose military experiences in many cases took them into remote parts of the world; when the music of such places is used in the classroom, these parents might well have something to contribute. Both the occupations and hobbies of parents may prove a source of community contact in the classroom. For example, the decreasing size of the world in terms of transportation and communication may affect music of the future through a broader exchange of musical ideas. The father who is an airlines, television, or radio employee may have something to say on this subject. And as with the children whose hobbies are collections which are international in scope, the parents' collections may have an indirect but enlightening relationship with the musical materials of the classroom.

CONCERT ATTENDANCE BY MUSIC CLASSES

We have been discussing bringing the community into the classroom. In addition to this, community resources outside of the classroom should be fully explored and utilized. It is now common practice to take busloads of children to concerts in the local community or more remote cities. Teachers should notice that the interest of children in music heard on these concert excursions is much higher if they are familiar with the music programmed, and have been told to watch and listen for features of special interest. It is often possible to obtain advance programs and stimulate interest in concert attendance by devoting a few moments of class time to their discussion. Evaluation of such concerts as a classroom follow-up is a worthwhile procedure.

MUSIC PROGRAM AND THE CHURCH MUSIC PROGRAM

The school music program can assist the church music program in developing young people's choirs by encouraging pupils to join such organizations and by reporting to church choir directors those boys and girls who may be interested in becoming members. Class talks by representative members of different faiths on the music of their respective churches may not only have musical value, but also develop religious tolerance. Some directors have taken choirs to sing at a service of each church in the community. Naturally, the co-operation of the clergy must be enlisted in such a project. Teachers should not overlook the fact that the church music program is a functional outlet for the school music program. Carry-over of the latter into community life is a real goal.

Church choir directors of young people's groups sometimes have difficulty scheduling their rehearsals because of extracurricular school activities. In one community, the supervising principal of the school solved this problem by clearing of rehearsals one afternoon a week — it was understood that no school music groups would be asked to meet after school on those afternoons. In very large school systems this may be difficult to do, but the idea is worth considering. The relationship between school and church in any community should be one of co-operation for the welfare of the child, not conflict.

PRIVATE TEACHERS AND THE SCHOOL
MUSIC PROGRAM

There are too few communities in which school music teachers and private music teachers work together for the good of the pupil. Yet, each can assist the other in developing interest. During the junior-high-school years, pupils sometimes acquire so many interests and activities that private music study is likely to be discontinued because the pupil does not see a practical use for it. The school music teacher can be of assistance here by seeing that the pupil has an opportunity to make functional use of his ability in the classroom or as a part of larger musical activities. The private teacher can be of assistance to the school music teacher by sharing with him information about the ability of the pupil and suggesting possible performance outlets. Many young pianists who are too reserved to offer their services as accompanists would enjoy this activity. The school music teacher with a heavy pupil load is unaware at times of some of the most important details concerning individual pupils; such information may be commonplace knowledge to the private teacher, who usually teaches one pupil at a time.

Meetings of private music teachers with school music teachers do much to bring about better relationships between the two groups and a better understanding of individual pupil behavior in two differing situations. It might be well to consider giving program credit to private teachers when their pupils appear in the capacity of soloists or accompanists in school situations and to recognize their efforts as having similar objectives to those of the school music program. Where music educators feel that these objectives differ it would be to the advantage of all concerned to talk over mutual problems and attempt to arrive at an understanding. Certainly the situation of the public schools in their goal of finding a place for music in the life of each child, interested or disinterested, talented or relatively less talented musically, and coming from homes of widely varying musical background, does differ somewhat from that of the private music teacher. But there are no irreconcilable differences, and with the interests of the child as the primary objective, common ground may be discovered as a basis of understanding.

COMMUNITY MUSICAL ORGANIZATIONS

Many music educators have found an excellent medium of public relationships in organizing and directing community bands, orchestras, choruses, and music study groups. In one community a resident came to the music director in the schools and said, "Some of us are wondering whether you could teach us to play instruments and have as much fun with music as the school children do. Would you take us on? Perhaps we could have an adult orchestra in time." A group of forty beginners was soon organized with ages ranging from 20 to 60. Great interest was displayed by the community in what was generally viewed as a somewhat hazardous experiment, but the project was carried on successfully, resulting in concerts both by the community group and by a combined parent and child group. Such organizations are useful in promoting good public relationships because they place the parent or taxpayer in the learner's situation. In the same way, the teacher faces community members who are adults, and should be able to demonstrate in actual practice much of the everyday philosophy of education in which he believes.

RADIO, TELEVISION, AND PUBLIC RELATIONS

Teachers should remember when they present junior-high-school groups through the medium of radio or television that they are invading a field in which professional standards are expected by listeners and viewers, and in which entertainment rather than educational experience is the paramount objective of the commercial broadcaster. Our justification for putting a student group in a performing situation here is that it may develop into an educational experience for the pupil. Unfortunately, for the most part this objective is not understood by the general listening public. Radio broadcasts, which focus the listener's attention on an aural experience, are particularly difficult to handle. Many of the common faults of relatively inexperienced musical organizations, such as imperfect intonation, faulty phrasing, and poor tone quality (and with choral organizations, inferior diction), are more noticeable on radio than in a situation where the attention of the audience is divided between listening and looking. Then, too, although it is common knowledge that the broadcast engineer plays an important role in radio performances, some stations do not have engineers sufficiently trained to make the most of young performing groups, or are handicapped by lack of time and/or lack of equipment necessary to do so. The music educator must take upon himself the responsibility of acquiring a working knowledge of broadcasting equipment and techniques, if he wishes to make a passable success of broadcasting junior-high-school groups.

Television presents the same situation as radio with regard to audience standards and commercial objectives. But it is ob-vious that audiences enjoy *seeing* boys and girls make music as much as hearing them and that imperfections are more likely to be overlooked while *watching* young musicians. Therefore, it would seem that television may offer greater success in the telecasting of school music groups than does radio.

Nevertheless, in television as in radio broadcasts, unless the teacher possesses enough "know-how" to safeguard the best interests of his pupils, they are likely to be disappointed in the results of a performance they have approached with great interest and enthusiasm.

The future of television in school-community relations may best lie in the possibility of bringing the public, through telecasts, into the actual classroom situation day by day and allowing it to watch the workings of the schools. This, with an explanatory background by educators who are articulate to a high degree in the matter of pointing out the objectives of today's schools in nontechnical language, may be one of the finest avenues yet devised for bringing about an understanding of today's schools. *The learning situation, rather than the performing situation, is in great need of public understanding.* But there still exists a wide disparity in commercial and educational aims in both broadcasting and telecasting, and until this gap is closed we cannot hope for too much from these media of public relations. However, considering the reverse face of the picture, that of bringing television into the classroom, we find a vastly different situation. One channel can bring into thousands of classrooms, if equipped for reception, the best of instruction through the use of great teachers and superlative materials of instruction, employing both aural and visual methods. Our children eventually may thus be able to see and hear the best in music performed by outstanding soloists, orchestras, and choruses, or to view art galleries and scientific laboratories hundreds of miles removed from the receiving classroom!

With the assignment of many telecasting channels to stations throughout the country, it is hoped that telecasters will find it worth their while to devote at least a small amount of time to the field of public instruction. It may not be unreasonable to hope that increasing numbers of wealthy philanthropic foundations will consider it a vital enough field to sponsor programs which may create as much interest on the part of classroom viewers as do such programs as "Captain Video" and "The Lone Ranger." With competent educational directors and *no strings attached*, this may become one of the most fertile fields yet discovered for superlative instruction in today's schools.

SUMMARY

Music is a powerful means of establishing good school morale because (1) its practical objective is enjoyment; (2) it is capable of being used to broaden the significance of other subjects; (3) it allows boys and girls to express themselves in terms of activity; (4) it is, through its organizations, an avenue for development of democratic understanding and self-government; and (5) it offers music organizations interested audiences, through which pupils may realize a sense of achievement and fulfillment.

Because it may be used in conjunction with every subject in

the curriculum, it is potentially a unifying subject. In this role music, rather than losing its identity and significance, assumes new authority and makes more sense to the pupil, as it becomes part of the fabric of everyday life.

In implementing this, it is necessary to maintain some degree of interclass activities both within the music department and between the music and other departments. Various subject teachers working in collaboration help the student to integrate his knowledge of different fields.

In arriving at a guiding philosophy regarding the performance level of pupils who individually or in organizations face audiences, teachers must bear in mind that professional standards of performance, often expected by audiences, are not necessarily those of school organizations. The difference, an obvious one, is that the pupil is both an immature learner and an amateur. Furthermore, teachers who have been misled into believing that they must "drive" pupils in an effort to attain perfection in performance should know that this is no longer commensurate with the goals of education in today's schools. The process of learning is as important as the end result, for it determines attitudes. Music educators are no longer trying to develop the capacities of the most talented few alone, but rather to make music vital in the lives of all children.

Children have a strong urge to make public appearances, as this satisfies certain needs. A good performance situation should not place an undue amount of strain upon the child, and understanding teachers will be careful to choose situations for public appearance in which the pupil performers will gain in confidence and ability through sharing their music with an audience. No child should be overtaxed in terms of public performance, and no child should be overlooked if he has the desire to be part of a performing group. Parents should be encouraged to accept and understand what each child or group of children has to offer at the prevailing level of maturity. Overrehearsing in an attempt to reach standards of performance which are too high has a strong flavor of exploitation where children are concerned. It also restricts the broad musical experience we believe to be vital in the junior high school.

Concerts should be more lifelike in that they should reflect the total music program. They should be *inclusive* of many children rather than *exclusive*. In building programs, the first consideration is the child; the choice of materials and arrangement of the program should be made with his welfare in mind rather than the entertainment of the audience.

School assemblies offer an opportunity to use music in a relaxed atmosphere. Much of the music learned in classes should be enjoyed again here. The cumulative song repertoire has a significant use in group singing. Small and large music ensembles should be encouraged to play for their fellow pupils.

The school activity program which is carried on in many schools may assist the music program by sponsoring music clubs. Because such clubs are voluntary, their members frequently develop an enthusiastic attitude, which may spark the entire music department. Since junior-high-school pupils are club-minded, the great potential of such clubs should be developed in every school.

Today's philosophy of music education and its practical application in the schools has not been sufficiently explained to the general public; in order to gain understanding and support from this source, teachers must wage a constant campaign to inform both parents and all interested persons (in general, the taxpayers) of today's educational objectives. Explanation is not enough, however; the public must be brought into the schools to see them at work, and the schools must be taken to the public. No system of education can make progress unless it is accepted by the taxpayers.

Community resources must be used whenever possible in the music program. This includes bringing into the classroom persons who can make contributions to the various projects being carried on, and trips by the class to relevant activities in the community.

Other possible avenues for the development of good school-community relations in the music program are through co-operation with church music directors and private music teachers. Both of the latter groups work with junior-high-school children to some extent, and, therefore, we can assume that the joint efforts of all concerned will work in favor of the child.

Television and radio, potent tools of mass communication, are also tools which may easily be mishandled. These are fields in which some technical know-how is essential. Because of the commercial slant of the majority of radio and television programs, listeners and viewers may not be greatly interested in the slower pace of the amateur school program. The future of television as a means of public orientation to the present-day practices of public schools may lie in extensive telecasting of many actual classroom situations instead of a few showcase activities.

Index